Holders of Extraordinary Imperium under Augustus and Tiberius

This volume focuses on special military and diplomatic missions in various provinces of the Empire that Augustus and Tiberius entrusted to selected members of the *domus Augusta*, granting them special prerogatives (*imperia extraordinaria*).

Sawiński compares and analyses various primary and secondary sources exploring special powers and missions in the provinces of the *domus Augusta* during the reigns of Augustus and Tiberius, from 27 BC to AD 23, from border regions on the Rhine and the Danube to client states such as Judaea and Armenia. It explores the legal aspects of these powers wielded in the provinces and how these missions and the subsequent honours helped to solidify power within a new hereditary system of power. The reader will also find in it a critical discussion of the current state of research on this subject.

Holders of Extraordinary Imperium under Augustus and Tiberius offers an important study of these powers and prerogatives of the imperial family that will be of interest to anyone working on the Augustan age, the early Empire and Principate, and the Roman imperial family. This volume should also prove useful to students of archaeology and art history.

Paweł Sawiński is Associate Professor at the University of Adam Mickiewicz in Poznań, Poland. His scholarly books and articles deal with various aspects of the history of ancient Rome. He is the author of, among other books, *The Succession of Imperial Power under the Julio-Claudian Dynasty (30 BC–AD 68)*, published in 2018.

Routledge Monographs in Classical Studies

Recent titles include:

Xenophon's Socratic Works
David M. Johnson

Dionysus and Politics
Constructing Authority in the Graeco-Roman World
Edited by Filip Doroszewski and Dariusz Karłowicz

Monsters in Greek Literature
Aberrant Bodies in Ancient Greek Cosmogony, Ethnography, and Biology
Fiona Mitchell

Antonio Gramsci and the Ancient World
Edited by Emilio Zucchetti and Anna Maria Cimino

Holders of Extraordinary Imperium under Augustus and Tiberius
A Study into the Beginnings of the Principate
Paweł Sawiński

Divination and Knowledge in Greco-Roman Antiquity
Crystal Addey

Travel, Geography, and Empire in Latin Poetry
Edited by Micah Young Myers and Erika Zimmermann Damer

Ancient History from Below
Subaltern Experiences and Actions in Context
Edited by Cyril Courrier and Julio Cesar Magalhães de Oliveira

For more information on this series, visit: https://www.routledge.com/Routledge-Monographs-in-Classical-Studies/book-series/RMCS

Holders of Extraordinary Imperium under Augustus and Tiberius

A Study into the Beginnings of the Principate

Paweł Sawiński

Translated by M. Jarczyk

Routledge
Taylor & Francis Group
LONDON AND NEW YORK

First published 2021
by Routledge
2 Park Square, Milton Park, Abingdon, Oxon OX14 4RN

and by Routledge
605 Third Avenue, New York, NY 10158

Routledge is an imprint of the Taylor & Francis Group, an informa business

British Library Cataloguing-in-Publication Data
A catalogue record for this book is available from the British Library

Library of Congress Cataloging-in-Publication Data
A catalog record for this book has been requested

ISBN: 978-0-367-72533-4 (hbk)
ISBN: 978-0-367-72534-1 (pbk)
ISBN: 978-1-003-15518-8 (ebk)

Typeset in Sabon
by Apex CoVantage, LLC

For my Grandmother Melania

Contents

Figures and tables

Figures

Tables

Acknowledgements

This book is a modified version of a study I published in Polish in 2005.[1] I would like to thank Adam Ziółkowski, with whom I have had the opportunity to again and again discuss the claims made in this book. His critical and discerning reading of the chapters has also influenced the final shape of this publication. I also want to thank Karol Kłodziński, who convinced me to have my book published with Routledge rather than elsewhere when we both stayed in Rome. Thanks are also due to the Dean's Office at the Faculty of Pedagogy and Fine Arts, Adam Mickiewicz University, Kalisz, for covering the cost of the translation. I am grateful to the De Brzezie Lanckoronski Foundation for granting me a scholarship in Rome in 2019, which made it possible for me to peruse the impressive collections of the libraries there.

Note

1 See Sawiński 2005.

Abbreviations

Ancient works

App.	Appian
B. Civ.	*Bella Civilia* (*Civil Wars*)
Hisp.	*Bellum Hispaniense* (*The War in Spain*)
Mith.	*Mithridatica* (*The Mithridatic Wars*)
Anth. Pal.	*Anthologia Palatina*
Cass. Dio	Cassius Dio, *Roman History*
Caes.	Caesar
Bell. Afr.	*Bellum Africum* (*The African War*)
B. Civ.	*Bellum civile* (*The Civil War*)
Cic.	Cicero
Att.	*Epistulae ad Atticum* (*Letters to Atticus*)
Brut.	*Epistulae ad Brutum* (*Letters to Brutus*)
Fam.	*Epistulae ad familiares* (*Letters to his friends*)
Flac.	*Pro Flacco* (*For Flaccus*)
Leg. Man.	*Pro lege Manilia* (*On the imperium of Cn. Pompeius*)
Phil.	*Orationes Philippicae* (*Philippic Orations*)
Prov. cons.	*De provinciis consularibus* (*On the Consular Provinces*)
Q. fr.	*Epistulae ad Quintum fratrem* (*Letters to his brother Quintus*)
Consol. ad Liv.	*Consolatio ad Liviam*
DPG	*Decreta Pisana Gaius* (*Decree of the town council of Pisa concerning commemorative honours for Gaius Caesar*)
DPL	*Decreta Pisana Lucius* (*Decree of the town council of Pisa concerning commemorative honours for Lucius Caesar*)

Eutrop.	Eutropius, *Breviarium Historiae Romanae* (*Abridgement of Roman History*)
Flor.	Florus, *Epitomae* (*Epitome of Roman History*)
HRR	*Historicorum Romanorum Reliquiae* (ed. H. Peter)
Hor.	Horace
Epist.	*Epistulae* (*Letters*)
Joseph.	Josephus
AJ	*Antiquitates Judaicae* (*Antiquities of the Jews*)
BJ	*Bellum Judaicum* (*The Jewish War*)
Liv.	Livius, *Ab urbe condita* (*History of Rome from its Foundation*)
Per.	*Periochae* (*Summaries*)
Mal.	Malalas, *Chronographia* (*Chronicle*)
Oros.	Orosius, *Historiae adversus paganos* (*History against the Pagans*)
Ovid.	Ovidius
Ars am.	*Ars amatoria* (*Art of Love*)
Pont.	*Epistulae ex Ponto*
Tr.	*Tristia* (*Sorrows*)
Plin.	Pliny
HN	*Naturalis historia* (*Natural History*)
Plut.	Plutarch
Luc.	*Lucullus* (*Life of Lucullus*)
Pomp.	*Pompeius* (*Life of Pompeius*)
RGDA	*Res Gestae Divi Augusti* (*The Achievements of the Deified Augustus*)
Sall.	Sallust
Hist.	*Historiae* (*Histories*)
SCPP	*Senatus consultum de Cn. Pisone patre*
Strab.	Strabo, *Geographica* (*The Geography*)
Suet.	Suetonius

Aug.	*Divus Augustus*
Cal.	*Caligula*
Claud.	*Claudius*
Tib.	*Tiberius*
Vesp.	*Vespasianus*
TS	*Tabula Siarensis*
Tac.	Tacitus
Ann.	*Annales* (*Annals*)
Hist.	*Historiae* (*Histories*)
Val. Max.	Valerius Maximus, *Facta et dicta memorabilia* (*Memorable Deeds and Sayings*)
Vell. Pat.	Velleius Paterculus, *Historia Romana* (*History of Rome*)

Modern works and collections

Act. Ant.	*Auctores Antiquissimi*
AEArq	*Archivo Español de Arqueología*
AE	*L'Année Épigraphique* (Paris 1888–)
AJA	*American Journal of Archaeology*
AJP	*American Journal of Philology*
AKB	*Archäologisches Korrespondenzblatt*
ANRW	*Aufstieg und Niedergang der römischen Welt*
Arch. Kor. RGZM	*Archäologisches Korrespondenzblatt des Römisch-Germanischen Zentralmuseums Mainz*
Arch. Class.	*Archaeologia Classica*
CA	*Classical Antiquity*
CCG	*Cahiers du Centre Gustave Glotz*
CIG	*Corpus Inscriptionum Graecarum* (Berolini 1828–1877)
CIL	*Corpus Inscriptionum Latinarum* (Berlin 1863–)
CJ	*Classical Journal*
CPh	*Classical Philology*
CQ	*Classical Quarterly*
GRBS	*Greek, Roman and Byzantine Studies*
HCC	A. S. Robertson (ed.), *Roman Imperial Coins in the Hunter Coin Cabinet University of Glasgow*, I: *Augustus to Nerva* (London, Glasgow, New York 1962)
HZ	*Historische Zeitschrift*
IG	*Inscriptiones Graecae* (Berlin 1873–)
IGR	*Inscriptiones Graecae ad res Romanas pertinentes*
IK	*Inschriften griechischer Städte aus Kleinasien* (Bonn 1972–)

Inscr. It.	A. Degrassi, *Inscriptiones Italiae*, 13: *Fasti et Elogia* (Rome 1937, 1963)
IvO	*Die Inschriften von Olympia* (Berlin 1896–)
JDAI	*Jahrbuch des deutschen Archäologischen Instituts*
JRA	*Journal of Roman Archaeology*
JRGZM	*Jahrbuch des Römisch-Germanischen Zentralmuseums Mainz*
JRS	*Journal of Roman Studies*
LCM	*Liverpool Classical Monthly*
LEC	*Les Études classiques*
LTUR	E. M. Steinby (ed.), *Lexicon Topographicum Urbis Romae* (Rome 1993–)
MDAI(R)	*Mitteilungen des deutschen archäologischen Instituts*
NZ	*Numismatische Zeitschrift*
PBSR	*Papers of the British School at Rome*
RE	*Realencyclopädie der classischen Altertumswissenschaft*
RGA	*Reallexikon der germanischen Altertumskunde*
RhM	*Rheinisches Museum für Philologie*
RIC	C. H. V. Sutherland, R. A. G. Carson (eds.), *The Roman Imperial Coinage*, I^2: *From 31* BC *to* AD *69* (London 1984)
RPC	A. Burnett, J. Amandry, P. P. Ripollès (eds.), *Roman Provincial Coinage*, I: *From the Death of Caesar to the Death of Vitellius (44* BC–AD *69)* (London 1992)
RSA	*Rivista storica dell'antichità*
SEG	*Supplementum Epigraphicum Graecum* (Leiden 1923–)
TAPhA	*Transactions of the American Philological Association*
ZPE	*Zeitschrift für Papyrologie und Epigraphik*

Introduction

Augustus's principate constitutes a critical point in the development of a new model of administering the provinces of the *Imperium Romanum*. In the system of ruling the state constructed by Augustus, and later Tiberius, a special role fell to the members of their immediate families, who received extraordinary powers and were assigned various tasks. The same persons were the primary executors of the expansionist policies of the first two rulers of Rome.[1]

This monograph deals with the various missions members of the *domus Augusta* carried out in the west and east of the Empire under Augustus and Tiberius.[2] Unlike ordinary provincial governors, they acted based on a special, or extraordinary (*extra ordinem*), *imperium*. That type of *imperium* was independent—as it gave the right to hold an ovation, triumph, or imperatorial acclamation in the event of a successful campaign—and superior relative to the *imperia* of provincial governors. In addition, its territorial extent was not limited to a single province, but usually covered a larger area. While carrying out the tasks assigned to them, members of the imperial family did not hold any official positions within provincial administrations, such as that of a *legatus Augusti pro praetore* or *proconsul*. Thus, the special character of their power—as in Augustus's case—separated it from the offices that had traditionally accompanied it: they held their *imperium* without being magistrates or promagistrates *cum imperio*. An analogy can be seen here to several special commands from the late Republican period: more on that subject below. Under Augustus, such prerogatives were granted to M. Agrippa, Drusus the Elder, Tiberius (the would-be princeps), and Gaius Caesar; under Tiberius, they were granted to Germanicus and Drusus the Younger. All of these were part of the reigning emperor's closest family, which leads to the assumption that entrusting them with important missions in the provinces was also a point in the dynastic policies of the first two *principes*.

In principle, the time span covered in this book extends from 27 BC to AD 23, determined at one end by the introduction of an important regulation that led to the provinces being divided into imperial ones and those of the Roman people (*populi Romani*)[3] and, at the other, by the death of Drusus the Younger, the last member of the *domus Augusta* to act in the provinces while equipped with an extraordinary *imperium*. The later emperors of the Julio-Claudian dynasty would no longer assign important missions in the provinces to members of the reigning family. It also bears emphasizing that neither did the Flavii. After Titus returned to Rome in 71, having taken over from his father as the supreme commander in the Jewish War, Vespasian did not entrust either of his sons with a mission in the provinces again.

In terms of territory, the book discusses the provinces of the Roman Empire, its border regions on the Rhine and the Danube subject to Roman expansion at the time, and the client states that were within the area of Roman influence—that is, Judaea and Armenia. In other words, all those lands where the above-mentioned members of the ruling dynasty were active. Their actions in Rome and Italy, on the other hand, fall outside the scope of my investigations here.

The principal aim of this monograph is to demonstrate the special role played by members of the *domus Augusta* as the main executors of the expansionist policies of the first two emperors and as their aides in administering the Empire at a delicate point in the development of the principate as a new political system of power. At this point, it should be noted that entrusting members of the reigning family with various tasks in the provinces while they held special powers (*imperia extraordinaria*) is a phenomenon characteristic only of the rule of Augustus and Tiberius, disappearing under the subsequent rulers of the Julio-Claudian dynasty. Therefore, in the book, I attempt to discover the reasons why that was the case.

The text comprises four chapters that I have additionally subdivided into sections for greater clarity. Chapter 1 deals mostly with analyzing the legal status of members of the *domus Augusta* in the provinces. I also list in it the most spectacular cases of extraordinary *imperia* during the Republic in order to demonstrate the Republican origins of the special prerogatives that granted Augustus and his family members their power in the provinces. Further into the chapter, I discuss the nature and scope of the *imperia* of the several members of the emperor's family during their missions and compare their legal standing with that of other governors. It should be stressed that the special rank of those persons was also determined by other, extra-legal factors, such as being part of the reigning dynasty, the emperor's support, or their own *auctoritas*, something I also deal with in the chapter.

In the two chapters that follow, I discuss individual missions of members of the *domus Augusta* according to their geography. In Chapter 2, I focus on military campaigns they led on the Rhine and the Danube—that is, in lands that, under Augustus and Tiberius, became the main target of Roman expansion. Chapter 3 moves on to their activity in the East, where they carried out various part-diplomatic, part-military missions, as well as inspecting the provinces there.

In Chapter 4, I present the various honours that could be accorded to members of the imperial family, concentrating on those granted to reward military and diplomatic success—that is, triumphs, ovations, and imperatorial acclamations. I also discuss those honours that commemorated their achievements in those areas materially—that is, triumphal and honorific arches.

Augustus's and Tiberius's principates are fairly well documented in the sources. Naturally, that does not mean all the issues touched upon by this monograph are treated in the sources in ways satisfactory to us today. Very often, the accounts are ambiguous, their interpretation quite controversial, and so, in many matters, we are forced to resort to hypotheses of varying likelihood.

Of course, literary sources form the core of our corpus of sources. Ancient authors devoted much attention to all the aforementioned members of the *domus Augusta*, which is quite understandable, considering their rank. Here, I shall limit myself to listing the works that were the most significant for the subject matter of this book. Chronologically, the first is *Roman History* (*Historia Romana*) by Velleius Paterculus (c. 19 BC–c. AD 30). In Book Two, Paterculus recounts the events of Augustus's principate and the most important aspects of Tiberius's. His text is significant in that it was written by someone familiar with military matters; as a legate of Tiberius, he was an eyewitness of that commander's campaigns on the Rhine and the Danube. However, considerable caution should be exercised when analyzing his account, as Velleius was an ardent supporter of Tiberius, and his reports of his superior's actions are, no doubt, often greatly exaggerated.

Another source is the *Annals* (*Annales*) by Tacitus (c. AD 55–120), dated to the end of Trajan's, or the beginning of Hadrian's, principate. The part crucial to my investigation comprises Books 1–3, where the author described in detail Germanicus's military campaigns on the Rhine (AD 14–16), his mission in the East (AD 17–19), and the actions of Drusus the Younger in Illyria. Moreover, Tacitus supplies us with precise information on Germanicus's legal status during his expeditions in Germania and the East. Many passages of his account are confirmed by two epigraphical texts: the *Tabula Siarensis* and the *Senatus consultum de Cn. Pisone patre*; thanks to them, we know the historian based his work on official state documents. For my analysis here, Tacitus's text is indubitably one of the most valuable.

Another ancient work I use in the book is *Roman History* (*Historia Romana*) by Cassius Dio (c. AD 155–235), a monumental account, in Greek, of the history of Rome from its beginnings up to the reign of Severus Alexander, or, more precisely, AD 229. Vital to my investigation here are Books 51–58, which the author devoted to the times of Augustus and Tiberius. As a senator and twice consul, Cassius Dio was an expert on the reality of Roman politics and administration, as well as the principles on which the Empire ran. He was also well versed in the workings of the Roman military. His work is of great importance, because he devoted much space to the administrative and military actions of the group of people of interest to me, recounting valuable information on their legal standing. On the other hand, the wide time gap between him and the era of Augustus and Tiberius does constitute a flaw; while analyzing his account, one has to be careful of possible anachronisms. Unfortunately, some passages of those books have only come down to us in epitomes made by the Byzantine authors Xiphilinos and Zonaras and in mediaeval excerpts. In spite of that reservation, Cassius Dio's text is beyond any doubt, along with Tacitus, one of the two largest and most vital historical works on the reign of the first two *principes*.

Occasional, but often important, information on the military activity and diplomatic missions of members of the imperial family can also be found in the *Antiquities of the Jews* (*Antiquitates Judaicae*) by Flavius Josephus, the *Twelve Caesars* (*De vita Caesarum*) by Suetonius, and the *Epitome of Roman History* (*Epitomae de Tito Livio*) by Florus.

Epigraphical sources are one other type I have used in writing the monograph. First, I must list a long inscription from Pisa (referred to below as *DPG*), which contains the text of the honorific edict issued by the authorities of that Italian town on the death of Gaius Caesar, the elder of Augustus's adoptive sons. The inscription was discovered at the beginning of the 17th century in the church of Santa Maria Della Spina in Pisa, where it had been integrated into the altar; it was preserved in two pieces, having been broken vertically. Its text provides detailed information on posthumous honours the inhabitants of Pisa accorded the prematurely dead son of the princeps, including some that commemorated his Parthian campaign, at the same time revealing how people who lived in Rome's colonies responded to the deaths of prominent members of the ruling family.[4]

Two monumental inscriptions deserve special attention: the *Tabula Siarensis* (referred to below as *TS*) and the *Senatus consultum de Cn. Pisone patre* (below, *SCPP*), discovered, respectively, in the 1980s and 1990s, near Seville in Spain.[5] The first of those contains extensive fragments of the decree of the senate posthumously honouring Germanicus adopted in December AD 19 (*senatus consultum de memoria honoranda Germanici Caesaris*) and a short passage from the law concerning the same matter passed by the people early in 20 after a *rogatio* by the consuls M. Valerius Messala and M. Aurelius Cotta (*lex Valeria Aurelia*); it also supplies valuable information on that commander's military work in Germania and his mission in the East. Its drawback is that some parts are only preserved in fragments, so that, for some matters, we have to rely on hypothetical reconstructions of the missing passages. The other inscription has survived to our times in six copies, the best preserved being copy A, with only a few letters missing. The *SCPP* contains the text of the decree adopted by the senate in December AD 20 in connection with the trial of Gnaeus Calpurnius Piso, officially charged with being involved in Germanicus's death. It provides precise information on the legal status of Tiberius's son at the time he was active in the eastern provinces of the Empire and makes it possible to look into the conflict between him and Piso, who was the governor of Syria. At the same time, it throws valuable light on the relationships between the *domus Augusta*, the senate, the equestrian order, the plebs, and the army.

The third category of sources made use of in this work contains coins, with the so-called official emissions being of special importance.[6] Those include the coins issued by the imperial mint, located in Lugdunum until Caligula, and later in Rome, as well as those issued by the mint in Rome which was formally administered by the senate. Also important are provincial emissions, the message of which tends to agree with that of imperial coins.[7] We have several emissions that celebrate the military and political successes of members of the *domus Augusta* and the way they were rewarded for their achievements. Some of those coins were only minted under Caligula or Claudius, to commemorate the successes of members of their own family.

Papyrological sources were likewise significant for my inquiry. I should mention the so-called Cologne papyrus, containing a fragment of a Greek version of the funeral speech (*laudatio funebris*) given by Augustus in 12 BC at the funeral of Marcus Agrippa, his son-in-law and closest associate;[8] a few of its lines are crucial for the discussion of the scope of Agrippa's *imperium*.

Finally, iconographic sources must be mentioned as well. Among other objects, I will analyze the images on Boscoreale *skyphoi*, the *gemma Augustea*, and the so-called Sword of Tiberius. However, it ought to be emphasized that any analyses based on that group of sources can only be regarded as hypothetical, for two major reasons. First, there is no certainty as to which members of the incumbent dynasty were depicted on any of those finds; and, second, it is not possible to precisely determine the dates when they were made.

The issues investigated in this monograph have been discussed in many works of literature; thus, my motivation for writing the book was not a lack of specialized publications, but rather because my point of view on many issues differs from those of other researchers. Among the aspects of my subject matter that have caused the most controversy, there are Agrippa's *imperium* (widely disputed in scholarship), the date of Germanicus's first independent *imperium* and his first imperatorial acclamation, and Tiberius supposedly criticizing Germanicus's Egyptian expedition. As the existing literature on the subject is massive, I shall only list the most important titles here.

Of the studies that take a comprehensive look at Augustus's and Tiberius's principate, one must certainly mention the works of R. Syme, R. Seager, D. Kienast, W. K. Lacey, J. Bleicken, W. Eck, J. S. Richardson, B. Levick, and W. Havener.[9] The subject of the *domus Augusta* taking shape and its role in the rise of the principate as a new political system of power has been investigated by, among others, F. Hurlet, M. H. Dettenhofer, and B. Severy.[10]

We also have at our disposal several biographies of those members of the reigning family who were entrusted with important missions in the provinces under Augustus and Tiberius, such as those of M. Agrippa by M. Reinhold and J. M. Roddaz, of Germanicus by B. Gallotta and Y. Rivière, and of Drusus the Younger by M. L. G. Shaw.[11] In addition, a number of multi-author works deal with Agrippa and Germanicus; those are collections published as a result of conferences, including conferences held on anniversaries of their births and deaths.[12]

Much has been written, too, on the military campaigns led by members of the *domus Augusta* and their diplomatic missions in the East. Here, the publications deserving of mention are primarily those by E. Koestermann, D. Timpe, F. E. Romer, K. Christ, B. Gallotta, M. Pani, A. Bernecker, G. A. Lehmann, R. Wolters, A. Luther, and W. Eck.[13]

The issues of the legal standing of the several members of the *domus Augusta* and the scope of the *imperia* based on which they carried out their special missions have been analyzed by such authors as E. W. Gray, L. Koenen, K. Bringmann, J. Bleicken, P. Arnaud, F. Hurlet, K. M. Girardet, C. Koehn, A. Dalla Rosa, and F. J. Vervaet,[14] and the honours accorded them are the subject of works by S. Weinstock, R. Syme, W. D. Lebek, and C. B. Rose.[15]

Notes

1 Contemporary researchers often use the term *co-regent* to refer to persons from that group. See, for example, Bringmann 1977: 219–238; Hurlet 1994: 255–289; Arnaud 1994: 221–253. In my opinion, that kind of terminology is unjustified, as, formally speaking, the only two co-regents were Agrippa (from 18 BC) and Tiberius (from AD 4).

2 The expression *domus Augusta* only explicitly comes up in the sources towards the end of Augustus's reign, in Ovid first (Ovid. *Pont.* 2, 2, 74; 3, 1, 135; 4, 15, 16). However, in this book, I shall use the term to refer to the emperor's family from the very beginning of Augustus's principate.

3 The provinces of the people of Rome are often referred to in literature as *senatorial*, but F. Millar (1989: 93–97) demonstrated that the practice was unjustified. See also Ferrary (2001: 109, note 35; 111), who refers to that category of provinces as *proconsular* ones.

4 The most important editions of the Pisan inscriptions are Rowe 2002; Segenni 2011; and Lott 2012.

5 For the most important editions of the two inscriptions, see Eck, Caballos, Fernández 1996; Sánchez, Gutiérrez 1999; Lott 2012.

6 In this book, I have mostly used the classic coin corpus, which is *The Roman Imperial Coinage,* I²: *From 31 BC to AD 69*, ed. C. H. V. Sutherland, London 1984.

7 The essential corpus of provincial coins from the times of the Julio-Claudian dynasty is *Roman Provincial Coinage,* I: *From the Death of Caesar to the Death of Vitellius (44 BC–AD 69)*, eds. A. Burnett, M. Amandry, P. P. Ripollès, London 1992.

8 For the *editio princeps* of that document, see Koenen 1970: 217–283.

9 Syme 1939; Seager 2005 (2nd edn); Kienast 2009 (4th edn); Lacey 1996; Bleicken 1998; Eck 2007; Richardson 2012; Levick 1999, 2013; Havener 2016.

10 Hurlet 1997; Dettenhofer 2000; Severy 2003.

11 Reinhold 1933; Roddaz 1984; Gallotta 1987; Rivière 2016; Shaw 1990.

12 See, for example, Ceresa-Gastaldo (ed.) 1990; Bonamente, Segoloni (eds.), 1987; Fraschetti (ed.), 2000.

13 Koestermann 1953: 345–378, 1957: 429–479, 1958: 331–375; Timpe 1967: 289–306, 1968; Romer 1974; Christ 1977: 149–205; Gallotta 1981: 293–316;

Pani 1987: 1–23; Bernecker 1989; Lehmann 1989: 207–230; Wolters 1990a: 7–15, 2014–15: 197–209; Luther 2010: 103–127; Eck 2010: 19–33.

14 Gray 1970: 227–238; Koenen 1970: 217–283; Bringmann 1977: 219–238; Bleicken 1993: 117–133; Arnaud 1994: 221–253; Hurlet 1994: 255–289, 1997; Girardet 2000: 216–227; Koehn 2010: 301–322; Dalla Rosa 2014; Vervaet 2014, 2020: 121–201.

15 Weinstock 1966: 891–898; Syme 1979: 308–329; Lebek 1987: 129–148, 1989a: 45–82, 1991a: 47–78; Rose 1997.

1 The legal foundations of the power held by members of the *domus Augusta* within the provinces

1.1 Terminological remarks

I use a number of terms in the book to refer to various categories of *imperia*. One of those is *imperium proconsulare*, a term I use to indicate the powers of commanders of proconsul rank. However, there has been a tendency in recent years to deny the term being applicable to late Republic or early Empire situations, as some historians believe proconsul commanders active then held *imperium consulare* of chiefly military nature (*imperium militiae*).[1] This opinion is primarily based on the interpretation of a number of passages by Cicero, who writes that provincial governors and commanders acting outside Rome held *imperium consulare*, and is also based on the lack of the notion of *imperium proconsulare* in Republican sources.[2] This term appears for the first time in Valerius Maximus, writing at the time of Tiberius.[3] I believe that opinion is open to discussion: if we were to accept this interpretation, it would mean that the proconsuls were vested with the same *imperium* outside Rome as the consuls and were of equal status to commanders. This assumption is obviously unacceptable. Reading texts by ancient authors demonstrates, for instance, that, in some situations, consuls could issue orders to proconsuls, which clearly indicates their *imperium* was superior (*maius quam*) to that of proconsuls.[4] Under the circumstances, I find the claim that proconsuls held *imperium consulare militiae*—that is, their power was equal to that of consuls—unjustified. I am also unconvinced by the notion that the term *imperium proconsulare* never coming up in sources from Republican and Augustan times means no such *imperium* existed at the time. Although Republican authors do not use the *imperium proconsulare* notion *expressis verbis*, their texts do contain the phrase *imperium pro consule*.[5] I do not believe these terms are diametrically different in meaning. It seems that we are dealing with the same model of authority, expressed only in a different grammatical form. The justification for such an assumption can be the fact that, in sources dating back to the Empire, both terms are used interchangeably to describe the prerogatives of the proconsuls. In the *SCPP*, written during the rule of Tiberius, the prerogatives of Germanicus, who was delegated to the East as a proconsul, were described as *imperium pro consule*.[6] Valerius Maximus, writing in the same period, uses the notion of *imperium proconsulare* in his description of the authority of P. Cornelius Dolabella, who, in 43, was proconsul of Asia.[7] However, when referring to the prerogatives of Pompey, who was delegated proconsul in 77 and sent to oppose Sertorius, he uses the term *imperium pro consule*.[8] An important addition to the records of Valerius Maximus is a mention by Livy, who writes that Pompey was sent to Spain with proconsular authority.[9] These two examples clearly show that both terms possessed the same meaning. The fact that both Livy and Valerius Maximus used the term *imperium proconsulare* when referring to the situation during the Republic is crucial. Taking into account the fact that these authors were writing during the principates of Augustus and Tiberius—and, therefore, in a period not so far removed from the events described—it is difficult to assume that we are dealing with an anachronism.[10] In this context, the mentions in Livy and Maximus can be a further argument to confirm that the use of the term *imperium proconsulare* is justified in the description of the prerogatives of the proconsuls. For that reason, I shall consistently apply the term to refer to the powers of commanders of proconsul rank, both in the late Republic and during Augustus's and Tiberius's principates.[11]

Another term I use in the book is *imperia extraordinaria*, although, unlike *imperium proconsulare*, it is not a technical term. I employ it to refer to the extraordinary powers held by some commanders under the Republic and, later, members of the *domus Augusta* who carried out special missions in the provinces in the reigns of the first two emperors. The term is in widespread use in scholarly literature in reference to the powers of commanders called *privati cum imperio*, meaning for the most part people who received their *imperia* as *privati*—that is, even though at the time they held no office *cum imperio* or even though they had skipped some rungs in the *cursus honorum*.[12] However, I do find objectionable the aforementioned term *privatus cum imperio*: it is my belief that this term, apart from the fact that it does not appear in ancient sources, is unfortunate and raises serious concerns. The context in which the notion of *privatus* appears in ancient sources indicates serious opposition to the term *imperium*. Sources show that a public person becomes *privatus* after *imperium* ceases, not at the moment when it is gained.[13] We also have source evidence indicating that the granting of *imperium* to an individual not holding a position in office means that this person ceases to be *privatus*.[14]

I use the term *imperium maius* quite often in the book, but it ought to be stressed that, unlike *imperium consulare* or *proconsulare*, it is not a technical term, merely a general one reflecting the hierarchy applying to any two types of *imperium* (such as a consul's *imperium* being superior to a praetor's). I mostly use the term to refer to the *imperia* held by the emperors and those members of the *domus Augusta* who, as proconsuls acting in the provinces, had *imperia* greater than (*maiora quam*) those of proconsuls governing public provinces on the senate's mandate.

1.2 Extraordinary commands during the Republic

Under the Republic, military campaigns were conducted by diverse categories of commanders.[15] Besides magistrates *cum imperio*—that is, consuls and praetors—there were proconsuls and propraetors—former consuls and former praetors, whose military *imperium* was, as a rule, prolonged after their term of office was over in the practice of *prorogatio imperii*.[16] Under special circumstances, a campaign would be entrusted to a dictator appointed for a term of 6 months; the dictator had *imperium maius* relative to the powers of other magistrates. Beginning with the Second Punic War, the Roman arena of war started to see the rise of commanders whose careers differed greatly from the traditional *cursus honorum* of most Republican generals. These new commanders were nominated *extra ordinem* and had *imperium*, although as a rule they did not hold any office *cum imperio*.

1.2.1 P. Cornelius Scipio (Africanus)

The first example of a spectacular command in Republican times I want to highlight is the case of P. Cornelius Scipio (later Africanus), granted special *imperium* in Spain in 210 BC. After the deaths of the commanders in charge in the region—incidentally, they were Scipio's father and uncle—the senate faced the necessity of nominating a new general in their place. From Livy, we learn the incumbent consuls convoked the *comitia centuriata*, which unanimously elected Scipio—incidentally, the sole candidate—the commander for Spain. The historian reports Scipio held his command in the rank of proconsul,[17] which some scholars took to mean he received *imperium consulare*. They reached that conclusion based on the assumption that, under the Republic, proconsuls had the same military powers (*imperium consulare militiae*) as consuls.[18] I have already argued above (in Section 1.1) that their viewpoint seems unconvincing to me. Thus, we may assume Scipio acted in Spain based on a proconsular *imperium*.[19]

Granting young Scipio (who was only 24 at the time he received the command) a proconsul's powers was not extraordinary in and of itself: many commanders had led, and would lead, military campaigns with proconsular rank. The unusual circumstance was that Scipio received *imperium proconsulare* without having held either a praetorship or a consulship before, as, until then, proconsular-rank commands had only been given to ex-consuls and ex-praetors, whose *imperium* would usually be prolonged after their term of office ran out. Scipio, however, had only held an aedileship by then (in 213 BC), and, as we know, that office did not come with *imperium*.[20]

1.2.2 Pompey

No doubt one of the most flamboyant military careers of the late Republic was that of Gnaeus Pompeius; here, I would like to take a closer look at his three extraordinary commands—the special *imperia* of 77 BC (for Spain), 67

BC (to fight the pirates), and 57 BC (when Rome faced difficulties regarding its food supply).

The long war with Sertorius and the poor results obtained by Q. Caecilius Metellus who fought him convinced the senate to pick a new commander, who was to finally put an end to the war in Spain. Originally, the senate intended to assign that task to the two consuls of 77 BC, D. Junius Brutus and Mam. Aemilius Lepidus Livianus; however, both refused. Under the circumstances, the senate decided to accept L. Marcius Philippus's proposal and entrust the high command in Spain to Pompey. Sources tell us he was to act there armed with *imperium pro consule*,[21] but not how long the *imperium* would be valid. Still, we do know he held the command based on those prerogatives until 71 BC. The extraordinary character of his command in Spain lay in his attaining proconsulship without having held any offices beforehand or even being a member of the senate;[22] most likely, there had been no precedent in the history of Rome.[23]

In 67 BC, Pompey received his second extraordinary command. That time it targeted the pirates who prowled the Mediterranean, going so far as to raid towns in Italy. As the situation was becoming increasingly inconvenient for Rome, the plebeian tribune A. Gabinius put forward the motion to nominate from among the former consuls a commander with extraordinary powers who would solve the problem. The plebs then decided to assign that function to Pompey despite resistance from the senate, which, as Cassius Dio reports, was against granting him such broad prerogatives.[24] The range of prerogatives granted Pompey with the *lex Gabinia* was staggering: he had at his disposal virtually all of Rome's fleet, the legions stationed in the provinces, and unlimited funds, as well as the right to recruit soldiers and appoint fifteen legates subordinate to him, all of propraetorian rank (*legati pro praetore*).[25] Again, it needs to be stressed here that allowing Pompey his own legates was unprecedented in Rome's history until that point.[26]

The most detailed information on the type and scope of the *imperium* granted Pompey by the *lex Gabinia* is to be found in Velleius Paterculus, from whose account it is known the *imperium* could be evoked in all the Roman provinces on the Mediterranean up to 50 miles (or around 75 kilometres) inland, and was equal (*aequum*) to those of the proconsuls governing them.[27] That information correlates well with Cassius Dio mentioning Pompey was accorded a proconsul's status (ἀντὶ ὑπάτου).[28] Therefore, based on the accounts of those two authors, we may assume it was *imperium proconsulare*.[29] It is striking that the territorial scope of Pompey's *imperium* significantly exceeded the borders of a single province.[30] Unlike with standard magistracies, where the *imperium* remained valid for 1 year, his powers were to hold for 3.[31] Interestingly, his *imperium* did not stem either from coming into a specific magistracy *cum imperio* or from a *prorogatio imperii* granted a magistrate; instead, the political power involved was separated from the office it would normally come with, as we have already seen in the case of Scipio Africanus discussed above.

K. M. Girardet believed equating Pompey's *imperium* with those of other proconsular governors was meant to make it possible for him to act freely and without obstruction in their provinces,[32] a view I find incorrect, as the solution adopted did potentially allow for misunderstandings between Pompey and other proconsuls. A conflict of that kind did occur later on Crete, where the local governor, Q. Caecilius Metellus Creticus, waged war against the pirates on his own, ignoring any orders Pompey issued.[33] Granting Pompey *imperium aequum* relative to other proconsuls' *imperia* placed him, legally, on the same level with them, but, in practice, there can be no doubt that, owing to the funds and forces at his disposal, his power was immense, and the most apt conclusions are those of Velleius Paterculus and Cassius Dio, who both state plainly that, owing to the *lex Gabinia*, Pompey took control of all the lands under Rome's rule.[34]

In 57 BC, disruptions in the shipping of grain to Italy and the resulting rise in its price led to serious unrest among the Roman plebs; the senate decided to entrust Pompey with solving that problem too. After a motion by the consuls (the *lex Caecilia Cornelia de Cn. Pompeio extra ordinem rei frumentariae praeficiendo*), he was granted the supervision of grain supply (*cura annonae*) throughout the Mediterranean for 5 years and assigned fifteen legates to help him.[35] Cassius Dio reports he was given proconsular powers to carry out that task.[36] In K. M. Girardet's opinion, the nature of Pompey's duties (*procuratio annonae*) indicates his *imperium* was not military in nature,[37] which is absolutely unacceptable, as we know that, under the Republic, a proconsul's powers always had a military dimension to them (*militiae*), regardless of what his duties were in the province assigned to him.

From Cicero, we find out that, at the same time, and also owing to the grain crisis, the plebeian tribune Gaius Messius laid another proposal before the senate, in which he postulated granting Pompey unlimited funds, fleet, and army, as well as *imperium maius* relative to those of other governors in the provinces of Rome.[38] Messius's intentions were for such broad powers to prevent potential conflict between Pompey and other proconsuls, such as had been the case during the war on pirates, when the above-mentioned conflict with Metellus occurred, but, in the end, Messius's project was not adopted.[39] However, it ought to be emphasized that was the first attempt noted in our sources to grant a Roman commander such broad prerogatives.

1.2.3 G. Cassius Longinus

The second attempt at granting a Roman commander *imperium maius* in relation to that of other provincial governors comes up in the context of the events that took place in Rome in February of 43 BC, when the senate convened to decide who should be entrusted with the special command in the East in the war against P. Cornelius Dolabella, who had been deemed an enemy of the state (*hostis publicus*). From the account of Cicero, who took part in that session of the senate, we know he suggested the task be entrusted to Cassius Longinus, one of those who had killed Caesar.[40] Cicero's proposal would have had Cassius granted the province of Syria, where he would govern as a proconsul, and the high command of all military units stationed in the eastern provinces. For the purposes of the war against Dolabella, within the provinces of Syria, Asia, and Bithynia and Pontus, Cassius would have also had unlimited access to their financial and military resources. In addition, Cicero's project included granting Cassius *imperium maius* relative to those of the provinces he would have entered as part of his campaign.[41] However, just as in Pompey's case before, the motion was rejected, because the senate feared Cassius's position would become too strong.[42] The ambitions of the consuls then in office, Hirtius and Pansa, were probably of some importance as well, as they wanted to conduct the campaign against Dolabella themselves. As we know, it was to them that the senate ultimately gave the command in that war.[43]

The issue of choosing the commander for the war with Dolabella came up again at the beginning of May, after the two consuls died unexpectedly in the Battle of Mutina. This time, the senate decided to entrust the command of the campaign to Cassius.[44] It should be stressed that Cassius was by then in Syria province and in charge of the legions stationed there,[45] and so, to an extent, the decree formalized the status quo. C. Koehn argues convincingly that the wording of the senate's decree that granted Cassius the high command in the war against Dolabella probably followed Cicero's motion mentioned above and rejected by the senate several months prior.[46] On those grounds, he supposes Cassius was then assigned the province of Syria and granted *imperium pro consule*, which was to be *maius* relative to those of the governors of the neighbouring provinces should he have to enter those.[47] Such broad prerogatives were to allow Cassius easy access to those provinces' resources during military operations against Dolabella. Thus, in his case, greater *imperium* was due to a specific mission in specific provinces.[48]

The cases discussed above demonstrate that, under the Republic, particularly in its final period, a new category of commanders armed with special powers appeared next to the commanders and governors who followed the standard procedure. Its rise resulted from the extraordinary circumstances that came about during the 1st century BC (civil wars and threats to the state, both internal and external). The scope of their power differed fundamentally from the prerogatives of other *duces* active in the Roman provinces, as they could exercise their *imperium* in an area larger than one province (Pompey in 67 BC, and Cassius in 43). In addition, unlike the typical governors and commanders, some of the members of the group held *imperium* without having ever held any offices *cum imperio* (Scipio Africanus in 210 BC and Pompey in 77–71). Finally, in one case, our sources expressly confirm that the *imperium* was *maius* relative to the power of other provincial governors (Cassius in 43).

1.3 The nature and scope of the *imperia* held by members of the *domus Augusta*

1.3.1 The nature of Augustus's imperium

At the famed senate session of 13 January 27 BC, Octavian[49] ostentatiously "renounced" political power and handed the management of all matters of the state over to the senate and the people. The senators, however, did not "accept" his decision, eventually "persuading" him instead to take over the control of part of the Empire. No doubt that development had been pre-arranged by Octavian and his closest associates. Out of gratitude for his having "restored" the Republic, the senate granted Octavian the proud cognomen of *Augustus* (meaning, *filled with divine power*) and entrusted into his care a large province including Spain (without Baetica), Gaul, Syria, and Egypt—that is, the territories where a large majority of the legions were stationed. Meanwhile, the Romanized areas largely devoid of military forces fell under the rule of the people of Rome.[50]

Sadly, the sources provide no information on the legal grounds for Augustus's power in the provinces assigned him. From Cassius Dio, we just know it was granted to the princeps for 10 years.[51] The nature of Augustus's *imperium* in the provinces between the years 27 BC and 23 BC causes much controversy in scholarship. Essentially, present-day researchers fall into two camps on the issue. In some historians' opinion, Augustus governed his provinces based on the consular *imperium* he had had continuously as consul since 31 BC. J. Bleicken defines his power as *imperium consulare extra pomerium*, whereas M. Dettenhofer and K. M. Girardet see it as *imperium consulare militiae*.[52] A similar view is held by A. Ziółkowski, who stresses that Augustus's *imperium*, unlike that of other consuls, who could only make use of it in Rome (*domi*), applied in the provinces too.[53] Furthermore, according to some researchers, consular *imperium* made Augustus superior to proconsuls in public provinces, allowing him to interfere with the running of those provinces if he deemed it necessary.[54]

Meanwhile, other scholars believe that, from the year 27 BC on, Augustus governed his provinces based on *imperium proconsulare*.[55] Their assumption here is that, from Sulla's time on, consuls could only evoke their *imperium* in Rome and Italy, a principle ignored during the civil wars of the Republic's final years and then brought back by Augustus in 27 BC.[56] Thus, the period from 27 BC until 23 BC was allegedly Augustus's unbroken consulship and proconsulship both.[57] However, this view is not convincing. As I have mentioned above, Augustus's *imperium*, unlike that of other consuls, was *militiae* owing to the provinces assigned to the emperor in 27 BC, and so it could be exercised away from Rome as well. Moreover, no sources confirm that the princeps governed his provinces as a proconsul before 23 BC. The powers conferred on Augustus in 27 BC gave him full civilian and military authority in the provinces assigned him. He could also appoint his own legates (*legati Augusti pro praetore*) to supervise his provinces in his name[58] and efficiently monitor public provinces, with all proconsuls subordinate to him as the supreme commander and the only holder of auspices.[59]

Towards the end of June of 23 BC, Augustus unexpectedly resigned from consulship.[60] In order to make up for the loss of *imperium consulare domi*, the senate granted the princeps tribunician power for life. At the same time, those prerogatives of his that had, until then, constituted the legal basis for his reign outside Rome were modified.[61] Key information on the subject is supplied by Cassius Dio:

> τήν τε ἀρχὴν τὴν ἀνθύπατον ἐσαεὶ καθάπαξ ἔχειν ὥστε μήτε ἐν τῇ ἐσόδῳ τῇ εἴσω τοῦ πωμηρίου κατατίθεσθαι αὐτὴν μήτ᾽ αὖθις ἀνανεοῦσθαι, καὶ ἐν τῷ ὑπηκόῳ τὸ πλεῖον τῶν ἑκασταχόθι ἀρχόντων ἰσχύειν ἐπέτρεψεν.[62]
>
> they also permitted him to hold once and for all and for life the office of proconsul, so that he had neither to lay it down upon entering the pomerium nor to have it renewed again, and they gave him in the subject territory authority superior to that of the governor in each instance.[63]

The historian reports Augustus was then granted proconsular powers (*imperium pro consule*) for life, greater than (*maius quam*) the *imperia* of all provincial governors. The significant new feature was that Augustus's *imperium* would not expire on his crossing the pomerium—unlike that of all other proconsuls—which was supposed to protect the princeps from having to have it renewed each time he left the city.[64] Many historians accept that information in Cassius Dio, assuming that, in 23 BC, Augustus received the so-called greater proconsular *imperium*, which at that point became, alongside the *tribunicia potestas*, one of the two major pillars of his power and a major component in the power of successive emperors later on.[65] J. L. Ferrary thinks Augustus could only use his greater *imperium* if he appeared in person in a province governed by a senatorial proconsul,[66] an opinion I do not find convincing, as the passage from Dio quoted above does not indicate that the emperor could only exercise his *imperium* after arriving in the province. In fact, such a solution would have no doubt been irrational. Therefore, I think Augustus was able to freely interfere with the affairs of proconsular provinces and issue *mandata* to their governors, both while visiting the provinces and without leaving Rome.

J. Rich believes that the granting of superior *imperium* to Augustus in 23 BC was closely connected with the plans for his journey to the East in 22 BC, when he would also visit proconsular provinces.[67] Considering that visit only took place the following year, his opinion is open to discussion, and I find myself more convinced by the view of C. Koehn, who thinks those prerogatives were conferred on Augustus chiefly to make up for his losing the *imperium consulare militiae*, which had formed the basis for his control over provinces since 27 BC. Thus, the point of the regulation was to redefine Augustus's formal status in the provinces after he had resigned from consulship.[68]

However, some scholars, especially in recent years, have questioned the reliability of Dio's account regarding Augustus being granted *imperium maius*. W. Ameling believes the senate granted Augustus a 5-year-long *imperium* equal (*aequum*) to the *imperium* of proconsuls in the public provinces and, to support his thesis, he cites the well-known passage from the *Res Gestae* in which the emperor emphasizes that he did not have any more power than his colleagues in the office. Ameling concludes that the princeps cannot have had *imperium maius*, as that would explicitly belie his own words. Instead, Ameling thinks that particular solution was dictated by the political crisis in Rome in 23 BC (with increased opposition to Augustus and Varro Murena's conspiracy), which supposedly convinced the princeps to curtail his own prerogatives (by resigning from consulship and adopting *imperium aequum*). Because, as Ameling claims, such prerogatives did not conflict with Republican tradition, they could not provoke the opposition.[69]

However, Ameling's view fails to convince. I do not believe the famous sentence from the *Res Gestae* he draws on has any bearing on the discussion of the nature of Augustus's power in the provinces, as the words refer primarily to his status as a consul in Rome. Augustus's goal was to convince the audience of his self-eulogy that, during his consulship, he had had—formally speaking—the same prerogatives as the consuls he shared the office with and had only been superior to them by virtue of his *auctoritas*.[70] Nor did granting him *imperium maius* necessarily have to violate Republican traditions, as indicated by the case of Cassius, who had been granted such powers in the eastern provinces in 43 BC.[71]

Therefore, I see no reason to reject Cassius Dio's information regarding Augustus receiving superior *imperium*, especially as the accuracy of his account is indirectly confirmed by other sources. On that subject, it is worth bringing up the testimony of Flavius Josephus, who quotes a letter written by Augustus to G. Norbanus Flaccus, the proconsul of Asia. In the letter, the princeps ordered that the rights of the Jews inhabiting the province be respected. Josephus also quotes the letter of that proconsul to the authorities of Sardes, also calling on them to respect the rights of the Jews living there, in which he invoked the directives (*mandata*) he had received from the princeps.[72] Thus, Josephus's account clearly proves Augustus could issue orders to governors of public provinces. I do not believe the situation recounted by him resulted merely from the emperor's *auctoritas*, being also an effect of him holding greater *imperium*.[73]

Another source to supply indirect evidence in support of Cassius Dio's version is the *SCPP*. The inscription expressly states that, as princeps, Tiberius had *imperium maius* to that of all the provincial governors in the Empire.[74] We know Tiberius gained that kind of power in AD 13, shortly before Augustus's death, when his *imperium* was made equal to that of Augustus in all the provinces by a decree of the senate, later approved by the people.[75] Therefore, if that regulation resulted in Tiberius having *imperium maius*, Augustus's *imperium* must have been the same.

Moreover, some historians believe Dio guilty of an anachronism where he refers to Augustus's *imperium* as *proconsulare* and so defines the powers granted him in 23 BC as *imperium consulare*,[76] a claim based on the controversial assumption that the *imperium* of proconsuls was in fact consular under the Republic. The same researchers emphasize that the term *imperium proconsulare* is only explicitly encountered in the reign of Tiberius and after, and so it should not be used in reference to Augustus's powers. I have presented my counter-arguments above (in Section 1.1) and so see no reason to correct Dio's account in that regard.

Another view held by some scholars does seem correct, however: namely, that Dio made a mistake in reporting Augustus was granted a proconsul's powers for life.[77] Instead, they believe the prerogatives were initially conferred on him for 5 years (a *quinquennium*). Thus, they were first renewed in 18 BC, and later regularly every 10 years—that is, in 8 BC, AD 3 and AD 13.[78]

In summary, we can say the legal aspects of Augustus's authority in the provinces were not established all in one go in a single act of law, instead evolving over time, the decisions of 23 BC being crucial. Between 27 and 23 BC, the emperor's power in the provinces and command of the army resulted from a consular *imperium militiae*; from 23 BC on, when he had resigned as consul, he was to govern his *provincia* as proconsul, and his *imperium* was defined as *maius quam* relative to those of all provincial governors. One specific feature of his power was its separation from the office that traditionally went with it: the princeps held *imperium*, even though he was neither a magistrate nor a promagistrate *cum imperio*.[79] Unlike other special *imperia* known from the late Republican period, which only covered a few provinces (such as Cassius's in 43 BC), Augustus's *imperium maius* applied in all the provinces of the *Imperium Romanum*. After the year 23, *imperium proconsulare* was, next to *tribunicia potestas*, one of the two most vital components of Augustus's imperial power. It should be emphasized that the title of *proconsul* is extremely rare in Augustus's titulature. It is actually only confirmed in the decree from El Bierzo in Spain, dated to 15 BC.[80] The model of controlling the army and the provinces worked out in the reign of the first princeps was then adopted by successive emperors of the principate era.

1.3.2 M. Agrippa

The first member of the imperial family to receive extraordinary prerogatives in the provinces was Marcus Agrippa. Although it is beyond discussion that Agrippa was Augustus's second-in-command and the second most important person in the state from the moment the principate was established until his death, specifying the exact nature of the *imperium* based on which he carried out various tasks in the provinces of the Empire has caused intense controversy. The reason is primarily the sparse and ambiguous character of what sources we have; whereas ancient authors provide us with a fair amount of information on Agrippa's actions in the provinces, they are extremely reticent and imprecise when it comes to the exact nature and scope of his *imperium*, because they were not particularly interested in complicated legal nuance. What is more, except for Velleius Paterculus, ancient historians, especially Cassius Dio, wrote a long time after the events on which they reported, which leads to more interpretation problems. A new incentive to research Agrippa's *imperium* was provided by the publication of the Cologne papyrus, which contains a fragment of a Greek version of the funeral speech (*laudatio funebris*) Augustus gave at his friend's funeral in 12 BC.[81] It is probably a Greek translation of the original *laudatio*, which was written down after Agrippa's death to then be circulated throughout the Empire. The papyrus is usually dated to the last decade of the 1st century;[82] only a version of it from Egypt, specifically Fayum, happens to survive to this day.[83] However, it is not known when exactly the papyrus was discovered, only that it comes from a private collection, the owner of which gifted it to the Institute of Ancient History at the University of Cologne.[84] Although the document does not explicitly mention Agrippa, we can be certain the honours listed in it refer to Augustus's friend and son-in-law, as first granting and then prolonging *tribunicia potestas* are mentioned, in 18 and 13 BC, respectively, leaving no room to doubt that it was Agrippa who was intended. For an investigation of the exact nature of his *imperium*, lines 7–11 are crucial, in which we read he was granted special powers in the provinces:

1 ἡ [γ]ὰρ τοι δημαρχικὴ σοι ἐξουσία εἰς πέντε
ἔτε κατὰ δόγμα συνκλήτου
Λέντ<λ>ων ὑπατευόντων ἐδόθη καὶ
4 πάλιν αὔτη εἰς ἄλλην Ὀλυμπιάδα
[ὑ]πατευόντων Τιβερίου Νέρωνος
καὶ Κυιν<τι>λίου Οὐάρου γαμβρῶν τῶν
σῶν προσεπεδόθη. καὶ εἰς [ς] ἅς δήποτέ
8 σε ὑπαρχείας τὰ κοινὰ τῶν Ῥωμαίων
ἐφέλκοιτο, μηθενὸς ἐν ἐκείναις
ἐξουσίαν μείζω <εἶναι> τῆς σῆς
ἐν νόμωι ἐκυρώθη.[85]

tribunicia enim potestas tibi in quinque
annos ex senatus consulto
Lentulis consulibus data et

rursus in alterum quinquennium
Tiberio Nerone et Quintilio Varo consulibus generis
tuis delata est. et quascumque te in
provincias res publica Romana
adhiberet, nullius in illis
ut esset imperium maius tuo,
per legem sanctum est.[86]

In whatever of the provinces to which the public affairs of the Romans might take you, it was established in law that no one's *imperium* in those places would be greater than yours.[87]

However, interpreting the passage is not without its difficulties, as it must be remembered it is not an official document we are dealing with, but rather a Greek copy of the Latin *laudatio*. Moreover, the papyrus is ambiguous in how it refers to Agrippa's powers relative to those of other governors, allowing for two interpretations.

The first problem we face is determining the date when Agrippa received the special prerogatives in the provinces that the Cologne papyrus mentions, as it only lists the consular date when he was granted tribunician powers, without, unfortunately, specifying when the *lex* was passed that conferred on him the extraordinary powers in the provinces. Assuming the prerogatives were listed in the text in the order they were granted, we may deduce the *lex* in question was adopted in 18 BC at the earliest—the year Augustus's son-in-law first attained *tribunicia potestas*—but perhaps only in 13 BC, when his tribunician powers were extended for another 5 years.[88] The latter option could be supported by Cassius Dio, who mentions Agrippa was granted *imperium maius* than that of other governors outside Italy and sees Agrippa's special prerogatives as connected to his mission in Pannonia in 13 BC:

Κἀν τούτῳ τὸν Ἀγρίππαν ἐκ τῆς Συρίας ἐλθόντα τῇ τε δημαρχικῇ ἐξουσίᾳ αὖθις ἐς ἄλλα ἔτη πέντε ἐμεγάλυνε καὶ ἐς τὴν Παννονίαν πολεμησείουσαν ἐξέπεμψε, μεῖζον αὐτῷ τῶν ἑκασταχόθι ἔξω τῆς Ἰταλίας ἀρχόντων ἰσχῦσαι ἐπιτρέψας.[89]

Meanwhile he increased the power of Agrippa, who returned from Syria, by giving him the tribunician power again for another five years, and he sent him out to Pannonia, which was eager for war, entrusting him with greater authority than the officials outside Italy ordinarily possessed.[90]

Again, that interpretation seems doubtful to me. First, I do not believe the papyrus has to list Agrippa's honours in the order they were granted; rather, it does so in the order of their importance. That is why it starts with tribunician powers (Tacitus's *summi fastigii vocabulum*),[91] placing special powers in the provinces second. Thus, we have no grounds to conclude with certainty that Agrippa had *tribunicia potestas* first, and the special *imperium* only later. Second, we must ask why Agrippa should have received extraordinary *imperium* for the military campaign in Pannonia, as the passage from Cassius Dio suggests. Had his previous missions in imperial and public provinces in both the West and the East of the Empire not required such prerogatives? After all, Pannonia was not subject to Roman administration at the time, and his actions there would not have involved interfering with the powers of other governors.[92] Therefore, at that point, he did not need such vast prerogatives, and I believe we ought to interpret Dio's account somewhat differently. Namely, I suspect he refers, not to Agrippa receiving special *imperium* outside Italy for the first time, but rather to his having it prolonged again, as with his tribunician powers.[93] In other words, despite not having strong evidence in the sources, I suppose the *lex* granting Agrippa special *imperium* in the provinces had been adopted earlier—most likely as early as 23 BC.[94] My guess would be it was done with his first eastern mission in mind (in the years 23–22 BC), which had among its objectives inspecting those provinces (particularly the public ones). That involved having special powers that would make it possible to interfere with the decisions of the governors there. I suspect Agrippa received such prerogatives in the provinces shortly after the senate conferred similar powers (the *imperium maius quam*) on Augustus when he had resigned from consulship in 23 BC.[95]

Ascertaining the territorial range of Agrippa's *imperium* is another matter. Both Velleius Paterculus and Cassius Dio mention Agrippa's departure for the East in their narratives of 23 BC, allegedly caused by his rivalry with Augustus's nephew Marcellus, but they differ in certain details: Paterculus lists Agrippa's destination as Asia, whereas Dio says it was Syria. He adds that, in the end, Augustus's son-in-law never got there, stopping in Mytilene on Lesbos:

> *Post cuius obitum Agrippa, qui sub specie ministeriorum principalium profectus in Asiam, ut fama loquitur, ob tacitas cum Marcello offensiones praesenti se subduxerat tempori ...*[96]
>
> After his death Agrippa, who had set out for Asia on the pretext of commissions from the emperor, but who, according to current gossip, had withdrawn, for the time being, on account of his secret animosity for Marcellus ...[97]

ῥαΐσας δ᾽ οὖν, καὶ μαθὼν τὸν Μάρκελλον οὐκ ἐπιτηδείως τῷ Ἀγρίππᾳ διὰ τοῦτ᾽ ἔχοντα, ἐς τὴν Συρίαν εὐθὺς τὸν Ἀγρίππαν, μὴ καὶ διατριβή τις καὶ ἀψιμαχία αὐτοῖς ἐν ταὐτῷ οὖσι συμβῇ, ἔστειλε. Καὶ ὃς ἐκ μὲν τῆς πόλεως εὐθὺς ἐξώρμησεν, οὐ μέντοι καὶ ἐς τὴν Συρίαν ἀφίκετο, ἀλλ᾽ ἔτι καὶ μᾶλλον μετριάζων ἐκεῖσε μὲν τοὺς ὑποστρατήγους ἔπεμψεν, αὐτὸς δὲ ἐν Λέσβῳ διέτριψε.[98]

> When he recovered, therefore, and learned that Marcellus because of this was not friendly toward Agrippa, he immediately sent the latter to Syria, so that no occasion for scoffing or for skirmishing might arise between them by their being together. And Agrippa straightway set out from the city, but did not reach Syria; instead, acting with even more than his usual moderation, he sent his lieutenants thither, and tarried himself in Lesbos.[99]

At first glance, the passages just quoted might imply Agrippa's *imperium* during his first mission in the East (23–22 BC) was limited to the province of Asia (formally under the rule of the senate) or the imperial province of Syria. Based on the passage in Cassius Dio, H. Siber put forward the claim that, during that time, Agrippa was merely *legatus Augusti pro praetore* for Syria.[100] However, that opinion is unconvincing. Considering that Agrippa was Augustus's second-in-command and the second most important person in the state, it seems unlikely he would be sent to the eastern provinces as a mere *legatus Augusti*.[101] However, the passages from Velleius Paterculus and Cassius Dio ought not be taken literally; neither author means a specific Roman province in the East, instead using those names metonymically for all of the Roman East.[102] It is in a similar sense that Flavius Josephus uses the term *Ἀσία* when writing about Agrippa's return from the East in 13 BC:

> Ἀγρίππου γε μὴν ἀνιόντος εἰς τὴν Ῥώμην μετὰ τὴν διοίκησιν τῶν ἐπὶ τῆς Ἀσίας δεκαετῆ γεγενημένην.[103]
>
> Agrippa was returning to Rome, after he had finished his ten years government in Asia.[104]

He certainly intends, not Asia as a specific province of the people of Rome, but the whole continent—that is, all Roman provinces in the East.[105] He is at any rate more precise when he says Agrippa governed all the provinces across the Ionian Sea:

> πέμπεται δ' Ἀγρίππας τῶν πέραν Ἰονίου διάδοχος Καίσαρι.[106]
>
> Now Agrippa was sent to succeed Caesar in the government of the countries beyond the Ionian Sea.[107]

The expression πέραν Ἰονίου renders the Latin *transmarinae provinciae*, which refers to all the eastern provinces.[108] That lets us deduce that, during his two missions in the East (in 23–22 BC and 17–13 BC), Agrippa held *imperium* that applied in all the provinces of the Roman East.

It is another question whether Agrippa's *imperium* was really limited to the eastern provinces, as the passage from Josephus suggests. In fact, that would be a wrong deduction to make. Josephus is not being quite exact when he writes Agrippa governed the East for 10 years, or from 23 to 13 BC;

actually, in the meantime (between the years 20 and 18 BC), he also carried out missions in western provinces of Rome, specifically in Spain and Gaul. Therefore, his *imperium* must have covered the western provinces of the Empire too, and Flavius Josephus only lists the provinces where Agrippa had *imperium* during his mission in the East. That does not justify the claim that it was confined to them.[109] Moreover, the Cologne papyrus does not indicate that Agrippa's *imperium* was territorially limited to a subset of provinces either (καὶ εἰς [ς] ἅς δήποτέ σε ὑπαρχείας τὰ κοινὰ τῶν Ῥωμαίων ἐφέλκοιτο), and the passage from Cassius Dio quoted above also clearly confirms Augustus's son-in-law could use his *imperium* in any province other than Italy (μεῖζον αὐτῷ τῶν ἑκασταχόθι ἔξω τῆς Ἰταλίας ἀρχόντων ἰσχῦσαι ἐπιτρέψας). Thus, we may assume that Agrippa's *imperium*, like Augustus's, extended to all the provinces of the *Imperium Romanum*.[110]

There is much debate among modern researchers primarily regarding the nature of Agrippa's prerogatives and, specifically, whether his *imperium* was *maius* relative to those of other governors. The reason for all that controversy is an ambiguous expression used in the text of the papyrus to refer to the relationship between Agrippa's *imperium* and the *imperia* of other provincial governors (μηθενὸς ἐν ἐκείναις ἐξουσίαν μείζω <εἶναι> τῆς σῆς). L. Koenen, who first edited and published the document, did not doubt *imperium maius* relative to the *imperia* of the proconsuls of public provinces and legates of imperial ones was meant,[111] but other scholars were sceptical, believing only *imperium aequum* was meant—that is, power equal to that of other governors.[112] In the opinion of E. Badian, one of the more significant supporters of that interpretation, Agrippa cannot have received *imperium maius*, because no commander had held such broad powers under the Republic, and, in his view, Agrippa's prerogatives cannot have outdone the Republican precedent known so far. Thus, he thought the passage in question ought to be read, "Your power was to be equal to that of anyone else in those provinces."[113] His opinion is largely shared by W. Ameling, who believes that, owing to the political crisis that occurred in Rome in 23 BC (with the Republican opposition becoming more active and tensions rising within the *domus Augusta* because of the supposed adoption of Marcellus), Augustus could not grant Agrippa such broad powers, lest the situation become even tenser. In Ameling's opinion, those circumstances also forced the princeps to reduce his own prerogatives; he allegedly resigned from the consulship he had held continuously since 31 BC, accepting proconsular *imperium* instead, equal to that of the proconsuls of the provinces of the people.[114] In other words, he believes that, if Augustus did not have *imperium maius*, Agrippa could hardly receive it.[115]

I find the claim about *imperium aequum* completely erroneous. After all, even regardless of how controversial it is to see conflict within the *domus Augusta* in 23 BC,[116] we have indirect evidence in the sources that Agrippa's *imperium* was, in fact, *maius* relative to the governors' powers. Namely,

Josephus quotes in his work letters Agrippa wrote to the authorities of Ephesus and Cyrene with instructions on respecting the rights and customs of the Jews living there,[117] mostly the right to send sacred money to Jerusalem and the right not to be called before a court of law on the Shabbat:

> Ἀγρίππας δὲ καὶ αὐτὸς ἔγραψεν ὑπὲρ τῶν Ἰουδαίων τὸν τρόπον τοῦτον:ʽἈγρίππας Ἐφεσίων ἄρχουσι βουλῇ δήμῳ χαίρειν. τῶν εἰς τὸ ἱερὸν τὸ ἐν Ἱεροσολύμοις ἀναφερομένων ἱερῶν χρημάτων τὴν ἐπιμέλειαν καὶ φυλακὴν βούλομαι τοὺς ἐν Ἀσίᾳ Ἰουδαίους ποιεῖσθαι κατὰ τὰ πάτρια. τούς τε κλέπτοντας ἱερὰχρήματα τῶν Ἰουδαίων καταφεύγοντάς τε εἰς τὰς ἀσυλίας βούλομαι ἀποσπᾶσθαι καὶ παραδίδοσθαι τοῖς Ἰουδαίοις, ᾧ δικαίῳ ἀποσπῶνται οἱ ἱερόσυλοι. ἔγραψα δὲ καὶ Σιλανῷ τῷ στρατηγῷ ἵνα σάββασιν μηδεὶς ἀναγκάζῃ Ἰουδαῖον ἐγγύας ὁμολογεῖν.[118]
>
> Agrippa to the magistrates, council and people of Ephesus, greeting. It is my will that the care and custody of the sacred monies belonging to the account of the Temple in Jerusalem shall be given to the Jews in Asia in accordance with their ancestral customs. And if any men steal the sacred monies of the Jews and take refuge in places of asylum, it is my will that they be dragged away from them and turned over to the Jews under the same law by which temple-robbers are dragged away from asylum. I have also written to the praetor Silanus that no one shall compel the Jews to give bond on the Sabbath.[119]

> Μᾶρκος Ἀγρίππας Κυρηναίων ἄρχουσιν βουλῇ δήμῳ χαίρειν. οἱ ἐν Κυρήνῃ Ἰουδαῖοι, ὑπὲρ ὧν ἤδη ὁ Σεβαστὸς ἔπεμψε πρὸς τὸν ἐν Λιβύῃ στρατηγὸν τότε ὄντα Φλάβιον καὶ πρὸς τοὺς ἄλλους τοὺς τῆς ἐπαρχίας ἐπιμελουμένους, ἵνα ἀνεπικωλύτως ἀναπέμπηται τὰ ἱερὰ χρήματα εἰς Ἱεροσόλυμα, ὡς ἔστιν αὐτοῖς πάτριον, ἐνέτυχόν μοι νῦν ὡς ὑπό τινων συκοφαντῶν ἐπηρεάζοιντο καὶ ὡς ἐν προφάσει τελῶν μὴ ὀφειλομένων κωλύοιντο: οἷς ἀποκαθιστάνειν κατὰ μηδένα τρόπον ἐνοχλουμένοις, καὶ εἴ τινων ἱερὰ χρήματα ἀφῄρηνται τῶν πόλεων τοὺς εἰς ταῦτα ἀποκεκριμένους καὶ τοῦτα διορθώσασθαι τοῖς ἐκεῖ Ἰουδαίοις κελεύω.[120]
>
> Marcus Agrippa to the magistrates, council and people of Cyrene, greeting. The Jews in Cyrene, on whose behalf Augustus has already written to the former praetor of Libya, Flavius, and to the other officials of the province to the effect that the sacred monies may be sent up to Jerusalem without interference, as is their ancestral custom, now complain to me that they are being threatened by certain informers and prevented (from sending these monies) on the pretext of their owing taxes, which are in fact not owed. I therefore order that these monies be restored to the Jews, who are in no way to be molested, and if sacred monies have been taken away from any cities, the persons in charge of these matters shall see that amends are made to the Jews there.[121]

Both those cities lay in provinces that were formally governed by the senate: Cyrene, in the remit of the proconsul of Crete and Cyrenaica, and Ephesus, in that of the proconsul of Asia. Therefore, Agrippa's letters prove he had the final word in matters that fell within the powers of the governors of those provinces. His being able to issue such orders (*mandata*) did not just follow from his *auctoritas*, as K. M. Girardet suggests, but rather primarily from his greater *imperium*;[122] it must be remembered in this case that Agrippa's *auctoritas* was not equal to Augustus's.

Of course, it is possible to question the authenticity of the letters quoted by Flavius Josephus and wonder if they might not be simply a fiction created by that author, but I do not believe we have grounds for such scepticism. Even if they are not literal copies of Agrippa's instructions, I see no reason to question the mere fact of Augustus's son-in-law interfering in the provinces of the people during his stay in the East. Furthermore, Josephus quotes a letter from the proconsul of Asia, Iullus Antonius, to the authorities of Ephesus, in which he confirms their duty to respect the rights and customs of the Jews of Asia province, invoking Augustus's and Agrippa's earlier orders on the matter.[123] Agrippa's interference in the matters of public provinces is also confirmed by epigraphical sources: an inscription exists containing part of his letter to the Gerousia of the city of Argos, which was in the jurisdiction of the proconsul of Achaea.[124] In it, Agrippa ordered that the old institution regain its lost powers and privileges, promising they would also be respected in the future. A hypothesis can be found in scholarship that the restored Gerousia was to take care of the imperial cult.[125]

While analyzing the text of the Cologne papyrus, we must also take into account its wider context: it has to be remembered it lists the powers of Agrippa, the second most powerful man of the state and Augustus's second-in-command. It is, thus, hard to imagine that man was granted *imperium* equal to that of other proconsuls, let alone ordinary imperial legates. Another indication that his prerogatives were exceptional is that they were conferred through an extraordinary procedure (on which see below). In my opinion, another argument for the text intending *imperium maius* is the passage, already discussed above, from Cassius Dio (54, 28, 1), who also writes Agrippa was granted such powers.[126]

The analysis of source material carried out above makes the following conclusions possible: as the closest associate of the princeps, Agrippa received special *imperium proconsulare*, which applied in all the provinces of Rome and was *maius* relative to the powers of the proconsuls of public provinces and of imperial legates. Most likely, he was already granted those prerogatives in 23 BC for his first mission in the East and then used them to carry out various tasks in both the western and the eastern part of the Empire between the years 23 and 12 BC. His *imperium* would remain valid for 5 years and was twice renewed afterwards, until 18 and 13 BC, respectively.[127] It is worth emphasizing Agrippa's *imperium*, like Augustus's, was not tied to him holding any specific office; neither did he have an official function in provincial administration. Thus, we see here separation of *imperium* from offices, which, as noted above, was specific to how Augustus and members of his immediate family wielded political power.

1.3.3 *Drusus the Elder*

The next member of the imperial family to receive extraordinary prerogatives was Drusus the Elder. After 12 BC, he conducted military campaigns in Germania, most likely in the rank of *legatus Augusti pro praetore*.[128] Suetonius and Cassius Dio report that, 1 year later, Drusus was rewarded for his successes in Germania with triumphal insignia (*ornamenta triumphalia*) and the right to hold an ovation, but also with *imperium proconsulare* (*ἀνθυπάτου ἐξουσίᾳ*), which was to apply from the moment Augustus's stepson resigned from praetorship—that is, from the beginning of 10 BC.[129] From then on and until his unexpected death in 9 BC, Drusus led his campaigns in Germania with the rank of a proconsul holding independent *imperium*. Dio's account is confirmed by an inscription from a dynastic monument erected in the reign of Claudius in Campus Martius, which attests to Drusus having held the title of proconsul.[130] The territorial extent of Drusus's *imperium* probably also included the provinces in Gaul, in order to give him free access to their resources during his expeditions against German tribes. Because Augustus's stepson died prematurely, it is difficult to tell for how long the *imperium* was granted. By analogy with other members of the imperial family, we can suppose it was for 5 years.[131]

1.3.4 *Tiberius*

Drusus's elder brother received independent military *imperium* at approximately the same time as he did, but researchers disagree on whether that happened already in 11 BC for his campaign in Pannonia and Dalmatia, or only in 8 BC, when, after Drusus's death, he took over the command of the legions in Germania.[132] In my opinion, a passage in Cassius Dio is crucial for determining the answer: the historian mentions that, in 11 BC, Tiberius was granted the same honours for his Pannonian and Dalmatian campaign as Drusus had been.[133] Although he does not explicitly mention proconsular *imperium*, it is quite likely it was among the honours meant, as Augustus's stepson received it at the time. Another important piece of evidence in favour of that investiture being dated to the year 11 BC is Tiberius's first imperatorial acclamation, which he won in 10 or 9 BC,[134] a clear indication that, at the time, he was no longer a mere *legatus Augusti*, but instead had independent *imperium* (as holding it was, along with the emperor's permission, a prerequisite for receiving the title of *imperator*).[135] As, in 11 BC, Tiberius, unlike Drusus, held no magistracy, he did not have to put off acting on his *imperium*.[136] It was probably set up to be valid for 5 years; between the years 11 and 9 BC, Tiberius acted based on it in Pannonia, and then, from 8 to 7 BC, in Germania. In 6 BC, it was extended, but would not be put to use, as Tiberius withdrew from political life and went to Rhodes.

He returned to Rome in AD 2, to be adopted by Augustus 2 years later and receive *tribunicia potestas* for 10 years, meaning he was officially designated the heir of the princeps.[137] In 4, he was once more dispatched to Germania to take command of the legions there. It is commonly accepted in scholarship that, at the time, he was also granted *imperium proconsulare*.[138] Even though no sources mention that explicitly, the view would seem absolutely correct, as we know that, shortly after his adoption, the princeps sent Tiberius on a new mission to Germania. As he was supposed to command the legions there, he must have had the military power necessary.[139] Like the tribunician powers, the *imperium* was conferred on him for 10 years. Armed with it, he conducted military campaigns in Germania in the years 4–6, in Pannonia and Dalmatia in 6–9, and again in Germania in 10–12.

In AD 13, Tiberius's prerogatives in the provinces were considerably increased in connection with his intended succession.[140] A *senatus consultum*, ratified then by the people as well, conferred on him *imperium aequum* relative to that of the princeps in all the provinces of Rome, meaning that, from then on, his *imperium* was *maius* in relation to those of all other governors and military commanders throughout the Empire.[141] From that point on, like Augustus, Tiberius had *summum imperium auspiciumque*, which applied in all of Rome's provinces.[142] It is worth noting that, this time, receiving such powers did not involve any specific mission; rather, it indicated that Tiberius was designated as Augustus's successor.

1.3.5 Gaius Caesar

At the beginning of 1 BC, possibly even as early as 2 BC, Augustus sent his grandson and adopted son to the East.[143] The objective of the mission was primarily to set the situation in Armenia in order and to normalize relations with the Parthian kingdom. Before he left Rome, Gaius Caesar received certain special prerogatives. From Cassius Dio, we learn they took the form of *imperium proconsulare*.[144] Ancient authors report that, geographically, Gaius's *imperium* extended to all the provinces of the Roman East. Suetonius refers to Augustus's son comprehensively as *praepositus Orientis*, and Tacitus writes that his post was *ad res Orientis*.[145] Both those historians' accounts correspond well with a place in *Fasti Praenestini* that specifies Gaius's remit as overseas provinces (*transmarinae provinciae*).[146] On those grounds, we may assume Gaius's *imperium*, like Agrippa's before, applied in all the provinces and regions under the rule of Rome to the east of the Ionian Sea. It was probably meant to remain valid for 5 years.[147]

Some scholars suppose Gaius's *imperium* was *maius* relative to those of all the governors in the East,[148] but that belief finds no confirmation in sources, which, in Agrippa's and Germanicus's cases, do mention such broad prerogatives being granted. That straightaway begs the question of why Gaius did not receive them. Perhaps it was owing to the specific character of his eastern mission, the main objective of which was to regulate Armenian and Parthian matters. As Gaius would mostly be active in the imperial province of Syria—where most of Rome's army present in the region was stationed—the vassal kingdom of Cappadocia, and Armenia, he did not need a greater *imperium* with which to interfere in the matters of provinces governed by senatorial proconsuls.

1.3.6 Germanicus

The next member of the *domus Augusta* who received extraordinary *imperium* was Germanicus, the adopted son of Tiberius and, alongside Drusus the Younger, a potential heir.[149] The moment Germanicus was granted his first independent *imperium* gives rise to some controversy among researchers, as the sources themselves disagree on that point. According to Cassius Dio, his investiture took place in AD 11, when he accompanied Tiberius on his mission to Germania. Dio clearly states Germanicus then received *imperium proconsulare* (*ἀντὶ ὑπάτου ἄρχων*).

> Μάρκου δὲ Αἰμιλίου μετὰ Στατιλίου Ταύρου ὑπατεύσαντος, Τιβέριος μὲν καὶ Γερμανικὸς ἀντὶ ὑπατου ἄρχων ἔς τε τὴν Κελτικὴν ἐσέβαλον.[150]
>
> In the consulship of Marcus Aemilius and Statilius Taurus, Tiberius and Germanicus, the latter acting as proconsul, invaded Germany and overran portions of it.[151]

However, Tacitus only mentions Germanicus being granted such powers in the context of Augustus's death, with the senate only conferring them at Tiberius's behest in the year 14:

> *at Germanico Caesari proconsulare imperium petivit* [Tiberius—P. S.], *missique legati qui deferent, simul maestitiam eius ob excessum Augusti solarentur.*[152]
>
> But he asked proconsular powers for Germanicus Caesar, and a commission was sent out to confer them, and, at the same time, to console his grief at the death of Augustus.[153]

The divergence in how ancient authors dated the event divides modern historians as well. F. Hurlet adopted Dio's chronology: Germanicus's first independent *imperium* was granted in 11, the evidence being Germanicus's first imperatorial acclamation, which Hurlet dates to AD 13/14.[154] P. Brunt and R. Syme in turn accept the content of Cassius Dio's account while rejecting his chronology and believe Dio made a mistake with his dating of Germanicus's first *imperium*. They argue that, as Tiberius was then the high commander of the Rhine army, and Germanicus necessarily fought under his command, the latter is unlikely to have been granted the status of proconsul at the same time. For that reason, they suggest that the date of the event should be moved to AD 13, when Germanicus replaced Tiberius as the general of the legions stationed on the Rhine.[155] In yet another view, K. Bringmann assumes, based on Tacitus, that Germanicus first received independent *imperium* only after Augustus's death and on Tiberius's clear orders. Thus, he decidedly rejects Dio's account, believing that either the author or a copyist made a mistake. Instead, he thinks that, until the death of the first princeps, Germanicus conducted military operations in Germania in the rank of *legatus Augusti*.[156] I find Brunt's and Syme's proposal unconvincing, however; Germanicus's becoming proconsul, which made his rank *de jure* equal to Tiberius's, need not have precluded the latter *de facto* holding the supreme command in Germania. The superiority of Tiberius stemmed in that case primarily from his greater military experience and *auctoritas*, because of which it was he who held the high command in Germania at the time. The informal hierarchy between them is, thus, well reflected in Ovid's choice of words, as the poet refers to Tiberius as *dux*, while calling Germanicus *proximus duci*.[157] Bringmann's perspective is difficult to accept as well, as one can hardly imagine Germanicus assuming the high command over eight legions stationed in Germania in the rank of a mere imperial legate after his consulship of AD 12. From Tacitus, we also know there were, at the time, two *legati Augusti pro praetore* under Germanicus's command, G. Silius and A. Caecina.[158] To summarize, I do not believe there are grounds to reject the version of Cassius Dio, who dates Germanicus being granted his first independent *imperium* to the year AD 11. A prime argument in favour of that date might be Germanicus's first imperatorial acclamation; as I indicate below, it most likely took place in the final years of Augustus's reign, which makes it legitimate to suppose that Germanicus obtained his first independent *imperium* before the first princeps died. Additionally, P. Swan rightly points out that earlier careers of members of the *domus Augusta* show they tended to be granted *imperium proconsulare* before attaining consulship, as the careers of Drusus the Elder and Gaius Caesar indicate.[159] I see no reasons to suppose that Germanicus's *cursus honorum* was different.

How, then, is one to interpret the Tacitus account? Th. Mommsen tried to reconcile the two narratives: he thought the mention in Cassius Dio was about Augustus conferring on Germanicus proconsular powers in AD 11, whereas Tacitus took note of the senate renewing that *imperium* after the first emperor's death, which, in Mommsen's opinion, automatically made Germanicus's prerogatives expire.[160] In my opinion, his views require a measure of verification, as I think Tacitus mentions not so much renewing Germanicus's *imperium* as extending it for another 5 years (*quinquennium*) at the behest of Tiberius as the new princeps.[161] Germanicus held a command in Germania *ex mandatis Augusti*, and, in my opinion, his position needed to be defined anew after Tiberius came to power, and so the senate granted him *imperium proconsulare* at the new emperor's express bidding. Thus, from that point on, Germanicus commanded the legions stationed in Germania *ex mandatis Tiberii*. Considering he had eight legions under his command, Tiberius's actions are fully understandable.

The issue of when Germanicus's *imperium* would expire is also somewhat controversial. Hurlet believes he would only hold independent *imperium* until AD 16, when he became a mere imperial legate (*legatus Augusti pro praetore*). As his evidence, he cites mentions in Tacitus of Germanicus's successes on the Rhine. Tacitus reports those were achieved under Tiberius's auspices, and, in Hurlet's opinion, the formula he uses, *auspiciis Tiberii*, clearly indicates Germanicus had by then lost independent *imperium*. It is further Hurlet's opinion that those passages in Tacitus actually refer to the campaign of AD 16 and mean that, while it lasted, Germanicus no longer had independent *imperium*. Another of Hurlet's arguments is that, after the Battle of Idistaviso, only Tiberius received the title of *imperator*, which supposedly indicates that Germanicus was by then just an imperial legate.[162] However, I believe Hurlet's opinion indefensible: the passages in Tacitus he draws on refer to all of Germanicus's actions on the Rhine between AD 14 and 16, not just the final year of his campaign, being a *sui generis* summary of his achievements during his time in Germania.[163] Thus in their light, we may suppose Germanicus was already in military command on the Rhine *auspiciis Tiberii* from AD 14 on. If we were to follow Hurlet's clues, we would have to conclude he was *legatus Augusti* from the beginning of his Rhine campaigns. That would, of course, be an incorrect conclusion, as it is contradicted by the accounts of Cassius Dio and Tacitus, who explicitly mention that Germanicus had independent proconsular *imperium*, all of which goes to show leading military campaigns under the auspices of the princeps need not have ruled out holding independent *imperium*: each Roman general, whether he was an imperial legate or a member of the *domus Augusta* holding extraordinary *imperium*, such as Germanicus here, fought under the auspices of the emperor as the supreme commander of all the armed forces.[164] That is clearly confirmed by the depictions on the *gemma Augustea*, which shows Augustus with an augur's staff (a *lituus*)—in that context, a symbol of the highest military command—and Tiberius before him in a triumphal quadriga. The image emphasizes that Tiberius's victories were achieved under the emperor's auspices.[165] Therefore, Tacitus's rhetoric is quite understandable and does not justify any conclusions about Germanicus having lost his *imperium*. His not being granted the title of *imperator* is no proof either. Although independent *imperium* was a prerequisite for an imperatorial acclamation, commanders holding it were not necessarily hailed *imperator*. The career of Tiberius himself provides an example: despite his many successes in Germania in AD 4–6, he only received one acclamation,[166] the same as Germanicus. Finally, the decisive counterargument is that, while Germanicus was active on the Rhine, the imperial legates in Germania were G. Silius (in Germania Superior, AD 14–21) and A. Caecina (in Germania Inferior, AD 14–16),[167] and Tacitus states clearly that they were direct subordinates of Germanicus.[168] One ought to agree, on the other hand, with Hurlet that Germanicus's *imperium*, like that of Drusus the Elder, covered the lands on the Rhine and the Gallic provinces, which let him freely use the military and material potential of Gaul during his campaigns against the Germans.[169]

In AD 17, Germanicus's powers were significantly increased as he was given a new mission in the East.[170] Our situation as historians is one of luxury this time, as the sources supply extremely detailed information on the specifics of his *imperium* and the procedure accompanying the appointment. Namely, in addition to Tacitus's text, we have two inscriptions, both mentioned above: the *TS* and the *SCPP*, as well as an Oxyrhynchus papyrus:

> *tunc decreto patrum permissae Germanico provinciae quae mari dividuntur, maiusque imperium, quoquo adisset, quam iis qui sorte aut missu principis obtinerent.*[171]
>
> There followed a decree of the Fathers, delegating to Germanicus the provinces beyond the sea, with powers overriding, in all regions he might visit, those of the local governors holding office by allotment or imperial nomination.[172]

> *lex ad populum lata esset, ut in quamcum(que) provinciam venisset, maius ei imperium quam ei qui eam provinciam proco(n)s(ule) optineret, esset.*[173]
>
> a law had been presented to the people that into whatever province he should go he should have greater authority than the proconsul governing that province.[174]

> *proconsul missus in transmarinas provincias ... ex mandatis Tiberii Caesaris Augusti.*[175]
>
> he had then been sent as proconsul to the overseas provinces ... according to the orders of Tiberius Caesar Augustus.[176]

> ὑπὸ τοῦ πατρὸς [ἐ]πὶ τὸ καταστήσασθαι τὰς πέραν θαλάσσης ἐπαρχίας.[177]
>
> he was sent by his father to restore the overseas provinces.[178]

It follows unambiguously from the sources quoted just above that Germanicus was to act in the East in the rank of a proconsul holding *imperium maius* relative to the powers of all the governors of the provinces in the region. Such broad prerogatives were meant to allow him to carry out the tasks entrusted to him unobstructed and to freely interfere in the affairs of each province of the Roman East should the need arise.[179] As had been the case with Agrippa and Gaius Caesar, territorially, his *imperium* applied in all the provinces across the Ionian Sea (*transmarinae provinciae*). There is much debate among researchers on whether the powers conferred on Germanicus gave him the right to enter Egypt, which had had a special status since Augustus's time, being reserved for the emperor, without whose permission no senator or *eques* could enter it: in Tacitus and Suetonius, we read that Tiberius criticized his son harshly for visiting Egypt without his leave.[180] Based on their accounts, some scholars believe that, unlike Gaius Caesar, who had been active in the East before him, Germanicus did not have a special mandate from the emperor permitting him to go to Egypt.[181] It is a very controversial opinion. From the formal point of view, we have no grounds to think the extraordinary prerogatives granted Germanicus in AD 17 did not enable him to enter that province:[182] the sources adduced above clearly indicate that the geographical extent of his *imperium* covered all the Roman provinces in the East (*transmarinae provinciae*), including Egypt.[183] At the same time, the view that Gaius Caesar actually received a special imperial mandate letting him enter Egypt is only based on an imprecise mention in Orosius, who reports that Augustus's son was sent to the East *ad ordinandas Aegypti Syriaeque provincias*.[184] As can be seen, Orosius mentions no special permit to enter Egypt issued by Augustus, merely mentioning two of the provinces where Gaius would act during his Oriental expedition. I believe that, in Gaius's case, the same as in Germanicus's later, no such permit was necessary, as the right to enter Egypt followed from the geographical scope of the *imperia* of those two members of the *domus Augusta*. Now, in that case, one should ask if the mention, preserved in ancient authors, of Tiberius berating Germanicus is even reliable, and, if so, what the reason for the criticism was. F. Hurlet thinks Tiberius scolded Germanicus not so much for entering Egypt as for entering Alexandria, deciding that, by doing so, Tiberius's son went beyond his prerogatives in that he visited the city without consulting the princeps first.[185] I find that opinion unconvincing, as Germanicus hardly could have waited for the princeps to permit him to enter the capital of Egypt when obtaining his permission would have taken a lot of time owing to the distance from Rome. Considering quick intervention was needed in Alexandria because of the unrest there, any such delay would have certainly been undesirable. Therefore, I believe the mentions in those two authors of Tiberius allegedly criticizing Germanicus to be fairly unreliable. The emperor was quite unlikely to criticize Germanicus's decision to go to Egypt when the orders Germanicus issued in that province prevented serious troubles.[186] Moreover, in my opinion, the picture transmitted by Tacitus of constant strife between Tiberius and his adoptive son, a picture Suetonius painted as well, reflects that author's resentment towards Augustus's successor: the first few books of the *Annals* paint a sullen princeps always critical of Germanicus's actions, first in Germania and then in the East. Meanwhile, Tacitus's account of Germanicus is clearly sympathetic, depicting him as one beloved of the people, his personality in total opposition to Tiberius's double-dealing character.[187] In other words, I share E. Koestermann's view that the ban on visiting Egypt with a special imperial mandate only applied to ordinary senators and equites, but was not needed in the case of members of the imperial family carrying out special missions ordered by the princeps.[188] At any rate, Tacitus himself clearly stresses in a passage in his *Histories* that Augustus reserved the province not just for himself, but for the whole *domus Augusta*.[189]

1.3.7 Drusus the Younger

In the case of Drusus the Younger, Tiberius's natural son and second major candidate for succession, the sources offer no information on the character of the *imperium* he held during his two missions in Pannonia, first in AD 14, and later in 17–20. Tacitus says only, in the context of discussing the *imperium proconsulare* conferred on Germanicus after Augustus's death, that Tiberius refrained from granting Drusus the same prerogatives, because Drusus had already been designated for consulship in the following year.[190] Based on that account, researchers suppose that, during his first Pannonian mission, the objective of which was to quell the mutiny of the Danubian legions, Drusus was acting as a simple *legatus Augusti*.[191]

In AD 17, the princeps entrusted his son with another mission on the Danube, in Illyricum according to Tacitus.[192] Although Tacitus does not mention Drusus receiving any special prerogatives then, it seems he must have been granted independent *imperium*; one strong argument in favour of that hypothesis is that, later, Drusus would be granted the right to hold an ovation as a reward for his diplomatic successes during the mission. Of course, holding independent *imperium* was among the conditions a commander had to meet in order to win that honour. Thus, scholars tend to believe Drusus was granted *imperium proconsulare* in 17, like Germanicus 3 years earlier.[193] The word Illyricum used by Tacitus means the *imperium* was valid in the provinces of Pannonia, Dalmatia, Moesia, Raetia, and Noricum.[194]

1.4 The procedure for conferring *imperium* on members of the imperial family

Under the Republic, decisions about conferring extraordinary military command were taken by the people and, under special circumstances (e.g. during civil wars), by the senate. In Pompey's case, two laws were passed by the people. The first, the *lex Gabinia* of 67 BC, granted him extraordinary powers so he could fight pirates; the other, the *lex Manilia* of 66 BC, involved special prerogatives in the East for the war against Mithridates and Tigranes. In both those cases, the officials behind the proposed laws were tribunes of the people, A. Gabinius and G. Manilius.[195] In 43 BC, the senate sanctioned the status quo, confirming extraordinary *imperium* in the East for Cassius and Brutus.[196]

That late-Republic model of granting special military powers was, with some modifications, adopted by Augustus, and then Tiberius, but our sources do not allow us to reconstruct the procedure of conferring extraordinary *imperium* for every member of the *domus Augusta*, doubtless because ancient historians were not particularly interested in complicated legal nuance. Epigraphic and papyrological sources are helpful, providing irreplaceable information on the legal trappings of the process that is of interest to us here, but, unfortunately, sources of that type only exist for Agrippa and Germanicus.

From the Cologne papyrus analyzed above, we know Agrippa was granted his tribunician powers by a *senatus consultum* (*κατὰ δόγμα συνκλήτου*), and his special *imperium* by a law (*lex*) adopted by the comitia (*ἐν νόμωι ἐκυρώθη*). F. Hurlet assumes the *lex* was then ratified with a *senatus consultum*.[197] Even though the text of the papyrus does not explicitly refer to the senate having any role in the process, Hurlet's guess would appear justified, except that it was the *senatus consultum* that had to be passed first, to be next confirmed by the people with a *lex*, as Roman legislative practice clearly shows the people sanctioning *senatus consulta* rather than the other way round. Therefore, the papyrus mentions the *lex* that sanctioned an earlier *senatus consultum* granting Agrippa extraordinary *imperium*.

There is one more piece of evidence for both the senate and the people taking an active role in the formal process of conferring special *imperia* on members of the *domus Augusta*: the later case of Tiberius, who received such powers in the provinces in AD 13 in close connection with his elevation to the rank of Augustus's co-ruler (*collega imperii*) and designation as the successor of the first princeps. Velleius Paterculus recounts that Tiberius was given those prerogatives at Augustus's behest and with a *senatus consultum*, which was then sanctioned by the people as well.[198] Suetonius lists the incumbent consuls as those who came forward with the motion.[199]

The procedure of special prerogatives being conferred is best attested to for Germanicus, in AD 17.[200] Crucial information is supplied by the two epigraphic texts mentioned above more than once, the *SCPP* and the *TS*, and by Tacitus. Owing to those sources, we know the first part of Germanicus's investiture was a decree of the senate (a *senatus consultum*) issued after Tiberius put it forward.[201] The second stage involved a law (*lex*) adopted by the people, most likely at the consuls' initiative (*rogatio*), which granted Germanicus special *imperium* in the eastern provinces.[202] Furthermore, prior to leaving Rome, he received special *mandata* from the princeps with instructions regarding his mission in the East.[203] Despite the silence of our sources on the subject, the procedure of conferring special *imperia* on Drusus the Elder, Gaius Caesar, and then Drusus the Younger should have been similar.

The participation of the senate and comitia in the procedure of conferring *imperium* on members of the *domus Augusta* went hand in hand with Augustus tending to keep up the appearances of respecting the Republican tradition and to strengthen the impression that his actions were legal.

Germanicus's case confirms that Tiberius continued his predecessor's policy in that regard.[204] However, there can be no doubt that the leading role fell each time to the emperor, who put forward the candidate and determined the nature and scope of the prerogatives to be granted, whereas the senate and the people only sanctioned whatever it was the princeps wanted. The extraordinary legal procedure involved in entrusting members of the *domus Augusta* with missions and granting them *imperium* served primarily to highlight their standing, which was special when compared with that of other provincial governors.

1.5 The nature of the *imperia* of provincial governors

1.5.1 The imperial provinces

Augustus's principate brought with it important changes in the system of administering the provinces. The most significant symptom of that process was the division of the Roman provinces into imperial (*provinciae Caesaris*) and public ones (*provinciae publicae* or *populi Romani*; Figure 1.1).[205] The latter had their governors appointed by the senate according to Republican principles. As a result of the division, two categories of governors developed, chosen through completely different procedures and for terms of differing lengths.

The governors of the highest status in the imperial provinces were the officials bearing the titles of *legati Augusti pro praetore* (literally, the emperor's envoys replacing a praetor).[206] They were selected from among ex-praetors and ex-consuls and, regardless of which of those two offices they had held, bore the same title of *legatus Augusti pro praetore*. Their appointment was each time decided by the princeps, from whom they received directives (*mandata*). Visually, the attributes of their power included military attire, a sword, and an escort of five lictors. Their term of office strictly depended on the emperor's will, but tended to be longer than 1 year.[207] Tiberius's reign offers many examples of long-term governorships in imperial provinces.

Even though, *de jure*, all the *legati Augusti* had the same status, whether they had held a praetorship or a consulship before, only former consuls were sent to provinces where significant military forces were stationed. That category included primarily the governorships of Germania Superior, Germania Inferior, and Syria, which had four legions each, and those of Hispania Tarraconensis and Pannonia, with three legions each. Meanwhile, former praetors were entrusted with provinces with no legions in them, where only small units might be stationed, intended for prevention. That group included Hispania Lusitania, Gallia Aquitania, and Galatia, among others.[208]

Determining the exact nature of the *imperium* those legates held runs into certain problems, however, as no detailed information on the subject can be found in the sources. Their official titles imply that, whether their office had been that of a praetor or consul, as imperial legates they held *imperium*

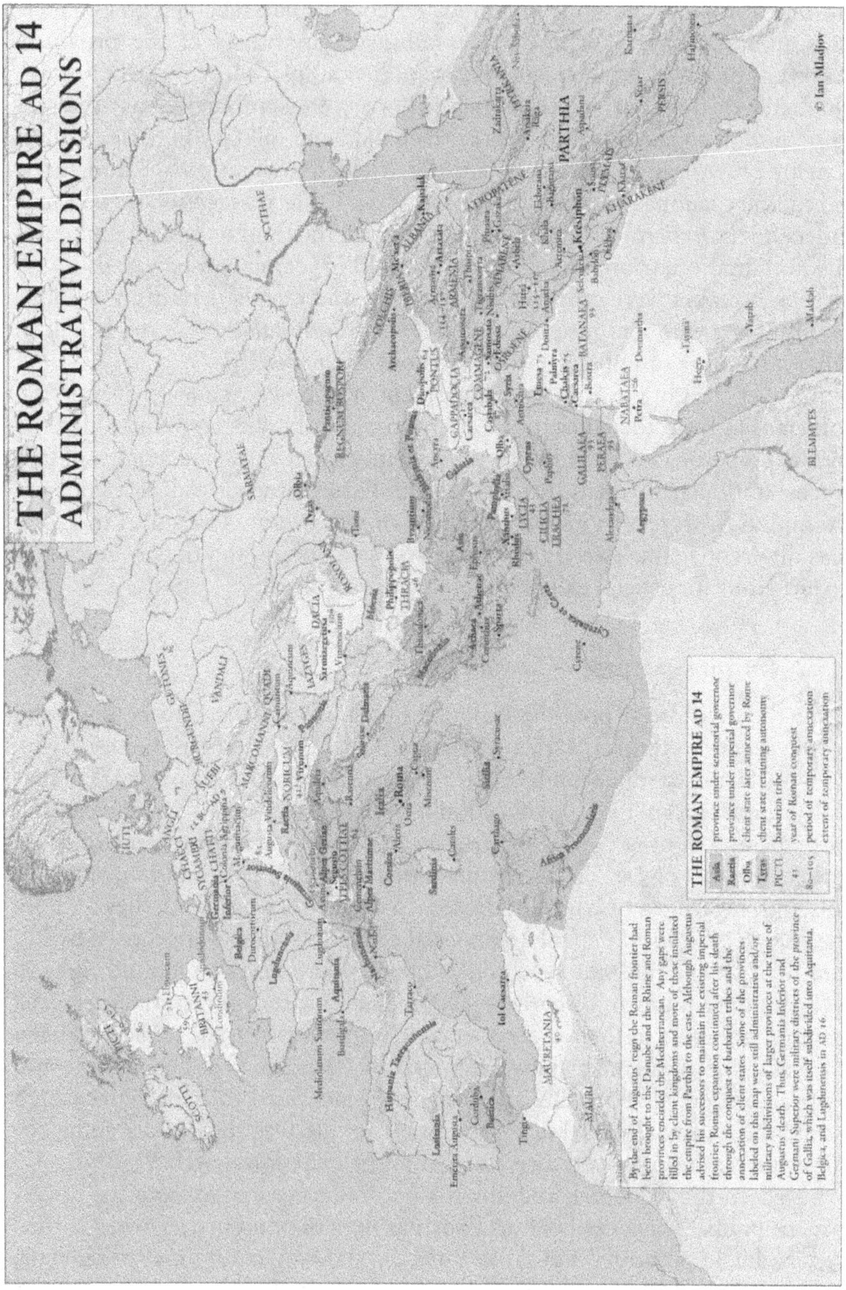

Figure 1.1 The Roman Empire under Augustus.

pro praetore. Thus, *de jure*, they had the same rank, and their *imperium* was *minus* relative to Augustus's proconsular *imperium*.[209] In practice, however, the *legati Augusti* chosen from among ex-consuls had much greater chances of a military career owing to the military importance of the provinces reserved for them. Germania offers a good example. Moreover, the specific character of the provinces in which legions were stationed meant that the *imperium* of consular legates was both civilian and military in nature, unlike that of praetorian legates, who mostly wielded civilian power and rarely led military campaigns. Still, there is no doubt that no *legatus Augusti* held independent *imperium*, which would give him the right to win an imperatorial acclamation, triumph, or ovation should his campaign be victorious,[210] as such honours were only due the emperor and members of his immediate family. The triumphal insignia (*ornamenta triumphalia*) were the height of what governors of imperial provinces could achieve.[211]

A lower class of governors of imperial provinces was made up of procurators chosen from the equestrian order. Procurators were appointed directly by the emperor and entrusted with provinces that only had small military forces stationed in them, usually of auxiliaries. Raetia and Noricum are examples: their governors bore the title of *procurator*. The status of Egypt was different again. Two legions were stationed there, and the province was governed by an official called the prefect (*praefectus*).[212]

1.5.2 *The provinces of the Roman people*

After the division of provinces carried out in 27 BC, those to be governed by the senate were Asia, Africa, Hispania Baetica, Gallia Narbonensis (from 20 BC), Sicily, Sardinia and Corsica (later an imperial province), Dalmatia (imperial from 11 BC), Macedonia, Achaea, Crete and Cyrenaica, and Bithynia and Pontus.[213] Analogously to imperial legates, governors of those public provinces were selected from among former praetors and former consuls, but, regardless of which of those two offices they had held, they all bore the title of *proconsul*.[214] Unlike imperial governors, they were chosen by lot, and their term could not last longer than 1 year. They also had no right to wear military uniform or carry a sword. In contrast to imperial legates, the number of lictors in their escort depended on whether their office had been a praetorship or a consulship. Ex-consuls were assigned twelve lictors, and ex-praetors, six.[215] Formally speaking, they answered to the senate, which issued them instructions, but there can be no question that, under some circumstances, they received directives from the emperor as well.[216]

Based on the titulature and Tacitus's account, we can assume the governors of public provinces held proconsular *imperium* no matter which office they had held before.[217] Thus, formally, the standing of all those proconsuls was the same. However, ex-consuls were entrusted with governorships in important provinces such as Africa or Asia, whereas the other provinces of the people were governed by ex-praetors. Senatorial proconsuls' *imperium* could only be exercised within the borders of the province assigned them.[218] A large majority of the proconsuls administered peaceful provinces with no military presence, so that their *imperium* was for the most part civilian in nature. The one exception could be the proconsul of Africa, who, in addition to administrative duties, also had military ones, because there was one legion stationed in Africa, and numerous wars were waged on the borders of his province.[219] From 19 BC on, proconsuls no longer held independent *imperium* and so could not apply for a triumph if they had led a victorious campaign; only *ornamenta triumphalia* were available to them. At the same time, it bears noting that governors of public provinces received them much less often than imperial legates; the honour would mostly fall to proconsuls of Africa, who were virtually the only governors of public provinces waging military campaigns.[220]

1.6 The legal standing of members of the reigning dynasty and the position of provincial governors

The work carried out by members of the *domus Augusta* in the provinces involved interfering with the remit of their governors; in order to prevent potential misunderstandings, they had the scope and nature of their powers precisely defined. The type of *imperium* they held depended on their mission and the character of the province. All the members of the ruling dynasty active in imperial provinces had *imperium proconsulare*, placing them above the imperial governors, who, as *legati Augusti*, had propraetorian *imperium*. Our sources clearly reflect that hierarchy and demonstrate that, whenever a member of the *domus Augusta* was active within an imperial province, its governor would be subject to his orders. It seems worthwhile to bring up a few representative examples of that. Velleius Paterculus reports that, during Tiberius's campaign in Germania in 4–6, he issued orders to Sentius Saturninus, the *legatus Augusti pro praetore* of that province.[221] The historian also mentions that Augustus moved two of his legates, Aulus Caecina and Plautius Silvanus, from eastern provinces to Pannonia to be under Tiberius's orders while the uprising was being suppressed (that is, in AD 6–9).[222] Tacitus in turn writes that, during Germanicus's Rhine campaigns, the *legati Augusti* of Germania Superior and Inferior, Gaius Silius and Aulus Caecina, served under him.[223]

Situations are also known when an imperial legate would not subject himself to a member of the *domus Augusta*. The most spectacular case is the behaviour of Gnaeus Calpurnius Piso during Germanicus's mission in the East. Between AD 17 and 19, Piso was *legatus Augusti pro praetore provinciae Syriae*.[224] We know from sources that, during his governorship, he ignored Germanicus's orders regarding the deployment of legions stationed in Syria and rescinded Germanicus's decrees regarding some of the towns in the province. He also supposedly tried to instigate war in Armenia and Parthia, as well as inciting the dethroned Parthian king, Vonones, to make a bid for the throne of Armenia, which may have contributed to serious unrest in the region.[225] As Piso was a *legatus Augusti* and had been assigned to Germanicus as his *adiutor*, those actions were evident disobedience towards a superior. Because Germanicus was present in the East on the authority of the senate and the people and as a direct representative of the princeps, who also held extraordinary *imperium*, Piso's actions were classified as an insult to the dignity of the *domus Augusta* and disregard of public law (*neclecta maiestate domus Augustae, neclecto etiam iure publico*),[226] and charges were brought against him before the senate. Piso, however, did not wait for the verdict to be announced, committing suicide instead.[227]

The situation was different when members of the ruling dynasty entered provinces of the people of Rome, whose governors had proconsular *imperia*. In that case, their *imperia* were defined as *maiora* relative to those of the proconsuls, which was to prevent potential conflict of powers. Agrippa's and Germanicus's cases are telling in that respect, in that they both had such prerogatives during their missions in the East, where some provinces had proconsular governors. Only Gaius Caesar stands out, as the sources do not confirm his powers were as broad.

The most important differences that appear when one compares the status of members of the *domus Augusta* with the position of provincial governors concern the territorial extent of their powers, the mode in which the *imperium* was granted, and the criteria based on which it was granted. Whereas a governor's *imperium* only applied within his particular province, that of members of the *domus Augusta* (Agrippa, Gaius Caesar, Germanicus, and Drusus the Younger) covered a larger area. The circumstances in which they received *imperium* differed as well. For governors, *imperium* stemmed from being appointed to the office of proconsul or imperial legate in a given province; for members of the *domus Augusta* (Agrippa and Germanicus), it stemmed from a special decree of the senate, later sanctioned by the people, without their holding any office of provincial administration. Additionally, some members of the imperial family did not have to climb the several rungs of *cursus honorum* in order to receive their proconsular *imperium*. Gaius Caesar's and Germanicus's careers provide the most spectacular examples, as they were both granted proconsular powers even though they had held neither consulship nor praetorship.

1.7 The *imperia* of members of the *domus Augusta* and the emperor's *imperium*

It is not easy to capture the differences between the emperor's *imperium* and those of some of his family members, as the line is extremely blurred. Whereas, in the case of persons who held *imperium proconsulare* (Drusus the Elder, Gaius Caesar, Tiberius before AD 13, and Drusus the Younger), it is known that their *imperium* was *minus* in relation to that of the princeps, the matter gets complicated for those members of the *domus Augusta* who were granted *imperium maius* to that of provincial governors (in their provinces).

To start with, I would like to compare Agrippa's extraordinary prerogatives in the provinces with those of the princeps and answer the question of whether the *imperium* of Augustus's son-in-law and second-in-command was the same as his own. It seems that, in spite of the reticence of the sources on the matter, it is possible to point to certain differences. First, we know that the greater *imperium* Augustus received in 23 BC was not explained by any specific mission in the provinces: it was granted to him, alongside the *tribunicia potestas*, as another component of his power as the emperor, after he had resigned from the consulship earlier the same year.[228] From then on, it was that *imperium* that defined Augustus's position relative to those of all the governors and military commanders in the provinces, allowing him to issue directives (*mandata*) to them at any moment if need be. Meanwhile, Agrippa's *imperium* was closely connected to his first mission in the East and, in the long run, was meant to make it possible for him to replace the princeps in carrying out various tasks in the provinces. Second, from Cassius Dio's account, we know Augustus's *imperium* remained in force when he crossed the pomerium,[229] an exemption intended to make it unnecessary to repeat the inconvenient process of renewing his *imperium* each time he left Rome for the provinces. However, there is nothing in the sources to indicate Agrippa was granted the same privilege.[230] It is impossible to determine if Augustus's *imperium* was actually *maius* relative to Agrippa's, as would be the case later with Tiberius and Germanicus, but, considering Agrippa held tribunician powers jointly with the princeps as his *collega imperii*, it would seem highly likely that, formally speaking, his *imperium* was also equal to that of Augustus.[231] There can, however, be no doubt that the crucial factor that placed the princeps higher than Agrippa was his imperial *auctoritas*.

Things were somewhat different still in the case of Tiberius, who, in AD 13, as our sources report (for which see above), was given the same *imperium* in the provinces as Augustus had. Unlike Agrippa's, it was not granted for a specific mission in the provinces, but rather signified Tiberius's official designation as Augustus's successor. From that point on, Tiberius had the same standing in the provinces as the emperor, only surpassed by him in terms of *auctoritas*.

Then there is Germanicus, a different case again. Thanks to the *SCPP*, we know that, during his mission in the East, his *imperium* had been clearly defined as lesser (*minus*) than Tiberius's.[232] It bears emphasizing that it is the first time, confirmed in the sources, that a clear hierarchy can be seen in the *imperia* of the princeps and a member of his family.[233] K. M. Girardet incorrectly interprets the text of the *SCPP*, assuming Tiberius was first granted *imperium maius* to that of proconsuls in public provinces at exactly the same moment as Germanicus received it for his mission in the East.[234] As I have said above, we do know Tiberius had actually been given such prerogatives already in AD 13, when he was granted the same power in all the provinces as that of Augustus, and, from that point on, his *imperium* was greater than that of other governors. Thus, the *lex* mentioned by the *SCPP* granted Tiberius no new prerogatives regarding proconsuls, merely specifying that his *imperium* would be *maius* relative to Germanicus's while the latter carried out his eastern mission.

One striking difference observable as one compares the *imperia* of the princeps and his family is their geographical scope. Unlike the emperor's *imperium*, which applied in all the provinces of Rome, the *imperia* of members of the *domus Augusta* tended to be limited to the specific set of provinces where they carried out their tasks. With Gaius Caesar and Germanicus, those were the eastern provinces (*transmarinae provinciae*); with Drusus the Younger, Illyricum.

1.8 The extra-legal aspects of the special position of members of the imperial family in the provinces

Holding special prerogatives (*imperia extraordinaria*) was not the only or the most important factor contributing to the special standing of members of the reigning dynasty. There were other, "extra-legal" ones, which determined their extraordinary position both in Rome and in the provinces. One of the more significant ones was certainly *auctoritas*, the charisma and popularity resulting from being part of the emperor's family as well as from individual traits and personal achievements, aspects that proved especially important when interacting with the army, border tribes, and foreign monarchs.

Certainly, Agrippa was the most notable of all the representatives of the *domus Augusta* active in the provinces. From the moment Octavian came into power in 30 BC until his death in 12 BC, he was Augustus's *de facto* second-in-command and the second most powerful person in the state. One important point in his career was his marriage of 21 BC to the emperor's daughter Julia, thanks to which he joined the inner circle of the *domus Augusta*. The union greatly affected how the inhabitants of the Empire saw Agrippa, which was reflected during his stay in the East in the extraordinary honours accorded him there.[235] His popularity also grew owing to his construction works, mostly in Rome, Syria, Spain, and Gaul, which resulted in many new public buildings.[236] Agrippa's successes in his many military campaigns, on the other hand, won him the reputation of an excellent general. A passage in Cassius Dio attests to Agrippa's charisma as a commander. The text concerns the outbreak of the anti-Roman uprising in Pannonia in 12 BC, the suppression of which Augustus entrusted to his son-in-law. As the historian reports, no actual intervention was necessary: it was enough for Agrippa to make an appearance, and the rebelling peoples gave up their revolt.[237]

Drusus the Elder and Tiberius were very popular too, particularly with the legions. After Drusus's unexpected death in 9 BC, the Rhine legions decided to cremate the corpse of their commander and laid the ashes in a tomb that was to be built in Mogontiacum (modern Mainz). When Augustus objected, serious unrest followed. Eventually, the emperor managed to disarm the tense situation by agreeing to a cenotaph being erected in Mogontiacum as a symbolic tomb in honour of his dead stepson.[238]

Velleius Paterculus, in turn, mentions the exuberant welcome given Tiberius by the Rhine legions in AD 4, when he had re-assumed command of them after a 10-year-long absence.[239] In this context, another interesting item in Velleius is a mention he makes regarding Tiberius's stay in Rhodes between 6 BC and AD 2: the historian reports that governors travelling east to the provinces assigned them visited Tiberius to pay their respects.[240] Now, Paterculus eulogizes Tiberius, so his account must be greatly exaggerated, but I believe that passage reflects well the difference in standing between members of the emperor's family and ordinary governors. Even though he had officially withdrawn from politics, Tiberius still enjoyed high esteem as a *privatus* because he belonged to the reigning dynasty.

Germanicus, too, is reputed to have enjoyed particular popularity with the army. Tacitus and Suetonius both write that soldiers of the legions stationed in Germania went so far as to see in him a candidate for the imperial purple after Augustus's death.[241] It appears that maybe that kind of popularity did not result simply from the young commander's virtues, but also from him being a son of Drusus the Elder, who had won huge respect from the Rhine legions during his work in Germania. According to Suetonius, an approachable personality and ease in winning people over earned Germanicus high regard and affection from the inhabitants of Rome and the provinces. The historian mentions that any return of Germanicus to Rome after a longer absence was vigorously celebrated, and his visits to provinces tended to receive very warm welcomes from the provincials.[242] His illness and premature death, on the other hand, caused heavy grief throughout the Empire. Both Tacitus and Suetonius describe a vehement reaction of the Roman plebs to news of Germanicus's death.[243] Gnaeus Piso's arrival in Rome only fanned the flames; Piso was officially charged with involvement in the death of Tiberius's son. In expressing their hatred of Piso, the people were stressing their affection for Germanicus. As the sources report, the situation was grave enough that there was even danger of Piso being lynched. Ultimately, Tiberius was able to lower the tension through an intervention from the Praetorian Guard.[244] As Suetonius writes, Germanicus's death left a mark beyond the borders of the Empire as well, so that a number of neighbouring barbarian tribes, as well as the king of the Parthians, went into mourning.[245]

In summary, it has to be said that, although the legal standing (that is, the scope and type of *imperium*) of members of the *domus Augusta* active in the provinces mattered for their relationships with representatives of provincial administration, the issue meant little to the remaining inhabitants of the province, unfamiliar with the nuances of Roman political power. For an average inhabitant of the Empire, what mattered most was that they were members of the reigning family and potential candidates for succession, and it was that factor, combined with personal merits and achievements, not any special *imperium* held, that made those persons exceptional in the eyes of the provincial population when compared with ordinary governors.

Notes

1 See Girardet 1990: 92; *id.* 1992: 179; *id.* 2001: 158; Bleicken 1993: 122 f.; Dalla Rosa 2014: 180 (note 12); Vervaet 2014: *passim*; Hurlet 2016: 583–584.
2 See Cic. *Flac.* 85 (Lucullus in Asia); Cic. *Prov. cons.* 15 (Gabinius in Syria); Cic. *Phil.* 11, 5 (Trebonius in Asia).
3 Val. Max. 6, 9, 7; 8, 1, 2.
4 See among others Cic. *Phil.* 4, 9; Liv. 23, 48, 1–2; 25, 15, 18–20; 26, 9, 10; 36, 37, 6; Cass. Dio 27, 91, 8. For a detailed analysis of individual cases, see Sawiński 2010: 36–38.
5 Sall. *Hist. fr.* 7; Caes. *Bell. Afr.* 97; Cic. *Phil.* 11, 30.
6 *SCPP* ll. 33–34.
7 Val. Max. 8, 1, amb. 2.
8 Val. Max. 8, 15, 8.
9 *Cn. Pompeius cum adhuc eques R. esset, cum imperio proconsulari adversus Sertorium missus est* (Liv. *Per.* 91). I rely on Teubner's editions (ed. O. Rossbach, Stuttgart 1959: 94) and Les Belles Lettres (ed. P. Jal, Paris 1984: 22). Loeb's publishers (ed. T. E. Page, London 1959: 114) suggest a reading of *consulare* that appears in one of the manuscripts.
10 In fact, the *Periochae* uprising is dated 4th century AD, but we cannot exclude the fact that the term *imperium proconsulare* was known to Livius.
11 I have put forward detailed arguments regarding the matter in an earlier paper; see Sawiński 2010: 29–44.
12 See Girardet 1992: 181; Bleicken 1993: 121; Vervaet 2014: 217 (note 10); Hurlet 2016: 586.
13 See Liv. 23, 23, 7; 30, 39, 3–4; 32, 7, 4; Cic. *Phil.* 8, 25. For an analysis of the cases described in those sources, see Sawiński 2010: 40.
14 Liv. 23, 34, 13–15; Caes. *B. Civ.* 1, 6. See also Sawiński 2010: 41–42.
15 For examples of various categories of commanders under the Republic, see Drogula 2015b.
16 For examples of the practice, see Liv. 28, 10, 11–12; 29, 13, 3–4; 30, 1, 3.
17 Liv. 26, 18, 2–10: *cum alii alium nominarent, postremum eo decursum est ut proconsuli creando in Hispaniam comitia haberentur; diemque comitiis consules edixerunt [...] Iussi deinde inire suffragium ad unum omnes non centuriae modo, sed etiam homines P. Scipioni imperium esse in Hispania iusserunt.* Other ancient authors are considerably less precise and more reticent in their descriptions of the procedure involved in appointing Scipio the commander in Spain, and they do not report any significant details regarding the type of *imperium* granted him. See App. *Hisp.* 18; Cass. Dio 57, 38–40.
18 See primarily Girardet 1992: 179; *id.* 2001: 168–169; Bleicken 1993: 122; more recently Vervaet 2014: 206 (note 25).
19 So e.g. Broughton (1951: 280), who refers to Scipio's prerogatives as *imperium pro consule*. See also Kloft 1977: 33.
20 See Broughton 1951: 263; Ridley 1981: 281.
21 Cic. *Leg. Man.* 62: *Quid tam inusitatum quam ut, cum duo consules clarissimi fortissimique essent, eques Romanus ad bellum maximum formidolosissimumque pro consule mitteretur? Missus est. Quo quidem tempore, cum esset non nemo in senatu qui diceret "non oportere mitti hominem privatum pro*

consule," L. Philippus dixisse dicitur "non se illum sua sententia pro consule, sed pro consulibus mittere." Cic. *Phil.* 11, 18: *Nam Sertorianum bellum a senatu privato datum est, quia consules recusabant, cum L. Philippus pro consulibus eum se mittere dixit, non pro consule.* Liv. *Per.* 91 (ed. O. Rossbach, 1959: 94): *Cn. Pompeius cum adhuc eques R. esset, cum imperio proconsulari adversus Sertorium missus est.* Val. Max. 8, 15, 8: *eques Romanus pro consule in Hispaniam aduersus Sertorium.* Plut. *Pomp.* 17, 3; Cass. Dio 36, 25, 3. *Contra* Girardet (2001: 167–168), who believes that Pompey, like all other commanders of proconsular rank, held *imperium consulare militiae.* Girardet also terms Pompey as *privatus cum imperio*, but I have already argued above that that choice of words is unfortunate.

22 Before, Pompey had only held a few military commands—for example, in the war against Lepidus and Brutus, assigned to him a few months earlier. It is supposed his actions then were sanctioned by an *imperium pro praetore.* See Broughton 1951: 90. Girardet (2001: 166) differs by suspecting Pompey was merely a *legatus pro praetore.*

23 See Girardet 2001: 168–169.

24 Liv. *Per.* 99; Vell. Pat. 2, 31,2; Plut. *Pomp.* 25, 1–2; Cass. Dio 36, 23, 1–5; 24, 1–4.

25 Plut. *Pomp.* 25, 3; App. *Mith.* 94; Cass. Dio 36, 37, 1, although the three authors differ a little in certain details. Plutarch reports Pompey had 300 warships at his disposal, whereas Appian mentions 270. Besides, unlike Plutarch and Cassius Dio, Appian writes that Pompey may have had twenty-five legates.

26 See Girardet 2001: 173.

27 Vell. Pat. 2, 31, 2: *A. Gabinius tribunus legem tulit ut, cum belli more, non latrociniorum, orbem classibus iam, non furtivis expeditionibus, piratae terrerent quasdamque etiam Italiae urbes diripuissent, Cn. Pompeius ad eos opprimendos mitteretur essetque ei imperium aequum in omnibus provinciis cum proconsulibus usque ad quinquagesimum miliarium a mari. Contra* Koehn (2010: 309–314), who thinks Pompey received *imperium maius* compared with that of other proconsuls, but could only evoke it if he appeared in a given province in person, a totally unacceptable opinion. All the authors cited above say Pompey came to wield great power owing to the *lex Gabinia*, but they are more likely to mean the vast financial and military potential he obtained and the geographical scope of his *imperium*, rather than his *imperium* being greater than that of other governors. Neither can I see a reason to reject the account of Velleius Paterculus, the only author to precisely specify Pompey's legal standing relative to other proconsuls, and one can hardly agree Pompey's ability to exercise his *imperium* depended on having to enter a given province. That would have been quite irrational owing to the huge scope of the military operations in question, and at any rate that was the purpose of the fifteen legates assigned to Pompey to pass his directives on.

28 Cass. Dio 36, 37, 1.

29 So e.g. Jashemski 1950: 93; Ehrenberg 1953: 119; Kienast 2009: 89. *Contra* Girardet 1992: 181–182; *id.* 2001: 173–174; and Vervaet 2014: 218, both of whom believe it was *imperium consulare militiae.*

30 The situation was similar in the case of M. Antonius Creticus, a praetor in 74, who was granted powers similar to those of Pompey, and also for a campaign against pirates; see Vell. Pat. 2, 31, 3. Ridley (1981: 295) calls Antonius's *imperium, infinitum.* See also Vervaet 2014: 218.

31 App. *Mith.* 94; Cass. Dio 36, 37, 1. See also Girardet 2001: 173.

32 Girardet 2001: 175.

33 Liv. *Per.* 99; Plut. *Pomp.* 29; Cass. Dio 36, 17a.

34 Vell. Pat. 2, 31, 2; Cass. Dio 39, 9, 3.

35 Cic. *Att.* 4, 1, 6–7: *legem consules conscripserunt qua Pompeio per quinquennium omnis potestas rei frumentariae toto orbe terrarum daretur*. Liv. *Per.* 104: *Cn. Pompeio per quinquennium annonae cura mandata est.* App. *B. Civ.* 2, 18; Plut. *Pomp.* 49, 4. Hurlet (2016: 588) is right to assume Pompey received the same prerogatives then as those granted him earlier by the *lex Gabinia*—*imperium aequum* relative to the powers of other proconsuls throughout the Mediterranean.

36 Cass. Dio 39, 9, 3. *Contra* Girardet (2000: 184), who uses as his starting point the controversial assumption that a proconsul's powers were of the same order as a consul's, which I have already mentioned above, and defines Pompey's *imperium* as *consulare*. Some researchers rely on Cicero (*Fam.* 1, 9, 7; *Q. fr.* 2, 3, 2) and believe Pompey was granted an exemption that allowed him as a proconsul to cross the pomerium without losing his *imperium* as a result and to smoothly carry out his duties in Rome itself if need be; see Koehn 2010: 310 (note 36); Vervaet 2014: 221. It is a controversial opinion, as the passage in Cicero (*Q. Fr.* 2, 3, 2) indicates something quite different. Namely, Cicero writes that, in February of 56 BC, the senate made a point of convening in the temple of Apollo in order to make it possible for Pompey to attend, and we do know the temple stood outside the pomerium, which suggests Pompey's *imperium* was not valid in Rome proper. Cass. Dio (39, 63, 3–4) likewise reports Pompey stayed outside the pomerium while carrying out his *cura annonae* duties, because, as a proconsul, he was forbidden from entering Rome.

37 Girardet 1992: 184; *id.* 2001: 189.

38 Cic. *Att.* 4, 1, 7: *alteram Messius qui omnis pecuniae dat potentatem et adiungit classem et exercitum et maius imperium in provinciis quam sit eorum, qui eas obtineant.* According to Vervaet (2014: 220, note 17), Messius's proposal was that Pompey be granted *imperius maius*, not in all the provinces (*in omnibus provinciis*), but only those he entered to carry out his mission.

39 Last 1947: 161–162; Ehrenberg 1953: 121; Bleicken 1993: 121; Girardet 2001: 188; Koehn 2010: 308.

40 Cic. *Phil.* 11, 7–30. See also Girardet 1993: 219.

41 Cic. *Phil.* 11, 30: *senatui placere C. Cassium pro consule provinciam Syriam optinere, ut qui optimo iure eam provinciam optinuerit, eum a Q. Marcio Crispo pro consule, L. Staio Murco pro consule, A. Allieno legato exercitum accipere, eosque ei tradere, cumque iis copiis et si quas praeterea paraverit, bello P. Dolabellam terra marique persequi. Eius belli gerendi causa, quibus ei videatur, naves, nautas, pecuniam ceteraque, quae ad id bellum gerendum pertineant, ut imperandi in Syria, Asia, Bithynia, Ponto ius potestatemque habeat, utique, quamcumque in provinciam eius belli gerendi causa advenerit, ibi maius imperium C. Cassi pro consule sit, quam eius erit, qui eam provinciam tum optinebit, cum C. Cassius pro consule in eam provinciam venerit.*

42 Cic. *Phil.* 11, 36.

43 Cic. *Fam.* 12, 7, 1; *Brut.* 2, 4, 2; Cass. Dio 47, 29, 4–5. Girardet 1993: 219, 222.

44 Cic. *Brut.* 1, 5, 1.

45 Cic. *Fam.* 12, 14, 4.

46 Among those sceptical about the claim is Hurlet 2016: 590.

47 A hypothesis confirmed, perhaps, by Appian (*B. Civ.* 4, 58, 1), who mentions a decree of the senate obliging the governors of eastern provinces to carry out Cassius's orders, as well as Brutus's.

48 Koehn 2010: 305–308. *Contra* Dalla Rosa 2014: 94–97; Vervaet 2014: 185–192; 262 (notes 157–158).

49 I call the not-yet Augustus Octavian here, even though we know he never used that name, going by Gaius Octavius until 44 BC, and by C. Iulius Caesar after being adopted by Caesar. See Kienast, Eck, Heil 2017: 53.

50 Strab. 17, 3, 25; Cass. Dio 53, 12, 3–7; Salmon 1956: 466; Ziółkowski 2004: 362; Wesch-Klein 2016: 37–39; Kienast, Eck, Heil 2017: 54.
51 Cass. Dio 53, 13, 1.
52 Rich 1990: 170; Girardet 1990: 108; Bleicken 1993: 130; Dettenhofer 2000: 78–79; Ferrary 2001: 109.
53 Ziółkowski 2004: 363.
54 Syme 1939: 315; Eck 2007: 64. Koehn 2010: 320. Somewhat differently, Rich (1990: 170) and Ferrary (2001: 133) believe that, in the years 27–23, Augustus may have issued orders to proconsuls not so much based on greater *imperium* as through his informal authority (*auctoritas*). Evidence for the princeps interfering with affairs of provinces governed by senatorial proconsuls is provided by an inscription from Cyme, which confirms the practice for the province of Asia. For an edition of the inscription with extensive commentary, see Sherk 1969: 313–320 (no. 61). On this subject, see esp. Giovannini 1999: 95–106; Ferrary 2001: 134; 137.
55 So e.g. Syme 1939: 314; Salmon 1956: 466–467; Kienast 2009: 87.
56 The view is based chiefly on the passages in Velleius Paterculus (2, 89, 3) and Cassius Dio (53, 13, 6). See also Salmon 1956: 463–464.
57 Syme (1939: 315) believes this to be a case of *cumulatio imperii*. *Contra* Rich 1990: 170.
58 With the exception of Egypt, governed by an equestrian prefect.
59 See Vervaet 2014: 263.
60 After that, he would only assume that magistracy twice in his reign, in 5 and 2 BC, respectively, when his adopted sons Gaius and Lucius Caesar donned their togas of manhood. See Suet. *Aug.* 26, 2–3.
61 Cass. Dio 53, 32, 3–5; Kienast, Eck, Heil 2017: 55. The *senatus consultum* which conferred on Augustus *tribunicia potestas* and *imperium proconsulare* was then sanctioned by the people in the comitia. See Vervaet 2014: 260 (note 151).
62 Cass. Dio 53, 32, 5–6.
63 Translated by E. Cary (Loeb Classical Library, 83).
64 As Rich (2012: 68) correctly emphasizes, the exemption did not entitle Augustus to exercise his *imperium* in Rome.
65 So, among others, Last 1947: 163; Salmon 1956: 469–470; Millar 1966: 156; Rich 1990: 170, 187; *id.* 2012: 68; Gruen 2005: 37; Kienast 2009: 105–106; Koehn 2010: 317–322; Galinsky 2012: 73; Levick 2013: 86; Dalla Rosa 2014: 185; Vervaet 2014: 261–263; *id.* 2020: 147.
66 Ferrary 2001: 137. Similarly Dalla Rosa (2014: 185; 250), who does not believe Augustus's *imperium* was *infinitum*, as Dio's text suggests. He thinks the princeps only received the privilege of carrying out his *imperium* in public provinces without having to visit them after AD 6. Dalla Rosa sees that supposed extension of the emperor's prerogatives as related to the military crisis caused by the anti-Roman uprising in Pannonia and Dalmatia. *Contra* Koehn (2010: 318, 321), who convincingly argues that Augustus's *imperium* applied in all provinces as early as 23 BC, regardless of whether he was there or not. Another scholar sceptical of Ferrary's claim is Vervaet 2014: 262–263 (note 158).
67 Rich 1990: 170; *id.* 2012: 68.
68 Koehn 2010: 318f.
69 Ameling 1994: 17–18; 20–21; 28. To a similar effect, Girardet (2000: 200–216), who consistently denies the existence of *imperium maius* before Tiberius's principate. Hurlet (2015: 79), in turn, opts for a neutral position, believing it is ultimately impossible to determine if Augustus's *imperium* was *maius* or *aequum* relative to the powers of other proconsuls.

70 As indicated by the formula *in magistratu* used in the text (*RGDA* 34, 3). See also Ziółkowski 2004: 363; Cooley 2009: 272.
71 See above.
72 Joseph. *AJ*. 16, 166; 171. Atkinson (1958: 319, 322, 325) dates Norbanus Flaccus's proconsulship to the years 18–17 or 17–16 BC. Somewhat differently, Pucci Ben Zeev (1998: 258–261; 281–283) places his governorship between 24 and 12 BC, suspecting Augustus's *mandata* and Norbanus Flaccus's letter to the authorities of Sardes were both sent around 12 BC.
73 Similarly Drogula 2015b: 362.
74 *SCPP* ll. 35–36.
75 Vell. Pat. 2, 121, 1. For more on that regulation, see below.
76 So esp. Ferrary 2001: 116, 141; Rich 2012: 68–69; Vervaet 2014: 261–263.
77 And then Vervaet (2014: 259–260, note 150) believes the term used by Dio, ἐσαεὶ καθάπαξ (*for life*), refers primarily to the exemption granted the emperor, which let him cross the pomerium without losing *imperium* in consequence.
78 See Ferrary 2001: 120–121; 141–143; Rich 2012: 69; Vervaet 2014: 272.
79 See Ziółkowski 2004: 366.
80 See Rich 2012: 68; Eck 2019: 485–486. For a basic edition of that inscription with commentary, see Alföldy 2000: 177–205. Still, some scholars incorrectly question the authenticity of the inscription. See Richardson 2002: 411–415.
81 For an interpretation of that document, see especially Koenen 1970: 217–283; Gray 1970: 227–238; Badian 1980: 91–107; Haslam 1980: 193–199; Ameling 1994: 1–28.
82 Koenen 1970: 222.
83 Ameling 1994: 1; Hurlet 1997: 42. It used to be believed the papyrus came from Oxyrhynchus. See Koenen 1970: 217.
84 Koenen 1970: 217.
85 I have used the text of the papyrus as found in Koenen 1970: 226.
86 The likely Latin phrasing of the *laudatio* following Girardet 2000: 217.
87 Translated by F. Drogula (2015b: 361).
88 So, for instance, Roddaz 1984: 347–348, who also thinks that the political climate in Rome in 23, bad for Augustus, was not conducive to granting Agrippa such broad prerogatives earlier than that.
89 Cass. Dio 54, 28, 1.
90 Translated by E. Cary (Loeb Classical Library, 83).
91 Tac. *Ann*. 3, 56, 2.
92 Although Dalmatia, a public province at the time, was next to Pannonia, nothing indicates Agrippa was supposed to undertake anything there.
93 The passage was similarly interpreted by Rich 1990: 206 and Ferrary 2001: 139.
94 For arguments in favour of that date, see Koenen 1970: 275–283.
95 *Contra* Ferrary (2001: 138–140), who assumes that, during Agrippa's first eastern mission, he acted as *legatus Augusti*. Ferrary does allow that Agrippa may have interfered with proconsular provinces then, but only based on an *imperium aequum*, believing he only received *imperium maius* than those of other proconsuls in the East in 18 BC. Ferrary sees this extension of Agrippa's powers as connected to his new position in the imperial family (including his becoming Augustus's son-in-law). Thus, he sees Agrippa's receiving superior *imperium* as meant for his second departure for the East. However, the idea that Agrippa was in 23 BC sent to the eastern provinces as a mere imperial legate seems unconvincing (on which see below).
96 Vell. Pat. 2, 93, 2. Woodman 1983: 280.
97 Translated by F. W. Shipley (Loeb Classical Library, 152).
98 Cass. Dio 53, 32, 1.

99 Translated by E. Cary (Loeb Classical Library, 83).
100 Siber 1940: 89–91.
101 See Roddaz 1984: 341; Richardson 2012: 98; Levick 2013: 86, who believe that, during Agrippa's first mission in the East, he was armed with an *imperium pro consule*.
102 One piece of evidence to prove that, in certain specific contexts, Cassius Dio uses "Συρία" as a synonym of the Roman East is the passage I quote above (54, 28, 1), where he writes of Agrippa's return in 13 from the eastern provinces to Rome.
103 Joseph. *AJ*. 16, 86.
104 Translated by B. Niese.
105 Roddaz 1984: 341; Hurlet 1997: 38–39.
106 Joseph. *AJ*. 15, 350.
107 Translated by B. Niese.
108 See Hurlet 1997: 38.
109 *Contra* Ferrary 2001: 142.
110 Dalla Rosa (2014: 183) thinks Agrippa, like Augustus, could exercise his *imperium* provided he came to the province in question—not a convincing opinion. Agrippa's letters to the authorities of Cyrene and Ephesus, quoted by Josephus (see below), indicate he could issue directives regarding public provinces without having to visit them in person.
111 Koenen 1970: 268–274. Similarly Rich 1990: 168; and, recently, Dalla Rosa 2014: 182–184; Drogula 2015b: 361.
112 So especially Gray 1970: 227–238; Badian 1980: 97–107; Ameling 1994: 1–28; Girardet 2000: 219.
113 Badian 1980: 105–106.
114 An assumption that is, however, clearly contradicted by Cassius Dio (53, 32, 5–6), who explicitly writes that Augustus's *imperium* would from then on be *maius* relative to those of other governors.
115 Ameling 1994: 27–28.
116 A claim made widespread in scholarship primarily by R. Syme (1939: 342–343). For my point of view on the matter, see Sawiński 2018: 26.
117 Generally, both letters are seen in connection with Agrippa's second visit to the East and dated to 14 BC. See Pucci Ben Zeev 1998: 270; 275–276.
118 Joseph. *AJ*. 16, 167–168.
119 Translated by M. Pucci Ben Zeev (1998: 263–264).
120 Joseph. *AJ*. 16, 169–170.
121 Translated by M. Pucci Ben Zeev (1998: 274).
122 See Girardet 2000: 219.
123 Joseph. *AJ*. 16, 172–173. Iullus Antonius was the proconsul of Asia, with a short break, in the years 9–3 BC. The letter to the authorities of Ephesus is usually dated to 4 BC. See Pucci Ben Zeev 1998: 285–290.
124 Ehrenberg, Jones 1955: 138 (no. 308); Sherk 1969: 323–324 (no. 63). The letter is generally dated to the years 17–13. See Roddaz 1984: 430; Pucci Ben Zeev 1998: 267.
125 Roddaz 2005: 403–404.
126 I believe the *imperium* in question was exactly the same as that granted to Germanicus in AD 17 for his mission in the East, more on which below.
127 See Rich 1990: 206; Hurlet 1994: 265; Kienast, Eck, Heil 2017: 65.
128 See Hurlet 1997: 86; Dalla Rosa 2014: 238; Rich 2015: 130; Kienast, Eck, Heil 2017: 61. *Contra* Vervaet 2020: 155, who believes that, from 12 BC, Drusus led the Rhine campaigns as a proconsul with independent *imperium*, an assumption contradicted by Dio's account quoted below, which only has Drusus gain those prerogatives in the following year.

129 Suet. *Claud.* 1. 3; Cass. Dio 54, 33, 5. *Contra* Vervaet (2020: 159), who believes Dio refers here, not to Drusus being granted proconsular powers for the first time, but to him having them renewed for another 5 years (*quinquennium*).
130 See Hurlet 1997: 87 (note 48).
131 Hurlet 1994: 271.
132 The former is favoured by such scholars as Bogue 1970: 145–147; Rich 1990: 224; *id.* 2015: 130; Hurlet 1997: 88–89; Seager 2005: 21; the latter, by Bringmann 1977: 235; Kienast, Eck, Heil 2017: 70—who believe Tiberius was in Pannonia as an ordinary imperial legate.
133 Cass. Dio 54, 34, 3.
134 More on that below.
135 See Rich 1990: 224; Hurlet 1997: 88; *id.* 2015: 147.
136 Hurlet 1994: 266.
137 See Sawiński 2018: 86.
138 Timpe 1962: 27; Woodman 1977: 210; Syme 1979: 315; Hurlet 1997: 141–146; *id.* 2015: 148; Severy 2003: 190; Rich 2012: 81.
139 But I reject the idea of Peter M. Swan (2004: 142), who claims Tiberius's *imperium* was *maius* in relation to those of other proconsuls, but *minus* than Augustus's; considering Tiberius was to act in Germania, I see no reason for such broad powers to have been granted him just then. Still, I cannot quite say on what Swan rests his claim.
140 I remain thoroughly unconvinced by the opinion of A. J. Woodman (1977: 210–211), who believes Tiberius's *imperium* was not increased (in the sense of becoming *maius* to those of other governors), merely extended geographically to now cover all the provinces of the Empire.
141 Vell. Pat. 2, 121, 1; Suet. *Tib.* 21, 1. See also Timpe 1962: 28, 47; Parsi 1963: 47; Levick 1999: 63; Seager 2005: 39; Rich 2012: 81; Stevenson 2013: 137; Hurlet 2015: 148; Kienast, Eck, Heil 2017: 71. Some researchers date that regulation to AD 12, e.g. Brunt 1977: 97; Woodman 1977: 211; Dettenhofer 2000: 204. The differences stem from ancient authors also dating the regulation variously, with Velleius Paterculus placing it in AD 12, before Tiberius's triumph, whereas Suetonius prefers AD 13.
142 See Vervaet 2014: 273.
143 The timing of Gaius Caesar's departure to the East is open to some discussion. I do just that below; see Section 3.3.
144 Cass. Dio 55, 10, 18.
145 Suet. *Tib.* 12, 2; Tac. *Ann.* 2, 42, 2. Somewhat differently, Orosius (7, 3, 4): *Gaium nepotem suum Caesar Augustus ad ordinandas Aegypti Syriaque provincias misit.* Still, he is wrong to limit the scope of Gaius's powers to the provinces of Syria and Egypt.
146 Although a fragment is missing at just that point, the reconstruction suggested by P. Herz (1980: 288) seems highly probable to me and has been adopted, with minor modifications, by others. See e.g. Arnaud 1994: 226–227; Hurlet 1997: 131–132.
147 Hurlet 1994: 271–272; Arnaud 1994: 229–232; Dąbrowa 1998: 203.
148 So e.g. Romer 1974: 93; Bringmann 1977: 228. Dalla Rosa (2014: 232) supposes such prerogatives were weilded by all members of the *domus Augusta* carrying out special missions in the East.
149 For Germanicus's place in Tiberius's succession plans, see Sawiński 2018: 111–120.
150 Cass. Dio 56, 25, 2.
151 Translated by E. Cary (Loeb Classical Library, 175).
152 Tac. *Ann.* 1, 14, 3.
153 Translated by C. H. Moore, J. Jackson (Loeb Classical Library, 249).

154 See Hurlet 1994: 274; *id.* 1997: 169. Similarly Swan 2004: 278. However, the date of Germanicus's first imperatorial acclamation is not certain. I discuss the issue in more detail in Section 4.1.
155 Brunt 1974: 180; 185; Syme 1978: 57–58, 63; *id.* 1979: 320.
156 Bringmann 1977: 227; in a similar vein, Lebek 1991b: 122. With some reservations, D. Kienast also accepts Germanicus had the status of *legatus Augusti pro praetore* until Augustus's death. See Kienast, Eck, Heil 2017: 73–74.
157 Ovid. *Tr.* 4, 2, 28. The word *proximus* is used in a similar sense by Velleius Paterculus (2, 71; 2, 127) to refer to Messalla Corvinus as being the closest in rank to Brutus and Cassius in the Republican camp, and to refer to Statilius Taurus, whom he describes as Augustus's second-closest aide (*adiutor*) after Agrippa.
158 Tac. *Ann.* 1, 31, 2.
159 See Swan 2004: 278. Drusus the Elder was granted *imperium proconsulare* in the year 11 BC and assumed consulship in 9 BC, whereas Gaius Caesar received *imperium proconsulare* in 1 BC and held his consulship in the following year. See Kienast, Eck, Heil 2017: 61; 67.
160 Mommsen 1888: 1158 (note 3).
161 See Vervaet 2014: 28 (note 43).
162 Hurlet 1994: 277–278.
163 See Tac. *Ann.* 2, 22, 1–2; 2, 41, 1–2.
164 See Syme 1978: 62; Dalla Rosa 2014: 240; Vervaet 2014: 28; 280 (note 207); Rich 2015: 133. *Contra* Hurlet (2006: 179), who believes members of the *domus Augusta* leading military campaigns with the rank of proconsuls had their own auspices.
165 See Zanker 1990: 232–233.
166 As discussed below.
167 Tac. *Ann.* 1, 31, 1–2; cf. also Eck 1985: 3; 107.
168 Tac. *Ann.* 1, 31, 1–2; 2, 6, 1; 25, 1.
169 Hurlet 1994: 275.
170 The guess made by Girardet (2000: 225)—that extending the scope of Germanicus's *imperium* was meant to make up for suddenly revoking his command in Germania—is not convincing. Instead, I believe it was mainly owing to entrusting him with a new mission in the East, during which he would visit public provinces.
171 Tac. *Ann.* 2, 43, 1.
172 Translated by C. H. Moore and J. Jackson (Loeb Classical Library, 249).
173 *SCPP* ll. 34–35.
174 Translated by J. B. Lott 2012, 143.
175 *TS* fr. 1, ll. 15–16.
176 Translated by J. B. Lott 2012, 89, 91.
177 P. Oxy. 2435, ll. 9–10. For an edition with meticulous commentary, see Weingärtner 1969: 73–90.
178 Translated by M. Jarczyk.
179 See Goodyear 1981: 323; Lebek 1991b: 103–124.
180 Tac. *Ann.* 2, 59, 1–3; Suet. *Tib.* 52, 2.
181 See primarily Weingärtner 1969: 44–46; Hennig 1972: 358–359; Drogula 2015a: 130. Goodyear (1981: 378–379) treats Germanicus's going to Egypt as deliberate insubordination, exceeding his prerogatives.
182 So Hurlet (1997: 204–205), who thinks Germanicus's *imperium* applied in Egypt as well.
183 For a long time, researchers stressed the special status of Egypt as a kind of private domain of the emperor, but that view was abandoned in the 1970s, and, since then, Egypt has been explicitly regarded as one of the eastern provinces of Rome. See Capponi 2013: 118.

184 Oros. 7, 3, 4.
185 Hurlet 1997: 206.
186 More on which below.
187 See e.g. Tac. *Ann.* 1, 33, 1–3; 2, 5, 1–2; 2, 26, 2–5; 2, 40, 1–3; 2, 43, 4–5; 6, 51, 3. For the manner in which Tacitus's narrative depicts Tiberius and Germanicus, see Shotter 1968: 194–214; Borzsák 1969: 588–600; Baar 1990.
188 Koestermann 1958: 350 (note 46).
189 Tac. *Hist.* 1, 11, 1.
190 Tac. *Ann.* 1, 14, 3.
191 See Hurlet 1997: 215; Kienast, Eck, Heil 2017: 75–76.
192 Tac. *Ann.* 2, 44, 1.
193 So e.g. Bringmann 1977: 236; Hurlet 1997: 215; Levick 1999: 130; Vervaet 2014: 85; Kienast, Eck, Heil 2017: 76.
194 Rogers 1943: 120; Goodyear 1981: 329; Hurlet 1994: 269; *id.* 1997: 216; Levick 1999: 130.
195 Vell. Pat. 2, 31, 2; 2, 33, 1; Plut. *Pomp.* 30.
196 Vell. Pat. 2, 62, 2; App. *B. Civ.* 4, 58, 1.
197 Hurlet 1997: 43.
198 Vell. Pat. 2, 121, 1: *senatus populusque Romanus postulante patre eius ut aequum ei ius in omnibus provinciis exercitibusque esset quam erat ipsi, decreto complexus est.*
199 Suet. *Tib.* 21, 1: *ac non multo post lege per consules lata, ut provincias cum Augusto communiter administraret.* See also Brunt 1974: 171.
200 For a detailed analysis of the process, see Hurlet 1997: 190–193.
201 Tac. *Ann.* 2, 43, 1.
202 *SCPP* ll. 33–35. See also Dalla Rosa 2014: 242.
203 As emphatically demonstrated by this formula in *TS* fr. 1, l. 16: *ex mandatis Ti(berii)Caesaris Au[g(usti).*
204 It ought to be noted that, later on, emperors would not observe that principle as rigorously.
205 See Vervaet 2014: 254; Wesch-Klein 2016: 39.
206 Cass. Dio 53, 13, 5. The existence of such titulature for governors of imperial provinces is also confirmed by inscriptions, which therefore verify the accuracy of Cassius Dio's text. See Ehrenberg, Jones 1955: 107–109 (nos. 199, 208, 211, 213).
207 Cass. Dio 53, 13, 5–8. See also Millar 1966: 157–158; Wesch-Klein 2016: 42–43.
208 See Schumacher 1988: 38.
209 See Rich 1990: 145.
210 See Eck, Caballos, Fernández 1996: 161; Rich 2012: 56; Vervaet 2014: 254. *Contra* Millar (1966: 157), who accepted Mommsen's view that *legati Augusti* held independent *imperium*.
211 The only exception being Aulus Plautius, who was given by Claudius the right to hold an ovation as an imperial legate, as discussed below.
212 Cass. Dio 53, 13, 2; Tac. *Hist.* 1, 11; Marquardt 1873: 134; 413–415; Schumacher 1988: 38; Wesch-Klein 2016: 43–45.
213 Marquardt 1873: 330–335; Schumacher 1988: 38; Sartre 1997: 22–25.
214 Cass. Dio 53, 13, 3–4. Also in this case Dio's version is confirmed by epigraphical sources; see Ehrenberg, Jones 1955: 106–110 (nos. 197–199 and 214).
215 Cass. Dio 53, 13, 2–4. See also Millar 1966: 157; Wesch-Klein 2016: 40–41.
216 As proven by a passage in Dio (53, 15, 4), who reports that, after the division of the provinces of 27 BC, the princeps could freely issue *mandata* both to legates he had appointed and to proconsuls of public provinces. See also Millar 1966: 164–165; Vervaet 2014: 255.

217 Tac. *Ann.* 1, 76, 2 (proconsuls of Macedonia and Achaea). Tac. *Ann.* 3, 58, 1–2 (a proconsul of Asia). Tac. *Ann.* 12, 59, 1; 13, 52, 1 (proconsul of Africa Proconsularis).
218 See Rich 2012: 68 (note 81).
219 Schumacher 1988: 38.
220 *Ornamenta triumphalia* for campaigns in Africa were, for example, awarded to L. Passienus Rufus, Cossus Cornelius Lentulus, and Junius Blaesus. See Vell. Pat. 2, 116, 2; 125, 5; Tac. *Ann.* 3, 72, 4.
221 Vell. Pat. 2, 105, 1; 109, 5; 110, 2.
222 Vell. Pat. 2, 112, 4; 113, 1–2.
223 Tac. *Ann.* 1, 31, 1–2: *duo apud ripam Rheni exercitus errant: cui nomen superiori, sub C. Silio legato, inferiorem A. Caecina curabat. regimen summae rei penes Germanicum.*
224 See Dąbrowa 1998: 32–34.
225 Tac. *Ann.* 2, 57, 1; 69, 1; *SCPP* ll. 37–45. See Drogula 2015a: 124.
226 *SCPP* ll. 29–35; Tac. *Ann.* 3, 12, 1–2.
227 Tac. *Ann.* 3, 15, 5. For Piso's trial, see esp. Eck, Caballos, Fernández 1996: *passim*; Eck 1997: 128–145; Bodel 1999: 43–63; Damon 1999: 143–162; Lebek 1999: 183–211. On Piso's conflict with Germanicus more recently, see Drogula 2015a: 121–153.
228 See above.
229 Cass. Dio 53, 32, 5.
230 L. Koenen's claim (1970: 273–274) that Agrippa received the same exemption is pure speculation. Similarly also Vervaet (2014: 85, note 53), who asserts that: "The permanent privilege to exercise *imperium* within the *pomerium* as proconsul was first granted to Augustus in 23, and must have been routinely granted to such privileged proconsuls as Agrippa, Tiberius and Germanicus, too, as all of these men are known to have stayed in Rome during their official terms for shorter or longer periods."
231 An interpretation indicated by a passage in Cassius Dio (54, 12, 4). See also Rich 1990: 168, 189. *Contra* Vervaet (2014: 273–274, note 187 and 2020: 147), who believes Agrippa's *imperium* was lesser than Augustus's.
232 *SCPP* ll. 35–36: *dum in omni re maius imperium Ti(berio) Caesari Aug(usto) quam Germanico Caesari esset.*
233 See Dalla Rosa 2014: 249–252.
234 Girardet 2000: 219–227.
235 Discussed below.
236 See below.
237 Cass. Dio 54, 28, 2.
238 *TS* fr. 1, ll. 26–28; Suet. *Claud.* 1, 3; Eutrop. 7, 13. See also Lebek 1989a: 52.
239 Vell. Pat. 2, 104, 4.
240 Vell. Pat. 2, 99, 4.
241 Tac. *Ann.* 1, 31, 1; Suet. *Tib.* 25, 2; *Cal.* 1, 1. For a discussion on the reliability of that report, see Sawiński 2018: 209–210.
242 Suet. *Cal.* 3–4.
243 Tac. *Ann.* 2, 82, 1–5; 3, 4, 1–2; Suet. *Cal.* 5–6.
244 Tac. *Ann.* 3, 14, 4; Suet. *Cal.* 2. See also Eck 1995: 7–9.
245 Suet. *Cal.* 5. Suetonius's report is also confirmed by the *SCPP* ll. 57–58.

2 Missions of members of the *domus Augusta* in the western provinces of the Roman Empire

Resorting regularly to members of the *domus Augusta* for part-military, part-diplomatic and administrative tasks was among the specifics of Augustus's principate and, later, in the early years of his reign, also of Tiberius's. Except for Gaius Caesar and Drusus the Younger, all the members of the imperial family active in the provinces as holders of extraordinary *imperium* had gained the necessary experience earlier by carrying out various other tasks. Before I present the several missions of members of the *domus Augusta* in the western part of the Empire, I want to briefly discuss the missions they had been assigned prior to receiving independent *imperium* that were important to their careers as being preparatory in a way for increasingly greater responsibilities.

In 20 BC, Augustus sent his stepson Tiberius to the East; Tiberius's orders were to strengthen Roman influence in Armenia. As Suetonius recounts, Tiberius's eastern expedition was the first independent task of his career.[1] Scholars generally assume Tiberius was probably sent to the East in the rank of *legatus Augusti pro praetore*.[2] His main achievement was setting Tigranes, who was friendly towards Rome, on the Armenian throne. According to the sources, Tiberius enthroned the new monarch himself.[3] Suetonius also mentions that Tiberius got back from the Parthians the legions' eagles the Romans had lost during Crassus's campaign.[4] That last piece of information is not confirmed elsewhere, however, so it is more likely the Parthians had by then handed over the *signa* directly to Augustus, perhaps while the emperor was in Syria in 20 BC.[5]

In 15 BC, Tiberius and his brother Drusus were given by the princeps the task of finalizing the conquest of the Alpine regions. Until recently, the consensus in scholarship has been that Augustus's stepsons led that campaign as *legati Augusti pro praetore*,[6] but now, F. J. Vervaet has proposed that their status during the expedition was that of proconsul with independent *imperium*. His arguments in favour of that claim include a passage in Dio (54, 22, 4) that says the two brothers waged the war in Raetia, partly themselves and partly through their legates (ὑποστρατήγοι). Vervaet supposes legates of praetorial rank (*pro praetore*) are meant, which allegedly means Augustus's stepsons held proconsular rank then, if subordinate *legati* fought under their command.[7] Now, that is in itself a controversial opinion, because the word Dio uses is not a technical term, instead referring in general to various subordinate commanders, and so it cannot be determined if the intended sense really is *legati pro praetore* as Vervaet would have it. Furthermore, even if Tiberius and Drusus did have other legates under their command, it does not necessarily follow they were proconsuls then. A passage in Velleius Paterculus is worth citing here that clearly demonstrates that *legati Augusti pro praetore* had other, lower-ranking legates at their disposal.[8] Another argument in favour of the brothers leading the Raetian campaign as *legati Augusti* may be seen in the fact they were not granted the titles of *imperator* for their successes, neither were they granted the right to hold a triumph. I find it unlikely that they would not have received those honours had they held independent *imperium*.[9]

As a result of the actions of Augustus's stepsons, the central Alps did fall under Roman rule, as did the northern foothills of the Alps, where the province of Raetia was subsequently created. Among the local tribes, the sources list the Raeti, the Vindelici, the Breuni, and the Ucenni.[10] The Alpine expedition was the first serious military undertaking Augustus entrusted to his stepsons. Maybe it is this campaign that is referred to by the emissions of *aurei* and *denarii* produced at the imperial mint at Lugdunum, dated to 15–12 BC.[11] Some researchers suppose the reverse side of those coins depicts Drusus and Tiberius in military attire, offering olive branches, which in that context symbolize victory, to Augustus seated in the *sella curulis*.[12] Still, with no legend, it is impossible to be sure.

In the year 7, Germanicus fought his first battle. Cassius Dio writes he was sent by Augustus to the Pannonian–Dalmatian front to help Tiberius suppress the uprising that had broken out there 1 year earlier. Apparently, Germanicus brought with him units made up of citizens and freedmen, which were to support the legions already engaged there.[13] There is little in the sources on Germanicus's part in the Pannonian–Dalmatian war; Velleius Paterculus only notes Tiberius sent him ahead of the main Roman force, whereupon he conducted several successful raids against the rebel tribes, but provides no details.[14] There is slightly more detail in Cassius Dio, who mentions a successful operation by Germanicus against the Dalmatian tribe of Mazaei in AD 7 and the capture by him 2 years later of two strategically important forts belonging to the rebels, Splonum and Arduba.[15] Germanicus was granted *ornamenta triumphalia* for his contribution to suppressing the uprising, which proves he did have the position of *legatus Augusti* during that time.[16] Germanicus's participation in the Pannonian–Dalmatian war was certainly an important stage in his military career, as it provided him with his first wartime experience under the eye of the seasoned Tiberius.

Besides military and diplomatic missions, Augustus entrusted members of his family with diverse civilian and administrative duties. The work carried out by Drusus the Elder in Gaul in 12 BC makes for an excellent example. His crucial achievement in that area was establishing the first centre of imperial cult within the western provinces. With the local tribes rebelling owing to a prescribed tax collection, Drusus decided to summon to Lugdunum the most eminent members of all tribes from the three Gallic provinces; then, in their presence, he established an altar to Roma and Augustus (*ara Romae et Augusti*). From then on, representatives of Gallic *civitates* convened each year at the altar, giving rise to the provincial assembly of Gaul (the *concilium trium Galliarum*). To begin with, the assembly only had a religious role, but, over time, it became the institution that represented the interests of the inhabitants of the provinces before the rulers of Rome. Establishing it was of major significance for integrating the recently conquered lands into the Empire, as well as for creating among the population an attitude of loyalty towards the emperor's political power.[17] Later, Drusus's foundation inspired and became the model for other similar provincial initiatives.[18]

The situations discussed above demonstrate that members of the reigning dynasty were, right from the beginning of their military and political careers, entrusted with responsible and prestigious undertakings. Even though, before obtaining independent *imperium*, they had, formally speaking, exactly the same standing as many other legates of Augustus, their tasks surpassed those of ordinary commanders in scale and importance. Additionally, those missions offered an excellent opportunity to prepare for ever more spectacular tasks.

2.1 Spain

Spain held an important place in Rome's foreign policy under Augustus. For the emperor, it was of top priority to subjugate the as yet unconquered northern and north-western parts of that province, which would make it possible to complete the conquest of the whole Iberian Peninsula. Augustus's campaign of 26–25 BC subjugated the warlike tribes of the Cantabri and Astures,[19] but, soon after the princeps left for Rome, the tribes rebelled against Roman rule. Because the campaigns of his legates had mediocre effect, in 19 BC Augustus decided to send Agrippa as his direct representative. Agrippa, right from the start, encountered strong resistance from the rebelling tribes, who had no prospects if they were defeated and so fought with particular determination. His undertaking was not helped either by the defeatism spreading through the Roman ranks, which was a result of a long campaign with no tangible successes. Thanks to the radical measures he took (which consisted in stripping one legion of its honorary epithet of *Augusta*), Agrippa was able to restore the weakened morale and discipline among the units. Gradually, the Romans took control of the situation, and, after much bloodshed, the uprising was at last quelled. The vanquished were treated with particular cruelty. All rebels able to bear arms were slaughtered, and the other members of the tribes that had revolted were deported from their mountain homes and settled on the plains.[20]

After the revolt had been smothered, Agrippa inspected the Spanish provinces;[21] first, he visited the colony of Emerita Augusta in Hispania Lusitania, founded earlier by Augustus, initiating there the construction of a theatre for the veterans that was eventually built shortly after 16 BC. The structure remains to this day, as does a monumental inscription bearing Agrippa's titulature, placed above one of the entrances. In return, the town's inhabitants honoured the emperor's son-in-law by erecting a statue of him.[22]

Next, Agrippa probably visited Ulia and Gades in Hispania Baetica, where he bestowed his patronage on both towns. In Gades, he also established a Roman navy base.[23] From epigraphic and numismatic sources, we know the inhabitants of the two towns honoured Agrippa with such titles as *patronus municipi* and *municipi parens*.[24] His achievements in Spain were certainly impressive. Thanks to his military talent and determination, the Romans managed to decisively break the resistance of the warlike Cantabri and Astures and to strengthen Rome's rule in north-western Spain.

2.2 Gaul

Representatives of the *domus Augusta* were also active in Gaul.[25] One of the more important tasks Augustus set himself was unifying the regions of Transalpine Gaul that Caesar conquered with the province of Gallia Narbonensis. Towards the end of 20 BC, the emperor sent Agrippa to Gaul. From Cassius Dio, we know he did that because of the revolt that broke out among the tribes, as well as the threat to the province from Germanic tribes. Agrippa managed to restore order with relative ease,[26] but the sources are silent on his military achievements in the area, concentrating instead on his construction work. Strabo tells us four important transportation arteries were built to connect Lugdunum, the administrative capital and main political and religious centre of Gaul, with other major towns of the province.[27] The significance of that undertaking was huge; besides its strategic importance (in that moving troops was now easier), the new system allowed for information to travel fast and favoured the growth of trade.[28]

Remnants of Agrippa's construction programme can be seen especially in the Roman colony of Nemausus (modern Nîmes) in Narbonne Gaul. From two fragmentary inscriptions, we know Augustus's son-in-law established a temple to Diana and baths in the city.[29] Older literature also attributed to Agrippa the establishment of the renowned temple of Maison Carrée,[30] but these days it is known the temple was actually only built after his death and dedicated to Gaius Caesar and Lucius Caesar, Augustus's prematurely dead grandsons.[31] We do not know for sure if the famous aqueduct of Pont du Gard was a public work of his. Although it is in fact dated to Augustus's time, it need not have been funded by Agrippa.[32] Agrippa's euergetism was appreciated by the inhabitants of the colony, who honoured him by issuing a special series of coins bearing his portrait on the obverse next to that of the princeps.[33]

Agrippa's construction work in the Gallic provinces resulted in various public buildings being erected and was extremely important for the cultural and civilizational development of the region. As it was a member of the reigning dynasty that ordered the construction, it was seen as reflecting the generosity of Augustus himself, which no doubt considerably strengthened the loyalty and gratitude of the local population towards Rome and its ruler.

In 9 BC, Drusus the Elder visited Gaul while on his way to Germania. The late-ancient chronicle of Cassiodorus reports he then consecrated a *templum Caesaris*, but D. Fishwick concluded that, writing several centuries later, Cassiodorus was wrong as to the character of the building. Rather, in Fishwick's opinion Drusus probably established an altar to Rome and Augustus, just as he had in Lugdunum. The altar was most likely erected at Andemantunnum (present-day Langres) in Gallia Belgica, in the area inhabited by the Lingones.[34]

In AD 11 or 12, Gaul was visited by Tiberius. His intervention was brought about by the unrest incited by the inhabitants of Vienna (modern Vienne) in Gallia Narbonensis. Our only source for that piece of information is Velleius Paterculus, who, unfortunately, does not say what caused the unrest and merely notes in a concise manner that Tiberius brought back order quickly.[35]

Towards the end of Augustus's reign, Germanicus, too, was active in the Gallic provinces. The sources report he inspected three of them, mostly to carry out a wealth census for the purpose of introducing new taxes.[36] It is widely accepted those were to fund the war in Germania being planned.[37] During his stay in Belgica, Germanicus received the news of Augustus's death and, under that circumstance, had the Belgae (*Belgarum civitates*) swear loyalty to Tiberius as the new ruler.[38]

2.3 Germania

2.3.1 The campaigns of Drusus the Elder (10–9 BC)

Modern historical literature gives an important place to attempts to determine the goals and specifics of Augustus's policy regarding Germania. Certainly, Drusus's campaigns on the right bank of the Rhine, begun in 12 BC, were the sign of a new phase in Roman policy for the region.[39] Diverse opinions abound among historians on the causes and character of Drusus's expedition. D. Kienast believes the aim of the campaign was to conquer the areas between the Rhine and the Elbe,[40] which I think is going too far—at that stage, a clear concept of conquest could hardly have crystallized. Moreover, we have no grounds to suppose that, before Drusus's campaigns, Augustus was already familiar enough with the geography of Germania to define the area to be brought under Roman rule so precisely. I find D. Timpe's opinion more convincing—that Drusus's expeditions were a remedy of sorts for the inefficiency of the system of treaties with Germanic tribes that had been in use until then. Thus, their purpose was not to conquer Germania, but to secure the borders of Gaul by creating a buffer zone and bringing the particularly "aggressive" German tribes under Roman control. If any plans for conquest were in fact made, then the idea took shape gradually as Drusus waged war on the right bank of the Rhine.[41]

Drusus was dispatched to Germania in 12 BC, to begin with, likely as a *legatus Augusti pro praetore*. Then, from 10 BC on, he led campaigns armed with proconsular *imperium*.[42] His first opponent in this year was the tribe of Chatti, who inhabited the lands on the upper Weser. Dissatisfied as the result of an earlier displacement and resettlement from their homelands to areas inhabited by the Sugambri, the Chatti had rebelled against the Roman decrees and drew the Sugambri into an anti-Roman coalition.[43] We do not have much information on Drusus's campaign against the Chatti and Sugambri. Cassius Dio, our main source, is uncharacteristically terse on the subject and not sure whether the tribes were conquered or only humiliated as a result of the Roman expedition.[44] Pointing out how scanty and ambiguous our source data are, D. Timpe suspected Drusus's campaign brought no decisive results, and so received little interest from ancient historians. What is more, in his opinion, the involvement of the Roman forces in the campaign against the Chatti made it possible for the Sugambri to destroy Oberaden, a strategically important fort on the right bank of the Rhine.[45] K. Christ even supposed that the legions were defeated by the units of the Chatti and Sugambri,[46] but his hypothesis is far-fetched. Although Dio is reticent in his account of Drusus's achievements there, that is far too little for us to assume that the Roman forces suffered defeat. We may, on the other hand, agree with those researchers' opinion that Drusus's campaign did not end in a spectacular victory, also borne out by the fact that Augustus's stepson did not receive any honours for his actions in Germania that year, in sharp contrast to his previous campaigns in the region, for which he was granted the *ornamenta triumphalia* and the right to hold an ovation.[47]

Therefore, after Drusus returned to Germania from Rome in 9 BC, his main goal was to ultimately subjugate the Chatti and Sugambri. The situation was unfavourable in that there was also anti-Roman sentiment among the Suebi, who included the Marcomanni, Quadi, and Hermunduri.[48] D. Timpe believed that, in the face of the enormous task that lay ahead, Drusus had to divide the Roman forces in two. One of those two armies, commanded by Drusus's legates, carried out a successful operation against the Sugambri from the Roman bases on the Lippe, while the other waged a victorious campaign against the Chatti and Suebi under the command of Augustus's stepson himself.[49] In the second part of the campaign, the Roman units crossed the Weser and attacked the Cherusci, a tribe who inhabited the land between the middle Weser and the Elbe. According to Cassius Dio, Drusus limited himself to devastating the lands of the tribe, which avoided facing the Roman force directly.[50] After a march through the territory of the Cherusci, the Romans reached the Elbe. Then, having tried to no avail to cross it, Drusus decided to retreat.

The problem of Drusus's retreat from the banks of the Elbe is quite controversial. In Suetonius and Cassius Dio, we read that the reason for the decision was a bad omen: allegedly, Drusus saw a vision of a larger-than-life Germanic woman who forbade him to march any further into Germania, and that episode made Augustus's stepson give up on his ambitious plans to continue the expedition beyond the Elbe.[51] D. Timpe read into that account a "veiled" sign of Drusus's senior staff and rank-and-file soldiers opposing their commander's ambitious plans;[52] A. Abramenko disagreed, rejecting the hypothesis of mutiny and believing Drusus's decision to retreat followed from his military failures.[53] Now, that opinion is difficult to share, especially as we do not know who may have been responsible for the supposed defeat: the Cherusci did try to avoid confronting the Roman legions. It is possible Drusus chose retreat because he was dismayed and discouraged by their tactics as they withdrew ever deeper into Germania. It cannot be ruled out that, as Timpe suggested, the course of the campaign—that is, forever chasing the enemy—displeased the soldiers, who convinced their commander to fall back. And there is one other option that I think must be kept open, namely genuine religious motivation. Perhaps Drusus interpreted the sign as a *prodigium*, which finally made him desist from marching on into Germania.

In order to commemorate the scale of the undertaking and the distance covered by the Roman expedition in Germania, Drusus decided to erect on the banks of the Elbe a *tropaeum*—a symbolic monument to victory, which in that case was to mark a line between the Roman world and the *Barbaricum*.[54] His victories are also featured on *aurei* minted in the reign of Emperor Claudius, who used them to commemorate his father's achievements. The obverse of that emission bears Drusus's portrait, with the legend "NERO CLAUDIUS DRUSUS GERMANICUS IMP," and the reverse depicts a *vexillum* standing between two shields and spears with the legend, *De Germanis*.[55]

Besides military operations, Drusus's important achievements included constructing buildings meant to strengthen Roman influence in Germania. Florus attributes to him numerous forts on the banks of the Rhine, the Lippe, the Weser, and the Elbe, and bridges across the Rhine.[56] Archaeological excavations did confirm the existence of two strategically important forts on the Lippe (Haltern and Oberaden), as well as other, smaller military bases, but telling precisely when they were created would be difficult, and so it is not quite certain they were Drusus's work.[57]

Meanwhile, Augustus's stepson did achieve one other important project by creating the Rhine fleet (the *classis Germanica*), stationed in what, today, is Bonn. The fleet made it possible to move troops instantly to threatened areas and to provision the legions efficiently.[58] Tacitus also mentions in connection with Drusus the start of the construction of a dam across the Rhine, which was supposed to stop the river from flooding.[59] Drusus's work in Germania was suddenly interrupted in 9 BC as a result of an ill-fated accident: owing to an unlucky fall from a horse, he broke his thighbone. The fracture led to complications, which eventually caused his death.[60]

Although the work he began was never finished, it does command respect. Drusus was the first Roman commander to reach that far into Germania, discovering places as yet unknown to Romans. No doubt that made it easier for other Roman commanders to campaign there later on. Tiberius's instant intervention in Germania in 8 BC demonstrates that the region had not been quite conquered, but it is an unquestionable achievement of Drusus that Tiberius was able to finish his work there in less than a year, and with little difficulty.

2.3.2 Tiberius's campaigns

2.3.2.1 The campaigns of 8–7 BC

Tiberius's arrival on the Rhine heralded a new stage in Rome's policy towards the German lands. In 8 BC, he was given the command of the legions stationed there, which had earlier been held by his younger brother.[61] His campaigns proved different in character from those of Drusus, who had sought direct confrontation with Germanic tribes, pillaging the territories of those that had revolted.[62] According to Tiberius's concept, the main instrument that would allow the unruly Germans to be reined in was deportation. Our sources report that, in 8 BC, he resettled 40,000 Sugambri on the left bank of the Rhine.[63] In R. Wolters's opinion, they were settled, as Roman colonists, near the Roman military camps of Castra Vetera (Xanten) and Novaesium (Neuss), where they were to grow crops, producing supplies for the legions.[64]

In practice, Tiberius's campaign of 8 BC crowned Drusus's earlier achievements, completing the process of "conquering" German lands,[65] or at least that was how his contemporaries saw the situation. Velleius Paterculus mentions that almost all of Germania was smoothly "subjugated" and made into a Roman province.[66] Aufidius Bassus, a historian of the Germanic wars, whose account only survives in short fragments, mentions that Tiberius actually conquered the whole area between the Rhine and the Elbe.[67] Then, in Cassius Dio, we read that, owing to the new territories Rome had gained, Augustus officially and ritually expanded the pomerium.[68] Tiberius's campaign was also commemorated in appropriate coin emissions. The obverse of the *aurei* minted on the occasion bore an image of Augustus wearing a laurel wreath; the legend read "AUGUSTUS DIVI F." The reverse showed a barbarian in Germanic dress—in that context, a personification of Germania—handing over to Augustus in the curule chair (*sella curulis*) a child, as a hostage and token of submission to Roman rule. The legend for the whole image is "IMP XIIII" (Figure 2.1).[69] Cassius Dio also mentions Tiberius intervening in Germania in the following year owing to unrest, but, with the sources being so reticent, we have virtually no information on the subject.[70]

The exact nature and extent of Roman rule over Germania are hotly debated in scholarship. The information provided by literary sources has been to some degree confirmed by archaeological investigations, which revealed many legion camps on the right bank of the Rhine (in the districts of Wetterau and Lippe), as well as lodgings of auxiliary troops from the

Figure 2.1 Aureus (8 BC)—Lugdunum. Obverse legend: AUGUSTUS DIVI F; a portrait of Augustus. Reverse legend: IMP XIIII; barbarian in Germanic dress, handing over a child to Augustus in the curule chair.

Source: *RIC* I², *Aug.* 200.

period in question.[71] However, those traces of Roman presence do not prove that the whole area between the Rhine and the Elbe was under Roman rule or subject to Roman administration. In J. Bleicken's opinion, Rome's power being fully extended over Germania was primarily obstructed by a lack of strong cities and aristocracy as the factors that normally solidified Rome's reign in newly conquered areas.[72] Thus, based on Dio's account referring to the governorship of P. Quinctilius Varus, we may assume only part of Germania was governed directly by Rome rather than all of it. Dio presumably meant the lands between the Rhine and the Weser.[73]

Perhaps it is to Tiberius's actions in the region that we ought to connect the establishment of the *Ara Ubiorum* (Altar of the Ubii), modelled on the Lugdunum institution.[74] The altar was probably erected in the vicinity of present-day Cologne, near the winter camp of the legions stationed there. It was intended as the main political and religious centre of Roman Germania; seen in that context, its establishment was mostly meant to serve quick Romanization and consolidation of the conquered Germanic areas. Unlike in the case of Lugdunum, the construction of the *Ara Ubiorum* did not entail the creation of a provincial assembly in the strict sense of those words, as, until Domitian's time, Germania was not formally a province.[75]

After recalling Tiberius in 7 BC, Augustus entrusted the governance of the conquered German lands to ordinary legates (*legati Augusti pro praetore*). Until AD 4, the region saw no major military undertakings, even though, soon after Tiberius's departure, Germanic tribes rebelled against Roman rule. Still, the legates active in Germania only carried out fairly insignificant offensive operations, focusing on defending the areas assigned to them.[76] With Tiberius in seclusion on Rhodes, and Gaius and Lucius Caesar too young, Augustus had no one by his side he could entrust with major military operations. That is, of course, not to say there were no talented commanders among the emperor's legates, but large-scale campaigns required great armies, and putting one in the hands of a legate would have run counter to Augustus's policy, which meant he consistently granted the high command of large forces to members of his immediate family.

2.3.2.2 *The campaigns of* AD *4–6*

Tiberius reappeared in Germania in AD 4, 2 years after his return from Rhodes, when his standing in the imperial family had changed. After being adopted by Augustus in AD 4 and receiving both *tribunicia potestas* and independent proconsular *imperium*, he had become *collega imperii* of the princeps and the primary candidate for succession.[77] His intervention in Germania was due to the long war that had broken out in the governorship of M. Vinicius (in AD 1).[78] In spite of Vinicius's response, the Romans were not able to restore order, and so Tiberius's direct intervention became necessary.[79] Velleius Paterculus, who is our main source of information on the matter, reports the military operations took two courses. More difficult ones were conducted by Tiberius, while the less crucial ones were carried out by Sentius Saturninus, Augustus's legate in Germania and a subordinate of Tiberius as the commander of the Rhine army. In AD 4, Tiberius led a victorious campaign against the Canninefates, Attuarii, and Bructeri; the Romans also crossed the Weser and accepted the surrender of the Cherusci. Velleius notes with satisfaction that, with the campaign over, Tiberius was the first Roman commander to allot to the victorious legions winter quarters in the very "heart" of Germania, at the springs of the Lippe.[80]

Velleius's account of the campaign of AD 5 is, in a sense, a eulogy of Tiberius. According to that historian, the Roman troops crossed all of Germania, reaching the Elbe. Among the defeated Germanic tribes, he lists the Chauci and the Langobardi, who inhabited the lands between the mouths of the Weser and the Elbe. He also mentions a large-scale operation of the Roman fleet, which circumnavigated the North Sea, reaching the mouth of the Elbe, from where it sailed upstream to join the army.[81]

In Augustus's autobiography, we read that a number of Germanic tribes were so impressed by Tiberius's campaign that they sent envoys to the emperor to solicit Rome's friendship,[82] but Cassius Dio is much more reserved in his evaluation of Tiberius's achievements, writing that, although the commander did reach first the Weser and then the Elbe, he had no notable successes. Even so, Dio reports, both Augustus and Tiberius received imperatorial acclamations again.[83] Velleius Paterculus disagrees, believing Tiberius's achievements in Germania so significant that the only Germanic people left unsubjugated were the Marcomanni, who lived near the springs of the Elbe. Under the leadership of the ambitious chieftain Maroboduus, the tribe created a tribal union whose actions were a serious threat to Roman interests in Germania. The Roman provinces that bordered on the lands of the Marcomanni—Raetia, Noricum, and Pannonia—were in danger too.[84] Tiberius planned a great campaign against the Marcomanni in AD 6, with as many as twelve legions participating. The troops were divided into two large forces. One, under Tiberius's command, was to strike against Maroboduus from Carnuntum in Noricum; the other, under Sentius Saturninus, would attack from Germania.[85] The plan failed right at the beginning because of the outbreak of the great anti-Roman uprising in Pannonia.[86] As Tiberius was, at the time, the only person in the imperial family Augustus could entrust with such a serious military operation, the emperor had to temporarily give up on any expansion plans regarding eastern Germania.

2.3.2.3 The campaigns of AD 10–12

In AD 9, Augustus gave the governorship of the Germanic lands to P. Quinctilius Varus, who ruled them with the rank of *legatus Augusti*. However, Varus's indolence and provocative policies caused the outbreak of an uprising led by the tribe of Cherusci. The Roman troops were ambushed and suffered crushing defeat in the Teutoburg Forest.[87] The effects of that *clades Variana* were grave; in order to keep Gaul safe from a possible Germanic invasion, Augustus decided to send Tiberius over again. However, our sources differ in how they evaluate Tiberius's actions in that period. Velleius enthusiastically reports that Tiberius concentrated for the most part on securing the bank of the Rhine and strengthening the strategically important points on the borders of Gaul, also attributing to him a raid into Germania, which allegedly ended in the destruction of the abodes of the tribes who lived there, after which Tiberius led the army to its winter quarters.[88] Cassius Dio contradicts that by simply not mentioning any offensive operations on the Roman side. According to his version, the Romans merely secured the bank of the Rhine to prevent a Germanic invasion of Gaul.[89] Although Suetonius, in turn, does mention Tiberius crossing the Rhine, he stresses that his actions on the other side were very cautious.[90]

As could be expected, when reporting on Tiberius's actions in the second year of the campaign (that is, in AD 11), Velleius depicts them as a single streak of significant military successes. He attributes to Tiberius various successful operations by both the legions and the fleet.[91] His version is, again, contradicted by Cassius Dio's account, where he writes the campaign was quite fruitless, as the Germans avoided facing Tiberius's legions directly, and the Romans, still affected strongly by Varus's failure, had not the slightest intention to venture into Germania.[92]

We have no sources at all for Tiberius's actions in Germania in AD 12. R. Wolters suspects that, in that year, he launched another expedition across the Rhine, where the Romans fought a victorious battle against the Bructeri.[93]

It appears the campaigns of the years 10–12 brought no important military achievements, not that such was their objective. Tiberius's actions succeeded primarily in cancelling out the negative results of Varus's defeat and securing the borders of Gaul against a possible invasion of Germanic tribes. He also enlarged and strengthened the fortifications on the Lippe, which connected the area to the Roman bases on the Rhine,[94] but potentially restoring Roman influence in Germania remained an open question.

2.3.3 Germanicus's efforts on the Rhine (AD *14–16)*

2.3.3.1 Suppressing the mutiny of the Rhine legions (AD *14)*

In the year 13, Tiberius was succeeded as the commander of the army stationed on the Rhine by Germanicus, who had already been active in the region 2 years earlier when he was sent to Germania in the rank of proconsul to gain appropriate military experience under Tiberius's eye.[95] In 12, Germanicus went back to Rome to assume a consulship; then after the consulship, he was again dispatched to Germania, where he took over as the commander-in-chief of the legions posted there.[96] In D. Kienast's opinion, Augustus's sending him there is proof that the princeps had not given up on his earlier ambitions—that is, to conquer Germany all the way up to the Elbe,[97] but it needs to be questioned, as it would be difficult to tell how far the emperor's plans for Germania went at that time. In Tacitus, we merely read:

> *bellum ea tempestate nullum nisi adversus Germanos supererat, abolendae magis infamiae ob amissum cum Quintilio Varo exercitum quam cupidine proferendi imperii aut dignum ob praemium.*[98]
>
> War at the time was none, except an outstanding campaign against the Germans, waged more to redeem the prestige lost with Quintilius Varus and his army than from any wish to extend the empire or with any prospect of an adequate recompense.[99]

I believe we can trust him as regards the priorities and goals of Roman policy in Germania in the final years of Augustus's reign; Rome's honour and prestige did have enormous importance in the matter. Thus Germanicus's primary objective must have been, not further conquest, but rather humiliating the Cherusci as chiefly responsible for the Roman defeat of AD 9, and getting back the lost legions' eagles. The latter was particularly important. Winning back standards lost on the battlefield was a matter of honour to the Romans. Let us not forget how punctiliously imperial propaganda had highlighted reclaiming the eagles lost by Crassus and Antony in the war against the Parthians and by Lollius in Gaul.[100]

There is little in the sources on Germanicus's activity in the provinces on the Rhine during the last 2 years of Augustus's reign. Velleius Paterculus merely reports that Augustus sent his grandson to Germania to deal with the remnants of the war there.[101] Ancient authors report no details of any military campaigns Germanicus may have led in the lands on the Rhine during that time.[102] Tacitus and Suetonius only note he was active then in the Gallic provinces, but it is not known exactly how much time he spent there. What we do know is that he was in Gaul when news reached him of Augustus's death.[103]

We know much more about Germanicus's campaigns on the right bank of the Rhine after Augustus died, as Tacitus writes about them extensively. The first task Germanicus had to deal with in AD 14 was quelling the mutiny of the legions stationed in Germania Inferior.[104] The revolt had many causes, including long service, which lasted between 30 and 40 years, poor pay, hard conditions, and strict discipline, brutally enforced by the officers. As another reason for the mutiny, Tacitus and Suetonius add the soldiers' dissatisfaction with Tiberius rising to the imperial purple, as they allegedly wanted to see Germanicus in his place.[105] As they report, the mutiny was mostly driven by veterans with 30 years of service behind them and urban plebs whom Augustus had join the Rhine army to strengthen the Roman contingent in Germania after Varus's defeat.[106] The time of the outbreak was not an accident; the army saw Augustus's death and the rise of a new emperor as a convenient moment to exact its demands.[107] Among those there were a pay rise, shortening the time of service to 16 years, suitable severance pay on leaving the ranks, and actually receiving the gratuities promised earlier by Augustus.[108] Tempers ran high enough that dangerous rioting ensued. According to Tacitus, the soldiers' anger was mostly directed at the hated centurions, who were cruelly beaten and then thrown either out of the camp or into the Rhine.[109] The situation was not helped by Germanicus's arrival at the camp, his highly emotional speech, or his staged, dramatic suicide attempt, as reported by Tacitus and Cassius Dio.[110] It is also from those two authors that we learn that, faced with the threat of the mutiny spreading, Germanicus decided to fabricate a letter from Tiberius in which the emperor promised the gratuities would be paid out and all who had served for 20 years or longer would be let go, while legionaries with 16 or more years of service would be transferred to reserve units.[111] With the rebels pressuring him, Germanicus had to start carrying out those promises immediately.[112] Forging Tiberius's letter means he had no directives from the emperor on how to act or what to concede to the mutinied legions, if anything. It was his own, independent decision to pay out gratuities from his own share, which he had not consulted with Tiberius on. Not that there was enough time for that; the circumstances called for radical appeasement measures.

Despite those measures working, they apparently—so suggest Tacitus and Dio—alarmed Tiberius, who was afraid Germanicus was soliciting the army's favour in order to take over as emperor.[113] After restoring calm, Germanicus travelled to meet the troops stationed on the Upper Rhine, whom he made swear loyalty to Tiberius as the new princeps, granting them the same concessions the Lower Rhine legions had already received.[114] After inspecting the legions in Germania Superior, he returned to the area on the Lower Rhine, where he met a deputation from the senate. The arrival of those senators in the camp caused renewed rioting, as the soldiers feared the purpose of the visit was to invalidate the concessions they had already been promised.[115] As it turned out, their fear was unfounded; news of the legions' mutiny had likely not yet reached Rome, and the senators came to offer Germanicus condolences on Augustus's death and to officially present him with the decree granting him proconsular *imperium*.[116] That time, the troops' aggression was mostly spent in attacking the senators. Tacitus and Dio write that the situation was bad enough that Germanicus decided to send his wife and son away from the camp for their safety;[117] in Tacitus and Suetonius, we read that his move made a strong impression. The soldiers, who held Caligula in particular esteem, considered it a dishonour to the legions that he left the camp and was left in the care of the Gaulish inhabitants of Trier.[118] According to Tacitus's account, Germanicus made good use of the mood of the army and, in return for having his son brought back to the camp, asked for the leaders of the mutiny to be named. His demand was accepted, and the leaders of the riots were executed.[119]

2.3.3.2 *The military campaigns of* AD *14–16*[120]

Almost as soon as the revolt in the army had been suppressed, Germanicus undertook an expedition into Germania. His first opponents were the tribe of Marsi. Ancient authors see that campaign in connection with the recently extinguished mutiny. Tacitus regards it as a *sui generis* occasion for the soldiers to "act out" after they spilled the blood of their comrades-in-arms,[121] whereas, for Cassius Dio, it was to keep idle legionaries from thinking of another riot.[122] A close connection between the expedition and the mutiny is indicated by the fact that only legions from Germania Inferior took part in it, as well as by the very choice of the place to attack, as the lands of the Marsi lay near the camp of the mutinied legions in Vetera. That is also how modern historians see Germanicus's first independent campaign on the right bank of the Rhine. D. Timpe believed it efficiently restored discipline in the Roman ranks, while also acknowledging its strategic aspect—namely, he thought it was also, in a sense, a scouting mission and one that prepared the army for a decisive offensive operation in Germania in the following year.[123]

The course of the campaign can be reconstructed from Tacitus's account.[124] Having crossed the Rhine, the Roman units attacked the lands of the Marsi between the rivers Lippe and Ruhr. They encountered little resistance, as the Marsi had not expected a Roman assault. Most of the Marsi were killed, and their homes were burnt down. The Romans also razed to the ground a local religious centre—a holy grove of Tanfana. The massacre of the Marsi apparently caused a vehement reaction from other Germanic tribes, such as the Bructeri, Tubantes, and Usipetes, who in turn attacked the returning

Roman troops. With some difficulty, Germanicus was able to fight them off, however, and led the army back to its winter lodgings.[125]

A thorough offensive campaign in Germania had been prepared for AD 15. In D. Timpe's opinion, the preparations and the choice of the moment to strike were significantly affected by strife within the coalition of Germanic tribes started by the Cherusci. Tacitus writes that a "pro-Roman" faction of Segestes fought with an "anti-Roman" one of Arminius,[126] and conflict among the Germans boded well for the Roman operation. According to Timpe's reconstruction, the campaign, originally planned for the summer of 15, was ultimately moved to spring, because the standing of the Rome-friendly Segestes gradually weakened, his faction losing influence in the coalition.[127]

During the first stage of the campaign, the Romans attacked the Chatti, the main ally of the Cherusci.[128] Thanks to lightning-fast troop movement, Germanicus managed to completely surprise the enemy. Most of the Chatti were slaughtered; the rest were enslaved. The Romans also pillaged the surrounding settlements and destroyed Mattium, the political and religious centre of the tribe. At the same time, another Roman force under the command of a legate of Germanicus once more crushed the Marsi.[129] The first part of the campaign resulted in neutralizing the Chatti—a mainstay of the anti-Roman coalition—and the Marsi, but not in weakening Arminius's authority and position among the Germanic tribes. Quite the contrary; Germanicus's brutal methods only aroused hostility in other Germanic peoples, making it easier for the Cherusci to expand and strengthen their coalition.[130]

Anticipating an attack, Germanicus decided to intervene. During the second phase of the campaign, the objective of the Roman army was principally to crush the Cherusci. Roman forces were concentrated on the Ems (ancient Amisia), where the legions were joined by the cavalry and fleet. They also succeeded in obtaining the support of the tribe of Chauci, who provided auxiliary troops. Germanicus then made a successful strike against the Bructeri, pillaging their homes in the process. Tacitus reports that, during the fighting, the Romans managed to recover the eagle of the 19th legion, lost in Varus's defeat.[131]

After defeating the Bructeri, the Roman troops reached the site of the defeat at the Teutoburg Forest, where Germanicus decided to bury the remains of Roman soldiers "strewn about" there, erecting a communal barrow for them.[132] We read in Tacitus that Germanicus's actions on the matter displeased Tiberius, who believed they weakened the army's morale and combat capability,[133] but the reason the historian quotes for the emperor's displeasure does not seem likely. The sight of corpses lying about unburied would have rather caused a spike of adrenaline in the legionaries, motivating them to avenge their comrades, which, in the context of the planned expedition against Arminius, would have certainly been useful. Instead, Tiberius's condemnation probably had ritual grounds, which actually does follow from Tacitus's text if one reads on: Germanicus was then an augur, and it was taboo for Roman priesthood to see or have any contact with a dead body.[134] Germanicus confronting Arminius directly did not yield the expected results. Even more, Varus's story nearly repeated itself, as Germanicus fell for Arminius's tactics and let Roman troops be drawn deep into Germania.[135] With no resolution achieved and with provisioning difficulties owing to the campaign being so long, he decided to retreat. Some units were sent by land along the coast of the North Sea, while others boarded ships. The setbacks suffered by the Romans were only made worse by powerful storms that dealt much damage to the legions marching along the coast. Eventually, the Roman troops reached the line of the Weser, from where they were moved to their winter quarters.[136]

Thus, the campaign of AD 15 did not bring Rome the expected effects. Arminius, Rome's primary opponent, had not been eliminated, and the Roman army had suffered serious losses in men. Its military potential had been reduced too (through losses in weapons and horses). Tacitus says that it was necessary to bring over extra contingents from Spain, Gaul, and Italy, and the same provinces were to provide more weapons and horses.[137]

Tacitus's text tells us Germanicus did learn the lesson the failures of that campaign carried, as the plan for the next year's operations was thoroughly prepared based on the experience drawn from the previous battles. The main undertaking was the construction of a large fleet (of around 1,000 ships), suited to carrying troops, horses, and food supplies. The fleet was to transport the Roman units by sea to the mouth of the Ems, from where they would sail upriver to charge into Germania. The plan would guarantee speed of movement and safe transport, while also preventing provisioning problems.[138] Thereafter, the legions marched until they reached the Weser, where, as E. Koestermann suspected, they conquered the tribe of Angrivarii.[139] The decisive battle with Arminius's army took place on the Middle Weser, near Idistaviso (although the exact site is uncertain). Tacitus reports the Romans had amassed a huge army—eight legions, two Praetorian cohorts, units of cavalry and mounted archers, as well as Gallic and Germanic auxiliaries.[140] According to his account, the battle ended in a massive and bloodless victory for the Romans.[141] After it was over, the legions hailed Tiberius as *imperator*, and Germanicus ordered the victory to be commemorated by the erection of a *tropaeum* made of weapons bearing the names of the defeated Germanic tribes.[142] Accepting Tacitus's account, Koestermann saw Idistaviso as a great military achievement of Germanicus, especially as it was won on a battlefield chosen by the enemy, with the Germans' later attack on the legions only a "desperate and futile attempt at turning the tide of the war."[143] One can essentially agree, while remembering that the Battle of Idistaviso did not prove decisive for the remaining course of the war; clearly, the Cherusci had not been completely broken if, soon after the defeat, they managed to mount another attack, which Germanicus only fought off with great difficulty and after heavy fighting.[144] After that successful defence, he decided to build another *tropaeum* made of arms.[145]

However, the Roman victory was overshadowed by a huge shipwreck and the deaths of some of the soldiers transported by the fleet. As Tacitus writes, the event spurred the Chatti and the Marsi to rise against the Romans again, although the rebellion was suppressed thanks to efficient and quick intervention by Germanicus and his legates. During the expedition against the Marsi, the Romans were also able to recover another eagle lost by Varus.[146]

Tacitus attributes to Germanicus a plan to continue operations in Germania in AD 17 too. They were to ultimately solidify the "conquest" of the lands between the Rhine and the Elbe, but, in the end, the plan was thwarted by Tiberius, who decided to recall his son from Germania.[147]

The fact of Germanicus being recalled from his high command in Germania causes much controversy.[148] Tacitus, who is our most important source on the subject, lists several reasons that supposedly affected Tiberius's decision:

> *sed crebris epistulis Tiberius monebat, rediret ad decretum triumphum: satis iam eventuum, satis casuum. prospera illi et magna proelia: eorum quoque meminisset, quae venti et fluctus, nulla ducis culpa, gravia tamen et saeva damna intulissent. se novies a divo Augusto in Germaniam missum plura consilio quam vi perfecisse. sic Sugambros in deditionem acceptos, sic Suebos regemque Maroboduum pace obstrictum. posse et Cheruscos ceterasque rebellium gentis, quoniam Romanae ultioni consultum es<se>t, internis discordiis relinqui. precante Germanico annum efficiendis coeptis, acrius modestiam eius adgreditur alterum consulatum offerendo, cuius munia praesens obiret. simul adnectebat, si foret adhuc bellandum, relinqueret materiem Drusi fratris gloriae, qui nullo tum alio hoste non nisi apud Germanias adsequi nomen imperatorium et deportare lauream posset. haud cunctatus est ultra Germanicus, quamquam fingi ea seque per invidiam parto iam decori abstrahi intellegeret.*[149]
>
> But frequent letters from Tiberius counselled the prince "to return for the triumph decreed him: there had been already enough successes, and enough mischances. He had fought auspicious and great fields: he should also remember the losses inflicted by wind and wave—losses not in any way due to his leadership, yet grave and deplorable. He himself had been sent nine times into Germany by the deified Augustus; and he had effected more by policy than by force. Policy had procured the Sugambrian surrender; policy had bound the Suebi and King Maroboduus to keep the peace. The Cherusci and the other rebel tribes, now that enough has been done for Roman vengeance, might similarly be left to their intestine strife." When Germanicus asked for one year more in which to finish his work, he delivered a still shrewder attack on his modesty, and offered him a second consulate, the duties of which he would assume in person. A hint was appended that "if the war must be continued, he might leave his brother, Drusus, the material for a reputation; since at present there was no other national enemy, and nowhere

> but in the Germanies could he acquire the style of Imperator and a title to the triumphal bays." Germanicus hesitated no longer, though he was aware that these civilities were a fiction, and that jealousy was the motive which withdrew him from a glory already within his grasp.[150]

Based on the passage quoted above, we may assume the most likely reason why Germanicus was called back was Tiberius's differing view on how to implement Roman policy regarding Germania. Whereas Germanicus, inspired by the glory of the victories of his father Drusus, intended to continue the war until the Germans caved in completely and the lands between the Rhine and the Elbe were conquered, the princeps believed the goals of the campaign as set by Augustus had been reached.[151] In Tiberius's opinion, the victory of Idistaviso, ravaging a greater part of Germania, and winning back the lost legions' eagles were compensation enough for the *clades Variana*;[152] moreover, the way Germanicus waged the war meant that Rome incurred heavy human and financial losses, and the effects were not commensurable.[153] His style of campaigning was certainly different from Tiberius's methods.[154] Recalling Germanicus did not mean Rome was giving up on its ambitions to control Germania;[155] still, Tiberius thought the key to the success there lay, not in bloody campaigns, but rather in instigating the Germanic tribes to act against one another according to the old Roman principle of *divide et impera*. Tacitus writes that the emperor did not rule out another military operation in the future, but it would have to happen in circumstances favourable to Rome,[156] and another factor that may have influenced Tiberius's decision to recall Germanicus was the unfavourable political situation in Armenia, as regulating it called for a representative of the *domus Augusta* to be sent east. With the inexperience of Drusus the Younger, Germanicus was the only candidate to consider.[157]

Germanicus's campaigns in the years 14–16, in spite of some measure of Roman success, did not bring Rome control of Germanic areas. The belief, ascribed to him by Tacitus, that all the peoples between the Rhine and the Elbe had been conquered, certainly does not reflect the facts, expressing rather the undying vitality of Roman aspirations to rule the region.[158] Roman efforts in Germania certainly seriously weakened the potential of some Germanic tribes, but did not break down Arminius, who, shortly after Germanicus's recall, could afford to take up arms against Maroboduus, and successfully too.[159] Even so, it was an important achievement of Germanicus that Gaul was protected against Germans' possible invasions through the creation of a safe buffer zone on the right bank of the Rhine.[160]

2.4 The Danubian areas (Pannonia, Dalmatia, and Dacia)

2.4.1 Agrippa's Pannonian campaign (13–12 BC)

After Germania, the second most important area of Roman expansion in Augustus's reign was the region on the Danube. The princeps intended to conquer the lands on the right bank of the river and set the border of the Empire on it, assigning the task of capturing that territory to members of his family. Towards the end of 13 BC, the emperor sent Agrippa to Pannonia, as the tribes there had risen up against Rome. Agrippa decided to start the campaign even though it was winter, but, if we are to believe Cassius Dio's account, no intervention was necessary: allegedly, his very arrival caused great panic among the Pannonian tribes, who decided to surrender. However, the campaign proved unlucky for Agrippa: on his way back to Italy, he contracted a serious disease, which ended in him dying.[161]

2.4.2 Tiberius's campaigns in Pannonia (11–9 BC)

Agrippa's work was then carried on by Tiberius, who had been sent to Pannonia in 12 BC, probably with the rank of *legatus Augusti*.[162] From 11 BC on, he already acted there as a commander holding independent *imperium*. The sources provide little information on his actions there during that time; Suetonius only mentions that Augustus repelled Dacian raids on Pannonia, which is probably a reference to an operation of Tiberius conducted in the region in 10 BC.[163] Suetonius's information is confirmed by Augustus, who reports in his autobiography that Tiberius crossed the Danube and successfully attacked Dacian tribes.[164] His retaliatory expedition was due to those peoples raiding Pannonia.[165] An interesting reconstruction of that campaign was put forward by A. Bernecker; in her opinion, after pushing the Dacians out of Pannonia, Tiberius invaded Dacia itself, ravaging the land and reaching its north-western outskirts. However, she does not see the campaign as a symptom of Roman expansion in the region, treating it instead as a punitive expedition the purpose of which was to retaliate for the earlier Dacian raids on Pannonia.[166]

Cassius Dio mentions two other successful campaigns that Tiberius conducted in 10 and 9 against Pannonian and Dalmatian tribes who had revolted against Rome because excessively high taxes were being exacted.[167] One direct result of Tiberius's efforts in the region was subjecting to Rome's rule the lands between the Save and the Danube, where the province of Illyricum was created.[168]

2.4.3 The uprising in Pannonia and Dalmatia suppressed by Tiberius (AD 6–9)

Combined with oppressive taxation, the strictness of the Roman administration in Pannonia and Dalmatia caused a massive anti-Roman uprising of tribes to break out there in AD 6.[169] Another important reason for the revolt was the forced enlistment of the local population into the Roman auxiliary units, which was widely implemented there. The spark was ignited by a recent wave of recruitment, carried out because of the intended campaign against the Marcomanni, and one other circumstance conducive to the outbreak was that Valerius Messalinus, then the governor of Illyricum, left this province with most of the legions stationed there to assist Tiberius in Germania.[170]

Among the rebel tribes, the sources list the Pannonian Breuci (from the Lower Save and Drave) under the command of Pinnes and Bato, the Dalmatian Daesitiates (from near modern Sarajevo) under Bato, and the Dalmatian Perustae and Mazaei.[171] Velleius Paterculus's estimates, no doubt exaggerated, indicate the insurgence managed to deploy an army of more than 200,000 men (200,000 foot soldiers and 9,000 cavalry).[172] The aggression of the rebels turned first against the Roman merchants and veterans present in the province, who were slaughtered; next, the insurgents attacked and pillaged the territory of the province of Macedonia. Velleius maintains that an attack on Italy was planned as well,[173] and, as Italy was not far from the areas where the uprising was going on, panic broke out in Rome. The fears we find expressed in the accounts of Roman historians were not groundless;[174] the sheer number of resources involved in suppressing the rebellion testifies to its scale. Suetonius reports fifteen legions and as many auxiliary units took part in the process,[175] and Velleius writes of ten legions, seventy cohorts, ten wings of cavalry, 10,000 veterans, and some units of royal cavalry provided by the Thracian ruler Rhoemetalces, a Roman ally.[176] Units made up of freedmen were also mobilized and used both to fight the insurgents and to protect strategically important points along the Italian–Dalmatian border.[177] Furthermore, to obtain the funds needed to finance the military operations, Augustus decided to levy a 2 per cent tax on the sale of slaves and to lock the payments that had been made until then from the treasury to the praetors so they could hold gladiatorial games.[178] The emperor gave the task of suppressing the rebellion to Tiberius, the only member of the *domus Augusta* who could possibly be up to it.[179]

The first part of the war brought no resolution. The insurgents avoided direct confrontation with the Romans, employing hit-and-run and scorched-earth tactics, which caused trouble for the Roman supply lines.[180] With the enemy using that kind of strategy, Tiberius could not mount a broad offensive operation and limited himself to protecting Italy from a possible attack.[181] The Roman legions also had to operate on difficult terrain, and Suetonius writes that the insurgents were able to ambush Tiberius, who only avoided a crushing defeat in that hopeless situation thanks to the gentlemanly attitude of Bato, one of the Pannonian leaders, who let him withdraw from unfavourable positions in a ravine.[182]

In AD 7, Augustus sent extra units under Germanicus's command to the Pannonian front. Drawing on Cassius Dio's account, E. Koestermann saw that as an expression of Augustus's distrust and impatience as regards Tiberius's efforts against the rebels, which had brought no apparent results. In other words, by dispatching Germanicus, the princeps hoped for some "fresh ideas" in the campaign.[183] That opinion would appear unfounded; Augustus hardly disbelieved Tiberius's military skill and experience, proven in many previous campaigns.[184] It is also unlikely the emperor thought the arrival of Germanicus, completely inexperienced in matters of war, could turn the tide.[185] Instead, we may assume Augustus sent Germanicus so that he could gain proper military experience under Tiberius's seasoned command, and, while he did that, he would bring more troops to the front, which would support the legions already engaged there.[186] The major breakthrough took place at the beginning of AD 8, when, owing to their supply problems, strength lost in the fighting, and a falling out among the leadership, most of the rebelling tribes decided to lay down their arms. The official surrender occurred on 3 August AD 8, on the Bathinus river (modern Bosna).[187]

Still, the insurrection went on in Dalmatia, where the tribes of Perustae and Daesitiates had revolted.[188] As Augustus's legates achieved mediocre results there, it proved necessary for Tiberius to intervene. On assuming the general command, he split the army in three. The first corps, commanded by him directly, was sent against the strongest rebel group led by Bato, known from previous battles in Pannonia.[189] After failing to provoke the Dalmatians to fight a decisive battle, Tiberius managed to lock Bato up in the well-fortified keep of Andretium near Salonae.[190] Even though the siege conditions and the ceaseless fighting caused dissatisfaction in the legions, he was able to restore discipline among the soldiers. After some heavy fighting at the foot of the fortress, at last the Romans won and captured it. The fall of Andretium and Bato's surrender were a breakthrough point of the war in Dalmatia. Having suppressed the uprising, Tiberius began the administrative reorganization of Illyricum. In the end, the region was divided into two provinces, Illyria Superior and Illyria Inferior, which would later be renamed Pannonia and Dalmatia.[191]

2.4.4 Tiberius's mission in Illyricum (AD *14)*

In 14, Augustus dispatched Tiberius to Illyricum again. The mission's objective was probably to reorganize the administration of the Illyrian provinces, which was intended to strengthen Rome's rule in the region, but it never succeeded because of Augustus's death, which made Tiberius turn back before he arrived.[192]

2.4.5 The mission of Drusus the Younger in Illyricum (AD *17–20)*

In Tiberius's reign, the Danubian provinces became the theatre of the actions of his natural son Drusus the Younger, then a main candidate to succession alongside Germanicus.[193] In 14, he was sent to suppress the mutiny of the legions stationed there, which broke out after Augustus died.[194] However, Drusus, unlike his brother Germanicus, did not then hold independent *imperium*, presumably acting instead as a *legatus Augusti*.[195]

Late in AD 17, Drusus was again sent to Illyricum, by then armed with independent *imperium*.[196] Tacitus claims Tiberius's son was expected to gain proper military experience there as well as win the sympathies of the army.[197] He took command of five legions, three of them stationed in Pannonia and the other two in Dalmatia.[198] The conflict that had flared between the factions of Arminius and Maroboduus provided a convenient opportunity for Roman intervention. Drusus's main task was to neutralize Maroboduus's kingdom, which posed a danger to Rome; he was to reach that goal not so much through direct military confrontation as by taking advantage of internal strife between Germanic tribes.[199] In that, he succeeded; Maroboduus was defeated, first by Arminius and second by Catualda of the tribe of Gotones (Goths), which in the end made him seek refuge in Roman territory.[200] Tiberius decided to detain him in Ravenna, where he spent the last years of his life.[201] In 19, Catualda met the same fate; defeated by the Hermunduri, he also had to seek Roman protection. He was then settled in Forum Iulium in Narbonese Gaul.[202] There can be no doubt the Hermunduri had acted at the behest of Drusus, who used them to get rid of another inconvenient adversary.[203] He ordered that Maroboduus's old warriors and followers be settled on the northern bank of the Danube, where the client state of *regnum Vannianum* was created, to be ruled over by Vannius of the Quadi.[204]

Shaw also sees Drusus's time in Illyricum in connection with important construction undertakings, attributing to him a stretch of the road from Aquileia to Carnuntum, and two roads that led from Salonae, the capital of Dalmatia province, to the Save, all of which made possible lightning-fast movement of troops and faster flow of information.[205]

Also in Tacitus, we read that Drusus left Rome for Illyricum two more times in AD 20, first after Germanicus's funeral, and then after Calpurnius Piso's trial. Unfortunately, there is nothing in the sources on what he did during that time.[206] We can only suspect that his missions were to keep consolidating Roman influence in the area.

Notes

1 Suet. *Tib.* 9, 1.
2 See Levick 1999: 26; Hurlet 1997: 84 (note 35); Kienast, Eck, Heil 2017: 70. *Contra* Vervaet 2020: 130–133, who puts forward the original claim that, at the time, Tiberius acted in the East as a proconsul with independent *imperium.* He thinks the powers granted Tiberius in 20 BC were similar to those earlier granted to Agrippa for his eastern mission of 23 BC. One of his main arguments is that, when Tiberius put a pro-Roman ruler on the Armenian throne, a *supplicatio* was decreed, as mentioned in Cass. Dio (54, 9, 5); in Vervaet's opinion, the honour could only be conferred on one who held independent *imperium.* However, the sources remain silent on the matter, and so it is ultimately impossible to determine Tiberius's legal standing during his mission to the East.
3 *RGDA* 27, 2; Vell. Pat. 2, 94, 4; Tac. *Ann.* 2, 3, 2; Cass. Dio 54, 9, 4.
4 Suet. *Tib.* 9, 1.
5 See Levick 1999: 234 (note 38).
6 See Syme 1979: 310; Hurlet 1997: 86; Kienast, Eck, Heil 2017: 61; 70.
7 Vervaet 2020: 145–146.

8 Vell. Pat. 2, 120, 3, who mentions L. Nonius Asprenas, a legate of Varus during his governorship in Germania. Of course, Varus held that post as a *legatus Augusti pro praetore.*
9 Although Augustus did receive his tenth imperatorial acclamation for Tiberius's and Drusus's successes in the Alpine campaign; see Syme 1979: 310; Kienast, Eck, Heil 2017: 58. *Contra* Vervaet (2020: 157 note 117), who supposes Augustus's stepsons were also hailed *imperatores* by the army then.
10 Vell. Pat. 2, 95, 1–2; Cass. Dio 54, 22, 1–5; Flor. 2, 22.
11 *RIC*, I², *Aug.* 164ab–165ab.
12 See Zanker 1990: 227; Severy 2003: 89–90. Vervaet 2020: 170f. Rose (1997: 15) is sceptical regarding that identification of the figure on the coin.
13 Cass. Dio 55, 31, 1.
14 Vell. Pat. 2, 116, 1.
15 Cass. Dio 56, 11, 1–2; 15, 1.
16 Cass. Dio 56, 17, 2. See Hurlet 1997: 167.
17 Agrippa had similar goals for the area in 20 BC; cf. below.
18 Liv. *Per.* 139; Cass. Dio 54, 32, 1; cf. also Deininger 1965: 21–24; Fishwick 1987: 97–99.
19 Cass. Dio 53, 25, 3–8; Suet. *Aug.* 20; 21, 1; Flor. 2, 33.
20 Our main source of information on Agrippa's actions in Spain is Cassius Dio (54, 11, 2–5), with sparse mentions in Velleius (2, 90, 1) and Horace (Hor. *Epist.* 1, 12, 26–27). For Agrippa's Spanish campaign, see Reinhold 1933: 92–93; Santos 1975: 538–539; Roddaz 1984: 402–410; Richardson 1996: 134.
21 To begin with, there were two provinces in Spain, Hispania Ulterior and Citerior. As a result of Augustus's later administrative reorganizations, three were created: Hispania Tarraconensis, Hispania Lusitania (imperial provinces governed by ex-consuls and ex-praetors), and Hispania Baetica (a province of the Roman people, administered by a former praetor). See Schumacher 1988: 38.
22 *CIL* II 474; Reinhold 1933: 94; Halfmann 1986: 164; Roddaz 1984: 416–418; Richardson 1996: 140–141.
23 Reinhold 1933: 94; Hanslik 1961: 1256–1257; Roddaz 1984: 412–418.
24 See *CIL* II 1527; *RPC* I 77–84.
25 Augustus divided Transalpine Gaul into three provinces: Aquitania, Lugdunensis, and Belgica. All three had the status of imperial provinces, governed by *legati Augusti* selected from among ex-praetors. See Schumacher 1988: 38.
26 Cass. Dio 54, 11, 1–2. See Halfmann 1986: 164.
27 Strab. 4, 6, 11.
28 Reinhold 1933: 89–90; Roddaz 1984: 389–392.
29 *CIL* XII 3153; 3154; see Reinhold 1933: 91.
30 See Reinhold 1933: 90–91.
31 See Roddaz 1984: 399.
32 Reinhold 1933: 91; Roddaz 1984: 400.
33 *RPC* I 523.
34 Fishwick 1987: 144–145.
35 Vell. Pat. 2, 121, 1. See also Wolters 2014–15: 206.
36 Tac. *Ann.* 1, 31, 2–3; 33, 1; *TS* fr. 1, l. 15.
37 See Koestermann 1957: 429; Timpe 1968: 38.
38 Tac. *Ann.* 1, 34, 1.
39 On the subject of Drusus's campaigns in Germania, see especially Christ 1956: 36–56; Schleiermacher 1960: 231–234; Timpe 1967a: 289–306; 1975: 142–147; Simon 1982: 38–42; Welwei 1986: 128–130; Lehmann 1989: 216–219; Wolters 1990b: 157–172; Callies 1993: 135–137; Deininger 2000: *passim.*
40 Kienast 2009: 362–363. See also Eck 2018: 12.
41 Timpe 1975: 147; see also Simon 1982: 47.

42 Rich 1990: 211, 213; Kienast, Eck, Heil 2017: 61.
43 D. Timpe (1975: 144–145) assumes there was a serious rebellion that year of tribes inhabiting the area between the Rhine and the Weser.
44 Cass. Dio 54, 36, 3.
45 Timpe 1967a: 296–297, 299–300; see also Welwei 1986: 129.
46 Christ 1956: 46–47.
47 Cass. Dio 54, 33, 5. See Rich 1990: 213, 217; Kienast, Eck, Heil 2017: 61.
48 Suet. *Claud.* 1, 3; Cass. Dio 55, 1, 2; Flor. 2, 30; Timpe 1967a: 300.
49 *Consol. ad Liv.* 17–18; Cass. Dio 55, 1, 2; Oros. 6, 21, 16; Timpe 1967a: 303.
50 Cass. Dio 55, 1, 2–4; Timpe 1967a: 304–305.
51 Suet. *Claud.* 1, 2: *hostem etiam frequenter caesum ac penitus in intimas solitudines actum non prius destitit insequi, quam species barbarae mulieris humana amplior victorem tendere ultra sermone Latino prohibuisset*; Cass. Dio 55, 1, 3–4.
52 Timpe 1967a: 294–295, 305.
53 Abramenko 1994: 377–378, 381.
54 Cass. Dio 55, 1, 3; Flor. 2, 30. See Timpe 1967a: 305; Christ 1956: 54. On Drusus's *tropaeum*, see more recently Castellvi 2015: 216.
55 *RIC* I², *Claud.* 73; *HCC* I, *Claud.* nos. 26–28.
56 Flor. 2, 30.
57 Gruen 1996: 181–182.
58 Flor. 2, 30; Christ 1956: 49.
59 Tac. *Ann.* 13, 53, 2.
60 Liv. *Per.* 142; Suet. *Claud.* 1, 3; Cass. Dio 55, 1, 4.
61 Cass. Dio 55, 6, 5; see Rich 1990: 224; Kienast, Eck, Heil 2017: 70.
62 On Tiberius's campaigns in Germania in the years 8–7, see especially Bernecker 1989: 271–302; Lehmann 1989: 219–220; Wolters 1989: 26–27; 30; 1990b: 173–229.
63 Suet. *Aug.* 21, 1; *Tib.* 9, 2; Tac. *Ann.* 2, 26, 3.
64 Wolters 2000: 37.
65 Bleicken 1998: 583; Deininger 2000: 767; Eck 2018: 13–14.
66 Vell. Pat. 2, 97, 4.
67 Aufidius Bassus in: *HRR* (H. Peter), 96.
68 Cass. Dio 55, 6, 6. See also Rich 1990: 224.
69 *RIC* I², *Aug.* 200; Wolters 1989: 32–34.
70 Cass. Dio 55, 8, 3.
71 Kienast 2009: 364–365.
72 Bleicken 1998: 582.
73 Cass. Dio 56, 18, 1.
74 The date it was established is uncertain. It is thought the altar may have been dedicated during Drusus's campaigns on the Rhine in 12–9 BC, Tiberius's expedition in the same area in 8–7 BC, or Tiberius's expedition in AD 5. See Fishwick 1987: 138.
75 Deininger 1965: 24–25; Fishwick 1987: 137–139.
76 Vell. Pat. 2, 100, 1; 104, 2.
77 See Sawiński 2018: 81–86.
78 Vell. Pat. 2, 104, 2.
79 The main source of information on Tiberius's campaigns in Germania at the time is Velleius Paterculus. However, his account, awed at Tiberius's achievements, needs to be treated very cautiously. Some details are also provided by Augustus in his *Res Gestae*, and then there are the laconic mentions in Cassius Dio, important in that, to an extent, they let us verify Velleius's panegyric regarding the results of Tiberius's campaigns. For the way Tiberius is depicted in Velleius Paterculus's narrative, see esp. Kuntze 1985: *passim*.

80 Vell. Pat. 2, 104, 3–5; 105, 1–3.
81 Vell. Pat. 2, 106, 1–3.
82 In that context, Augustus lists the tribes of Cimbri and Charydes (on the coast of the North Sea) and Semnones (on the right bank of the Elbe). See *RGDA* 26, 4; Cooley 2009: 224.
83 Cass. Dio 55, 28, 5–6.
84 Vell. Pat. 2, 108–109.
85 Vell. Pat. 2, 109, 5.
86 Vell. Pat. 2, 110, 1–2.
87 Vell. Pat. 2, 117–119; Suet. *Aug.* 23, 2; Cass. Dio 56, 18, 3–5; 19–21. On the subject of the battle itself and the latest locations proposed for it, see Wolters 2009: 100–124; Timpe 2012: 593–652; Baltrusch *et al.* 2012.
88 Vell. Pat. 2, 120, 1–2.
89 Cass. Dio 56, 24, 6.
90 Suet. *Tib.* 18, 1–2.
91 Vell. Pat. 2, 121, 1.
92 Cass. Dio 56, 25, 2–3.
93 Wolters 2000: 56.
94 See Welwei 1986: 136; Wolters 2000: 56.
95 Cass. Dio 56, 25, 2; see also Wolters 2014–15: 201.
96 Suet. *Cal.* 8, 3; Kienast, Eck, Heil 2017: 74.
97 Kienast 2009: 374–375. See also Eck 2018: 28.
98 Tac. *Ann.* 1, 3, 6.
99 Translated by C. H. Moore and J. Jackson (Loeb Classical Library, 249).
100 As demonstrated by coin emissions and iconographic finds. See *RIC* I^2, *Aug.* 131, 359; Wolters 1989: 32; Zanker 1990: 190–196.
101 Vell. Pat. 2, 123, 1. See also Tac. *Ann.* 1, 3, 6.
102 Neither is it known exactly what campaigns of Germanicus's are mentioned in the epigram attributed to Crinagoras (*Anth. Pal.* IX, 283), where we read of that commander's alleged victories somewhere between the Alps and the Pyrenees, as the fragment is difficult to interpret. See Barnes 1974: 25; Syme 1978: 58–59; Goodyear 1981: 84 (note 1).
103 Tac. *Ann.* 1, 31, 2; 33, 1; 34, 1; Suet. *Cal.* 8, 3. See also Wolters 2014–15: 206–207.
104 Four legions were stationed there; see Schumacher 1988: 38.
105 Tac. *Ann.* 1, 31, 1–4; Suet. *Tib.* 25, 1–2; *Cal.* 1, 1. However, I find that an unlikely reason; we should remember that, as their commander of many years, Tiberius must have enjoyed the sympathies and support of the Rhine legions. Thus, coming forward with a potential counter-candidate to the purple would have been not a realistic postulate of the mutinied legionaries, but more of a way of exerting pressure meant to exact their demands, which were mostly socio-economic in nature. *Contra* Eck 2018: 28. For a recent discussion of the mutiny, see Salvo 2010: 138–156.
106 Tac. *Ann.* 1, 31, 4; 35, 1–2.
107 Tac. *Ann.* 1, 16, 1.
108 Tac. *Ann.* 1, 31, 4; 35, 1–3; Vell. Pat. 2, 125, 1–2.
109 Tac. *Ann.* 1, 32, 1.
110 Tac. *Ann.* 1, 34–35; Cass. Dio 57, 5, 2–3.
111 Tac. *Ann.* 1, 36, 1–3. Cass. Dio 57, 5, 3.
112 Tacitus (*Ann.* 1, 37, 1) reports Germanicus paid some of the money promised from his own funds, borrowing some from close associates. See also Goodyear 1972: 267–268.
113 Tac. *Ann.* 1, 52, 1; Cass. Dio 57, 6, 2. His fears turned out to be utterly groundless; Germanicus's actions prove he was completely loyal to the new emperor. See also Timpe 1968: 27–28; 38–40.

114 Tac. *Ann.* 1, 37, 3.
115 Tac. *Ann.* 1, 39, 1–2.
116 See Levick 1999: 74.
117 Tac. *Ann.* 1, 40, 3; Cass. Dio 57, 5, 6–7.
118 Tac. *Ann.* 1, 41, 1–3; Suet. *Cal.* 9.
119 Tac. *Ann.* 1, 43–44.
120 Much has been written on Germanicus's campaigns in Germania in AD 14–16. See primarily Knoke 1922: *passim*; Christ 1956: 74–102; Koestermann 1957: 429–479; Akveld 1961: 35–70; Timpe 1968; Gallotta 1981: 293–316; Lehmann 1989: 227–230; Wolters 1990b: 229–245; 2000: 7–15; Rivière 2016: 189–233; Kehne 2018: 31–95.
121 Tac. *Ann.* 1, 49, 3–4.
122 Cass. Dio 57, 6, 1.
123 Timpe 1968: 24–30; in a similar vein, Christ 1956: 86.
124 Tac. *Ann.* 1, 49, 4; 50–51.
125 Tac. *Ann.* 1, 51, 1–4. See also Kehne 1998b: 441.
126 Tac. *Ann.* 1, 55, 1–2.
127 Timpe 1968: 67–68; Wolters 1989: 37–38.
128 Timpe 1968: 71.
129 Tac. *Ann.* 1, 56, 1–4.
130 Tac. *Ann.* 1, 59–60; Christ 1956: 90; Timpe 1968: 71; Kehne 1998b: 442.
131 Tac. *Ann.* 1, 60, 1–3.
132 Tac. *Ann.* 1, 60, 3; 61–62; Suet. *Cal.* 3, 2; Cass. Dio 57, 18, 1. Tacitus (*Ann.* 2, 7, 2) reports the barrow was later destroyed by the Chatti.
133 Tac. *Ann.* 1, 62. 2.
134 Tac. *Ann.* 1, 62, 2. See Sawiński 2018: 45.
135 Tac. *Ann.* 1, 63–68; Koestermann 1957: 445.
136 Tac. *Ann.* 1, 70, 1–5.
137 Tac. *Ann.* 1, 71, 2.
138 Tac. *Ann.* 2, 5, 2–4; 6, 1–2; Koestermann 1957: 448–449.
139 Koestermann 1957: 451.
140 Tac. *Ann.* 2, 16, 3.
141 For the description of the course the battle took, see Tac. *Ann.* 2, 17, 1–6.
142 Tac. *Ann.* 2, 18, 2. It was Tiberius's eighth and final acclamation; see Kienast, Eck, Heil 2017: 72. On the *tropaeum*, see Castellvi 2015: 216.
143 Koestermann 1957: 459–461.
144 The heavy fighting being reported by Tacitus (*Ann.* 2, 19–21).
145 Tacitus (*Ann.* 2, 22, 1) says the monument bore the following inscription: *debellatis inter Rhenum Albimque nationibus exercitum Tiberii Caesaris ea monimenta Marti et Iovi et Augusto sacravisse.*
146 Tac. *Ann.* 2, 23–25. E. Bickel (1943–44: 302–318) found Tacitus reliable only as regards recovering the eagle of Legio XIX, but data from numismatic and epigraphic sources do confirm Tacitus's version; see *TS* fr. 1, ll. 14; 28–29; *RIC* I^2, *Cal.* 57.
147 Tac. *Ann.* 2, 26, 4–5.
148 On that subject, see esp. Telschow 1975: 148–182.
149 Tac. *Ann.* 2, 26, 2–4.
150 Translated by C. H. Moore and J. Jackson (Loeb Classical Library, 249).
151 On Germanicus's *imitatio Drusi*, see Tac. *Ann.* 2, 8, 1; 14, 4; Wolters 1990a: 9; 1990b: 239–240.
152 Tac. *Ann.* 2, 26, 2; *TS* fr. 1, ll. 14–15.
153 The calculations carried out by P. Kehne (1998b: 444) indicate that, in the course of Germanicus's 3-year-long campaigns, between 20,000 and 25,000 soldiers died, a number roughly equivalent to four legions.

154 We can read about the way Tiberius conducted campaigns in Velleius Paterculus (2, 115, 5): *Nihil in hoc tanto bello, nihil in Germania aut videre maius aut mirari magis potui quam quod imperatori numquam adeo ulla opportuna visa est victoriae occasio quam damno amissi pensaret militis, semperque visum est gloriosum quod esset tutissimum, et ante conscientiae quam famae consultum, nec umquam consilia ducis iudicio exercitus sed exercitus providentia ducis rectus est*. The passage quoted indicates Tiberius avoided risky manoeuvres that could have cost his army too heavy losses. See also Timpe 1968: 74; 1971: 281.
155 Kienast 2009: 375; Lehmann 1991: 86–87.
156 Tac. *Ann*. 2, 26, 3–4.
157 Tac. *Ann*. 2, 5, 1; 43, 1; Kehne 1998b: 445.
158 Tac. *Ann*. 2, 22, 1.
159 Tac. *Ann*. 2, 44, 2; 45–46.
160 *TS* fr. 1, ll. 13–15; Kehne 1998b: 444.
161 Cass. Dio 54, 28, 1–3; Reinhold 1933: 125–126; Miltner 1937: 221; Roddaz 1984: 478–484.
162 See Kienast, Eck, Heil 2017: 70. *Contra* Vervaet (2020: 155), who believes Tiberius led military campaigns in Pannonia as early as 12 BC, as a proconsul with independent *imperium*. He fails to convince, because we know Augustus did not agree to Tiberius holding the triumph granted him that year and neither did he approve his imperatorial acclamation, which demonstrates his stepson did not hold independent *imperium* at the time. Moreover, the princeps himself emphasizes Tiberius was only an imperial legate during the Pannonian campaign. See *RGDA* 30, 1: *Pannoniorum gentes, qua[s a]nte me principem populi Romani exercitus nunquam adit, devictas per Ti. [Ne]ronem, qui tum erat privignus et legatus meus, imperio populi Romani s[ubie]ci, protulique fines Illyrici ad ripam fluminis Dan[u<v>]i. Contra* Vervaet 2020: 167. Now, Vervaet thinks the word *legatus* is not used here in its technical sense, instead generally meaning any person sent. He also suggests the word *legatus* is sometimes used in sources, including the *Res Gestae*, to refer to Augustan-era commanders of proconsular status, but his claim cannot be confirmed by analyzing the text of the *Res Gestae*.
163 Suet. *Aug*. 21, 1.
164 *RGDA* 30, 2. Cooley 2009: 248.
165 One such situation is mentioned by Cassius Dio (54, 36, 2).
166 Bernecker 1989: 128–132. See also Miltner 1937: 222–223.
167 Cass. Dio 54, 36, 2–3; 55, 2, 4; Liv. *Per*. 141.
168 *RGDA* 30, 1. See also Eck 2010: 19–33.
169 The attitude of the local population to Roman rule is best reflected by the words Cassius Dio (56, 16, 3) put in the mouth of a leader of the anti-Roman rebellion.
170 Cass. Dio 55, 29, 1–2. See also Swan 2004: 196–198.
171 Vell. Pat. 2, 110, 4; 115, 4; Cass. Dio 55, 29, 2–3; 32, 4; see also Koestermann 1953: 347–348; Swan 2004: 199–200.
172 Vell. Pat. 2, 110, 3; see Bleicken 1998: 593.
173 Vell. Pat. 2, 110, 4–6; Cass. Dio 55, 29, 2–4.
174 Suetonius (*Tib*. 16, 1) estimated the rebellion to be *gravissimum omnium externorum bellorum post Punica*.
175 Suet. *Tib*. 16, 1.
176 Vell. Pat. 2, 112, 4; 113, 1. Woodman 1977: 172; J. Bleicken (1998: 594) estimates the Roman forces at 150,000 men, not including the Thracian troops.
177 Vell. Pat. 2, 111, 1; Cass. Dio 55, 31, 1; Suet. *Aug*. 25, 2.
178 Cass. Dio 55, 31, 4.
179 Vell. Pat. 2, 111, 2; See also Woodman 1977: 161.

180 Cass. Dio 55, 30, 5.
181 Koestermann 1953: 354.
182 Suet. *Tib*. 20. After suppressing the insurrection, Tiberius rewarded Bato handsomely for his earlier actions.
183 Cass. Dio 55, 31, 1; Koestermann 1953: 358.
184 There is evidence for Augustus evaluating Tiberius's military skill highly in a passage in Suetonius (*Tib*. 21, 3).
185 The campaign in Pannonia was Germanicus's first military expedition. See also Swan 2004: 204.
186 Cf. Vell. Pat. 2, 129, 2. See Bleicken 1998: 593.
187 *Inscr. It*. XIII.2, 208, 491; Cass. Dio 55, 33, 1; Vell. Pat. 2, 114, 4; Koestermann 1953: 367. See also Woodman (1977: 178), who believes the surrender took place earlier.
188 Vell. Pat. 2, 115, 4.
189 Cass. Dio 56, 12, 1–2.
190 The siege is recounted in detail by Cassius Dio (56, 12–16).
191 See Ziółkowski 2004: 396; Kienast 2009: 371; Bleicken 1998: 595–596; Šašel Kos 2011: 115.
192 Vell. Pat. 2, 123, 1; Suet. *Tib*. 21, 1.
193 See Sawiński 2018: 116–120.
194 For a detailed description of the mutiny, see Tac. *Ann*. 1, 16–30.
195 Tac. *Ann*. 1, 14, 3. See Kienast, Eck, Heil 2017: 75–76.
196 See Shaw 1990: 172.
197 Tac. *Ann*. 2, 44, 1.
198 Shaw 1990: 176.
199 Tac. *Ann*. 2, 44, 2; Shaw 1990: 175, 178.
200 Tac. *Ann*. 2, 46, 1–5; 62, 1–3; 63, 1. Shaw 1990: 179–180.
201 Tac. *Ann*. 2, 63, 4.
202 Tac. *Ann*. 2, 63, 5.
203 Shaw 1990: 187.
204 Tac. *Ann*. 2, 63, 6; Rogers 1943: 122; Shaw 1990: 187–188.
205 Shaw 1990: 177–178.
206 Tac. *Ann*. 3, 7, 1; 11, 1; 19, 3; Rogers 1943: 124–125; Shaw 1990: 190.

3 The missions of members of the *domus Augusta* in the East

The victory over Antony in 31 BC at Actium gave Octavian power over the eastern reaches of the Roman Empire, but also meant he now needed to take a position regarding the order established there by Antony. Generally speaking, he preserved the system introduced by his rival, characterized by areas that were diverse in terms of status and methods of control co-existing under Rome's rule. Alongside provinces administered by Roman governors, the East included vassal kingdoms and principalities dependent on Rome, such as Cappadocia, Commagene, Judaea, Emesa, and Iturea.[1] Among the most important issues of Augustus's eastern policy, there was certainly the problem of Armenia and Parthia. The primary objective was to control Armenia and recover from the Parthians the legions' eagles lost by Crassus during his Parthian expedition. Another significant matter was to normalize the relations with the rulers of the vassal states who had chosen Antony's side in the war, and to ensure the loyalty of the inhabitants of the eastern provinces to the new regime. Agrippa's mission in the East in 23 BC must certainly be seen through that lens.[2]

3.1 Agrippa's first mission (23–22 BC)

However, most of our sources draw a connection between Agrippa's mission in the eastern provinces and his rivalry with young Marcellus, Augustus's nephew. According to those accounts, Agrippa felt offended that the emperor favoured Octavia's son, and so withdrew from political life to settle on Lesbos. Pliny and Cassius Dio write that it was Augustus who sent Agrippa away, whereas Velleius Paterculus, Tacitus, and Suetonius claim it was Agrippa's own decision to leave Rome,[3] but the perspective provided by all those sources is unacceptable, as we have absolutely no reason to suspect there was any conflict between Agrippa and Marcellus. No doubt, in suggesting that there was, ancient historians drew on the later case of Tiberius and his withdrawal to Rhodes in 6 BC as a result of his rivalry with Augustus's sons, Gaius and Lucius; most likely, they saw Agrippa's being sent away in the same light.[4] The only author who disagreed was Flavius Josephus, from whose text we learn that, as a direct representative of the emperor, Agrippa would govern all the provinces of Rome east of the Ionian Sea.[5] With that in mind, Agrippa's journey should not be seen in terms of an exile of honour, especially as, before his departure, he was granted special powers.[6]

Among present-day researchers, diverse opinions are represented on the reasons for Agrippa's mission. S. Jameson thought it was indirectly caused by the conspiracy of Varro Murena, a consul in 23 BC and a close aide to the princeps; Agrippa's main task would then have been to dismiss from his position the governor of Syria, probably a brother of the consul conspirator, and to make sure the Syrian legions remained loyal. Indeed, any military support he could have offered the conspiracy may have led to serious trouble.[7] D. Magie's approach to Agrippa's first mission was different: in his opinion, the goal was to conduct secret political negotiations with the Parthians about recovering the legions' eagles lost during Crassus's and Antony's campaigns, and the parley was to be held on Lesbos.[8] No doubt the problem of getting back those standards was paramount to Augustus's authority and position in the eyes of Roman society, which demanded he avenge the dishonour to the Roman soldiers, and, besides, the Parthian question held a special place in the imagery that Augustus was constructing of a new "golden era", which would only commence once the Parthians were humbled.[9]

Both those ideas are interesting, but it does not seem right to reduce the reasons behind the mission to one problem. Rather, I am inclined to see dispatching Agrippa to the East as being part of Rome's broader spectrum of policy there and connected to Augustus's inspection trip to that part of the world, planned for 22 BC. In other words, Agrippa may have been responsible for preparing the ground for that visit, as well as dealing with a number of issues—the Parthian question, Rome's relations with the rulers of the vassal kingdoms, the administrative machine of the eastern provinces, and ensuring the locals were loyal to the new regime.

According to Cassius Dio, Agrippa was to carry out his duties in Syria, the most vital province of the Roman East if looked at from the military point of view, but he chose to stay at Mytilene on Lesbos instead, sending his legates to Syria.[10] His choice of Lesbos as the place from which to govern the East was certainly no accident, as the island's convenient location enabled efficient control of most of the eastern provinces, primarily Asia, Achaea, and Macedonia.[11]

Not much source information is available on Agrippa's actions during that first mission in the East, and so it is impossible to tell exactly what he did while there. Only Flavius Josephus transmits a modicum of information, reporting on Herod visiting in Mytilene in 23/22. The aim of the visit was probably to strengthen the friendship (*amicitia*) between the Jewish ruler and Rome and to confirm he was loyal to the emperor. Although the sources do not mention it, we may suspect other client kings also took advantage of Agrippa's sojourn in Mytilene to visit and reassure him they were faithful to the reigning dynasty. Besides, Flavius writes that a delegation arrived from the inhabitants of Gadara in Judaea, a town given over to Herod after the Battle of Actium. Now, the relations between the inhabitants and Herod were strained, and the deputation arrived to make an official complaint about the Jewish king; however, Agrippa denied the envoys audience and sent them back to Herod.[12] He remained in the East until the end of 22 BC and, at the beginning of the new year, set off for Rome, stopping over in Sicily, where he met Augustus and reported back to him.[13]

3.2 Agrippa's second mission (17/16–13 BC)

Towards the end of 17 or early in 16 BC, Agrippa left for the East again to assume governorship of all the eastern provinces of the Roman Empire.[14] Compared with his previous stay in the region, his standing had changed fundamentally. In 21, Augustus had had his only daughter, Julia, marry Agrippa, making him, from that point on, the second most important person in the *domus Augusta* after the emperor. Moreover, in 18, Agrippa had been granted tribunician powers (*tribunicia potestas*), making him formally Augustus's co-ruler. Some historians believe it meant designating him as the emperor's successor as well.[15] His new status in the imperial family was primarily reflected in how the inhabitants of the eastern provinces honoured him.

His first destination after leaving Rome was Greece, where he stayed until the end of 16 BC. Regrettably, we know little about his actions there; literary sources are virtually silent on the subject, and inscriptions remain our main evidence. Unfortunately, with few exceptions, those mostly tell us the ways in which Greek cities honoured the emperor's son-in-law, while devoting less space to what he actually did in Greece. Such inscriptions are known from Athens, Corcyra, Taenarum, Gythium, Sparta, Corinth, and other places. Thanks to them, we know the inhabitants of all those towns honoured Agrippa with such prestigious titles as *εὐεργέτης*, *σωτήρ*, *κτίστης*, and *συγγενής*.[16] I do not share the optimism of those modern historians who believe we can use them to precisely determine his route in Greece,[17] as I do not think an honorific inscription irrefutably proves Agrippa had visited a given town; rather, it seems logical to assume he visited the most important towns of the province of Achaea, such as Athens, plus Sparta, where tangible traces of his presence remain anyway (for which see below). In fact, it is likely he visited those Greek cities that had, to use modern parlance, tourist appeal,[18] and, in the case of the less important Greek centres, we may only speculate on whether Augustus's son-in-law went there.

As has been mentioned above, little is known of Agrippa's achievements during his stay in Greece, although we do know he established an odeon in Athens to the south of the agora, called the Agrippeum in honour of the founder.[19] His visit was also commemorated by the Athenians by their erecting a colossal statue, placed opposite the propylaea leading to the Acropolis. Only the base of that monument remains, 9 metres high. M. Reinhold suspects it used to bear a sculpture depicting Agrippa riding in the triumphal quadriga. From the inscription preserved on that plinth, we know the construction was ordered by a decree of the Athenian assembly and honoured Agrippa as the city's benefactor.[20] Athenians erected another statue for him too, this one set in the renowned temple of Apollo on Delos. Its honorific inscription indicates it was paid for by the Athenian Areopagus Council.[21]

We can also be sure Agrippa visited the Peloponnese. His main destination was certainly Sparta, where he met the local notable Gaius Julius Eurycles (*Λακεδαιμονίων ἡγεμών*), who had fought at Actium on Augustus's side. The visit was commemorated in a series of coins beaten at Eurycles's behest and bearing an image of Agrippa.[22] Meanwhile, a local college, renamed the *Agrippiastai* in his honour, had a statue erected to him. In that way, the Spartan elite confirmed, in the new political landscape, their loyalty towards the *domus Augusta*.[23] Also attributed to Agrippa is the official establishment, most likely in 16 or 15 BC, of a veteran colony in Patras, where ex-soldiers from Antony's disbanded legions were settled. The official name of the settlement was *Colonia Augusta Aroe Patrensis*.[24] Epigraphic sources also inform us that Agrippa was in contact with the city of Argos. I have already indicated he wrote to the Gerousia at Argos, bringing that ancient institution back. During his stay in the Peloponnese, he also visited the famous sanctuary of Asclepius in Epidaurus. There is a tangible trace of his presence there in the form of a votive statue he dedicated to the god;[25] his visit to the sanctuary, known throughout the ancient world for its healing powers, should probably be seen as related to the rheumatic leg pains that ailed him, as mentioned by Pliny.[26]

Crossing the Hellespont, Agrippa left Greece for Asia Minor, where he presumably arrived at the beginning of 15 BC, likely touring Troy along the way. Perhaps it was during his stay in the Troad that another colony was founded, this one called *Alexandreia Troadis*, but, in this case, unlike with Patras, the matter is unclear, as the colony may have been founded at any point between 27 and 12 BC.[27]

The next place visited by the son-in-law of the princeps was Syria, where he probably arrived halfway through the year 15. Some sparse information on what he did there can be found in Strabo and in the Byzantine chronicler John Malalas. We need to be cautious regarding the latter, though, as he wrote in the 6th century, and much of what he reports is considered unreliable. In Strabo, we read Agrippa founded in Berytus the first Roman colony in Syria (*Colonia Iulia Augusta Felix Berytus*), settling in it veterans of two disbanded legions.[28] We also have an inscription from Berytus, dedicated to Jupiter for Agrippa's fortune, most likely an expression of gratitude for granting the town colony status.[29] While in Syria, Agrippa visited Antioch, the largest city of the province, twice, if Malalas is to be believed.[30] The first time, he allegedly established new baths, which were given his name, and enlarged the local theatre by adding a new section, among other projects; during his second visit, he was supposed to fund the reconstruction of the local hippodrome, damaged in an earthquake.[31]

From Syria, Agrippa went to Judaea, where Herod welcomed him with great pomp. Some interesting information on that visit can be found in Josephus. He reports that Agrippa visited Sebaste, Caesarea, and Jerusalem, among other places; the inhabitants of Jerusalem greeted him in festive attire, and Agrippa sacrificed a hecatomb in the Jerusalem temple and held a grand feast for the inhabitants.[32] In addition, Herod honoured his Roman protector by naming after him a town that used to be called Anthedon and had his name carved on one of the temple gates he had built.[33]

Having left Judaea, Agrippa sailed for Lesbos to winter there,[34] and it was on Lesbos that news reached him of the unrest that had broken out in the Bosporan Kingdom (a client state of Rome) owing to a certain Scribonius who usurped the throne. Under the circumstances, Agrippa decided to send Polemon, the king of Pontus—an ally of Rome—to depose the usurper and restore order. In spite of some measure of success, however, Polemon was not able to bring back peace, so that Agrippa had to intervene himself. In spring of 14 BC, he set out by sea through the Bosporus, arriving in Sinope on the Black Sea. As it turned out, no intervention was needed. If Cassius Dio is to be trusted, the mere news of Agrippa's arrival made the rebels lay down their arms.[35] After suppressing the rebellion, Agrippa set the aforementioned Polemon on the throne of the Bosporan Kingdom, which would now have to provide the Roman army with auxiliaries.[36] His intervention was then commemorated by the naming of Phanagoria, one of the capitals, after him. Moreover, on the orders of Queen Dynamis, gold staters were minted bearing Augustus's portrait on the obverse and Agrippa's on the reverse.[37] It is worth noting that, once he was done in the Bosporan Kingdom, Agrippa sent a report, not to the senate, but directly to Augustus, creating precedent for future commanders, who would, from then on, report on their military campaigns to the princeps.[38]

Having put the affairs of the Bosporan Kingdom in order, Agrippa decided to go to inspect the Roman provinces in Asia Minor. He visited Cappadocia, Bithynia and Pontus, Galatia, and Asia, where he stayed in Ephesus for a while.[39] The Ephesians honoured him with a coin emission bearing his image and that of his wife, Julia;[40] a statue of him was erected too as part of a larger statuary group funded by two freedmen of Augustus and Agrippa in honour of the *domus Augusta*. Sculptures of members of the imperial family were placed on top of a triple arch that acted as a gate leading to the local agora. There were statues of Augustus and Livia above the left-hand archway and statues of Agrippa and Julia over the right-hand one. Placing an image of Venus Genetrix, the patron goddess of the *gens Iulia*, above the central passageway indicates the whole monument was erected in honour of the *gens*. It is dated to the years 4–3 BC.[41]

Agrippa then left Ephesus for Samos, where he met a delegation of Jewish inhabitants of Greek cities who took the opportunity to accuse the Greeks of breaking the rights and privileges of the diaspora it had been granted by Augustus. He confirmed the concessions made earlier to the Jews, issuing two edicts addressed to the officials in Ephesus and Cyrene, telling the authorities there to respect the cult and rights of the Jewish community.[42] Afterwards he went to Mytilene again for the winter, to sail back to Italy in spring of 13 BC.[43]

From the information preserved in our sources, it would seem the 4 years Agrippa spent in the East were fairly intense. During that time, he visited a large majority of the provinces and vassal kingdoms in the region, leaving behind traces of his work there. For the local elite, his stay was a great occasion to emphasize their loyalty to the princeps and his family, proving it primarily through the prestigious honours heaped on Agrippa. In that way, locally prominent people could, in the future, count on the protection and support of Augustus's closest associate and the second most powerful man in the state, which would guarantee that their standing in their own communities would not be questioned.

3.3 Gaius Caesar's expedition (2/1 BC–AD 4)

Armenia held a special place in Roman eastern policy. The objective was for Rome to regain control of that state, which was a kind of a buffer zone between the Roman Empire and the Parthian Kingdom. Any Roman intervention in Armenian affairs had to cause a conflict with the *Imperium Parthicum*, which considered Armenia as important as Rome did. Augustus did not favour the plan, put forward during the late Republic and realized through the campaigns of Crassus and Antony, to solve the Armenian–Parthian problem through direct military confrontation, leaning instead towards diplomacy,[44] and Tiberius's eastern mission of 20 BC had already exemplified that. By following that policy, it was possible to set the Roman vassal, Tigranes, on the Armenian throne. After his death around 6 BC, Armenia again came under the Parthian sphere of influence, but Augustus could not react immediately. He was getting old and probably did not feel up to personally journeying to the East, and, with Tiberius on Rhodes, there was no one at the time in the imperial family who could have properly represented the princeps in any negotiations with the Parthian ruler. Thus, he had to wait for Gaius, the elder of his adopted sons, to reach the age to be dispatched there.[45]

We do not know the exact date when Gaius Caesar left for the eastern provinces.[46] Two views on the matter exist among researchers.[47] Some believe he set out in May of 2 BC, shortly after the official dedication of the Forum of Augustus, arguing mostly from numismatical sources;[48] others think it only happened in the following year (or, more precisely, on 29 January), a date based on a reconstruction of a missing fragment of the *Fasti Praenestini*, identified by P. Herz as a reference to Gaius Caesar's eastern mission.[49]

Our sources report that Gaius's main task was to settle the Armenian–Parthian question. Ovid writes that the aim of the expedition was to conquer all of Parthia, thus crowning Rome's reign over the whole world. Of course, that is mere *licentia poetica* and flattery typical of Augustan poets; it seems unlikely the emperor had plans that reached so far and were actually so unrealistic. Pliny mentions that Gaius Caesar was expected to put things in order on the Arabian Peninsula.[50] The mission also provided an excellent opportunity to advertise him among the inhabitants of the eastern provinces and the legions stationed there, while, for Gaius himself, it was a chance to gain important experience administering the state and leading military campaigns. By carrying it out successfully, he could also prove he was a worthy candidate to taking over from Augustus in the future—no doubt a matter of paramount importance for his image as that of the future successor. The expedition was prepared most thoroughly. As his son was completely unfamiliar with affairs of war, the princeps appointed a special staff of experienced advisors who would accompany the young man. Of particular importance among them were M. Lollius (consul in 21 BC) and P. Sulpicius Quirinius (consul in 12 BC).[51]

His first destination was Greece, where he probably visited Athens. The Athenians honoured Agrippa's natural son with even more pomp than the father before him, no doubt because they saw him as Augustus's would-be successor. A temple was built in the agora dedicated to Ares, and Gaius's statue was placed in it. Interestingly, the temple was made of materials from the demolition of a 5th-century temple to Ares in one of the Attic demes.[52] From an inscription found at the Theatre of Dionysus, we also know the Athenians surnamed Gaius *the New Ares*.[53] Drawing on Ovid, we may see the creative way they honoured Augustus's son as connected to the consecration of the temple to Mars Ultor in 2 BC—that is, shortly before Gaius Caesar left for the East; the poet clearly does consider the dedication and Gaius's expedition related. Also from Ovid, we know the youth was made out to be the new scourge of the Parthians and avenger of all the insults the Romans had suffered from them: his campaign was expected to continue Augustus's earlier victories.[54] In the context of Gaius Caesar's prospective succession, that kind of presentation was very important. It is not known how much time exactly Augustus's son spent in Greece, or which cities he visited. From there, he sailed towards Asia Minor, stopping along the way on Samos, where he met Tiberius, who had been staying on Rhodes. It is probably on Samos that Gaius spent his first winter in the East.[55]

From Samos, he crossed to the coast of Asia Minor; again, his sojourn in the region inspired its inhabitants to offer him honours. We know the town of Assos celebrated him as the prospective successor by erecting an inscription containing the title he was granted by the equites, *princeps iuventutis* (*ἡγεμόνα τῆς νεότητος*).[56] Having inspected the provinces of Asia Minor, in AD 1 he reached Syria, where he commenced preparations for the Arabian expedition.[57] Then he went to Egypt,[58] where, as D. G. Weingärtner supposes, he inspected the Egyptian ports on the Red Sea.[59] From there, he conducted a raid on Arabia (*Arabia Petraea*), but the sources have little to say on the subject. The only source to mention that campaign explicitly is Pliny, who merely notes it took place, without reporting any details on its course.[60] Unfortunately, the treatise on Gaius's Arabian expedition written by Juba II, the monarch of Mauretania who accompanied Augustus's son during his stay in the East, does not survive.[61] On the one hand, modern scholars treat Gaius's expedition as carrying on Augustus's policy towards the region, as exemplified earlier by the expedition led by Aelius Gallus, the prefect of Egypt, in 25–24. On the other hand, it is regarded as stemming from Gaius's wish to imitate Alexander the Great (*imitatio Alexandri*), as plans to conquer the whole Arabian Peninsula were attributed to him.[62] With the Arabian expedition over, Gaius returned to Syria, visiting Jerusalem along the way, but, unlike Agrippa, he did not sacrifice in the temple. Suetonius stresses that it won him Augustus's approval.[63]

After a short stay in Syria, halfway through AD 2, Gaius set out for Armenia. There, he had a "summit" meeting with the Parthian ruler, Phraataces, which took place on an island on the Euphrates. Velleius Paterculus, who witnessed the event himself, writes that both Gaius and the king of the Parthians were accompanied by large retinues and military units. The meeting reached its climax in two feasts, one organized by the Romans in Phraataces's honour, and the other by the Parthians in Gaius Caesar's.[64] Cassius Dio reports that the meeting made Phraataces give up all Parthian claims to Armenia and agree to accept a Roman candidate for the Armenian throne. In return, Rome officially acknowledged him as the king of Parthia. The Parthian monarch could not afford a military confrontation with Rome, as the situation in his state was not stable.[65] As a direct result of the agreement, Gaius set the Roman vassal Ariobarzanes on the throne of Armenia;[66] however, the pro-Parthian faction in Armenia did not accept the puppet king, and, in AD 3, an anti-Roman rebellion broke out, which forced Gaius to stage a military intervention. The sources tell us the campaign went well, reaching its high point in the siege and capture of Artagira, the main fortress of the insurgents.[67] During the fighting at Artagira, Gaius was wounded in an insidious manner; Velleius claims that it affected the young commander greatly, and so he decided to withdraw from public life.[68] Still, the wound was severe enough that Gaius died during his return journey to Italy, in February of AD 4, in Limyra in Lycia.[69] The Limyrans paid him posthumous honours by erecting a symbolic tomb (a cenotaph).[70]

Gaius Caesar's Armenian campaign is referred to by an interesting coin emission produced at the Pergamum mint: the obverse shows Gaius's head and the legend "Γ ΚΑΙΣΑΡ ΠΕΡΓΑΜΗΝΩΝ," and the reverse contains the image of an Armenian holding a spear and an arrow, with the legend "Α ΦΟΥΡΙΟΣ ΓΥΜΝΑΣΙΑΡΧΩΝ."[71] References to the Armenian–Parthian expedition can also be found in the ornamentation of the armour of a statue that most likely depicts Gaius Caesar, found in Caesarea in Mauretania (originally Jol, modern Cherchell). It is supposed the statue was put up shortly after Gaius's death by the Mauretanian king Juba II, who had accompanied Gaius during his eastern expedition.[72] In the centre of the image on the *lorica*, there is a half-naked figure, identified with Gaius, who presents Venus, the patron deity of the *gens Iulia*, with Victory with a *tropaeum*. The goddess is, here, Venus Victrix, herself in armour, with a sword and shield. Behind Augustus's son, there is another Victory, holding the oak-leaf crown (*corona civica*) above his head. Below that central scene, two centaurs are depicted, one holding the horn of plenty, and the other, a ship's helm, clear references to the results, propitious for Rome, of Augustus's victory at Actium. In that context, as P. Zanker was right to observe, Gaius's success was highlighted as a continuation of the blessed age commenced by that victory. At the top of the whole, there is an image of a helmeted and armoured Mars, and, on the tassets of the armour, there are heads of bearded barbarians, which stand for the defeated Parthians and Armenians.[73]

Ultimately, Gaius Caesar's mission brought no lasting effects; soon after he left Armenia, the Rome-appointed ruler was deposed, and the Parthian faction regained its influence. Still, Gaius can hardly be blamed for that, as he was merely carrying out the task the princeps had entrusted him with. The failure of the mission was caused, not by Gaius's incompetence, but rather by an incorrect choice of candidate for Armenian kingship, who did not win his subjects' approval.

3.4 Germanicus's mission (AD 17–19)

The developments in Armenia were not good for Rome, encouraging Tiberius to send Germanicus to the East.[74] Tacitus writes that was only an excuse to deprive him of his command over legions in Germania, endangering him anew in the restless Armenia and Parthia,[75] but, in this case, his opinion is not trustworthy; as I have said above, the image created by that historian and fixed by him in literature, of a growing conflict between Tiberius and Germanicus, is not reliable. The emperor's decision to send his adoptive son to the East followed quite simply from the fact he was the only person who could be entrusted with the mission.[76] After all, elsewhere in his narrative, Tacitus himself states clearly that, with the princeps so old and Drusus the Younger so inexperienced, Germanicus was the only member of the *domus Augusta* who could journey to the East.[77] The primary aims of his mission were to set a new king on the vacant throne of Armenia and to normalize relations with the Parthians.[78] Affairs also needed putting in order in the client kingdom of Commagene, where, after Antiochus's death, two factions were warring, one that wanted to keep the monarchy and another that supported transforming the state into a Roman province. Germanicus was also supposed to calm things down in the provinces of Syria and Judaea, which had asked the princeps to reduce their taxes.[79]

The route of Germanicus's tour of the East can be reconstructed fairly accurately based on Tacitus's text.[80] We also have many honorific inscriptions put up by certain towns in the provinces there. However, as with

Agrippa and Gaius Caesar, the inscriptions do not prove beyond all doubt that Germanicus did visit those places.[81] He probably left Rome in early autumn of AD 17, sailing across the Adriatic Sea to Dalmatia, where he had a meeting with Drusus, then active in the area.[82] From there, he followed the coastline to Greece, where, early in AD 18, he reached Nicopolis to assume his second consulship and see the place where the Battle of Actium was fought. His next destination was Athens, where he was welcomed with great honours;[83] then he sailed on to Lesbos, where, as Tacitus notes, Agrippina gave birth to Julia, the couple's last child.[84] The journey continued through Thrace and along the northern coast of Asia Minor, where Germanicus visited such cities as Byzantium, Perinthus, and Troy. According to Tacitus, he also inspected the province of Bithynia and Pontus, where he put an end to Roman officials abusing their power. One other place he visited during his stay in Asia Minor was the renowned oracle of Apollo at Claros, which allegedly had an inauspicious prophecy for him.[85]

On leaving Anatolia, Germanicus headed by sea, via Rhodes, to Syria and then Armenia, where he arrived in summer of AD 18. In Artaxata, he made Zeno, a son of the ruler of Pontus, the king of Armenia; having been crowned, Zeno took the name of Artaxias.[86] The choice of the new king proved apt, as he won the acceptance of both aristocracy and the lower classes and went on to rule uninterrupted until AD 34.[87] The coronation ceremony was then commemorated on didrachms and drachms produced at the mint in Caesarea in Cappadocia. The obverse of those emissions bears a depiction of Germanicus accompanied by the legend, "GERMANICUS CAESAR TI AUG F COS II"; the reverse shows Germanicus holding in his left hand a spear (symbolizing the Roman rule), while, with his right, he puts a tiara on the head of the Armenian elect standing beside him. The scene also has a legend, this one reading "ARTAXIAS GERMANICUS." The date of the emission is a point of some contention. Some researchers believe the coins were minted under Tiberius, whereas others date them to the reign of Caligula or even Claudius.[88]

Having solved the Armenian problem, Germanicus returned to Syria to meet a Parthian embassy sent by King Artabanus II. At the Parthian ruler's request, he renewed in Rome's name the friendship (*amicitia*) and alliance (*foedus*) with Parthia, also agreeing to deport from Syria Vonones, who had been seeking the Armenian throne and inciting the Parthians to revolt against Artabanus. In the end, Vonones was imprisoned in Pompeiopolis in Cilicia.[89]

At the beginning of AD 19, Germanicus visited Egypt; the first city on his route was Alexandria,[90] and the reason for the visit was a major crop failure, which, as Egypt was an important granary region of the Empire, could have led to a crisis in Rome itself.[91] Tacitus recounts that Germanicus ordered the granaries to be opened and grain distributed to the inhabitants of the city, lowering its price considerably.[92] In their gratitude, the Alexandrians wanted to confer divine honours on him; in response, he issued a special edict refusing them categorically. His argument was that such honours were only due to Tiberius and Livia.[93]

After the time spent in Alexandria, he set out upriver along the course of the Nile to visit the most important cities in Egypt;[94] from Tacitus, we know his route included Memphis and Thebes, were he saw the pyramids and the Colossi of Memnon, as well as Elephantine and Syene (Aswan) in the southern reaches of Egypt.[95] Having done his sightseeing tour of Egypt, Germanicus returned to Alexandria and sailed for Syria,[96] but soon fell unexpectedly ill and, in October of AD 19, died in Daphne in the suburbs of Antioch.[97] At the behest of the senate, two tombs were then erected in Syria to commemorate him: one in the forum in Antioch where his corpse had been cremated, and the other in Daphne, where he had died. It is supposed that the first of those, called *sepulchrum* by Tacitus, was actually a cenotaph similar to that the inhabitants of Limyra built after Gaius Caesar's death; the other, explicitly referred to by Tacitus as a *tribunal*, may have had the form of a huge sarcophagus.[98]

Germanicus's eastern journey was a good occasion for the inhabitants of the provinces in the region to shower him with prestigious honours, including statues, which we know were erected for him in Olympia, Lindos on Rhodes, and Palmyra, among other places. In Olympia, Germanicus's statue was most likely put up after a team he owned won the quadriga race during the games, although he was also celebrated as an *euergetes* (benefactor).[99] In Lindos, a statue of his stood in the company of statues of Tiberius, divus Augustus, and Drusus the Younger on the local Acropolis. Like the two emperors, the current one and the deceased, the two brothers were honoured there as *euergetai*. From the preserved dedication inscription, we know the whole statue group was set up by a decree of the assembly of Lindos.[100] In Palmyra, statues of Germanicus and Drusus were placed next to one of Tiberius in the courtyard of the local temple to Bel; later, they were moved to the *cella*. They had been funded by a certain Minucius Horatius Rufus, a legate of *legio X Fretensis*, stationed in Syria.[101]

All the foundations listed above bear a relationship to Germanicus's stay in the East, and it is worth noting that, while conferring honours on Germanicus, the locals would do the same for Drusus the Younger, even though he had never visited those parts. That is quite understandable, considering his standing within the *domus Augusta* and rights to succession from Tiberius were the same as Germanicus's. Honouring only Germanicus would have been a serious faux pas, which the local authorities must have known perfectly well. A loose analogy can be seen here to the earlier honours granted Gaius Caesar and Lucius Caesar as Augustus's intended successors.

Notes

1 See Sartre 1997: 16.
2 On Agrippa's first mission in the East, see Magie 1908: 145–152; Reinhold 1933: 79–85; Hanslik 1961: 1251–1253; Roddaz 1984: 319–328; Halfmann 1986: 25–26, 163; Dąbrowa 1998: 201.

3 Cass. Dio 53, 32, 1; Plin. *HN*. 7, 149; Vell. Pat. 2, 93, 2; Suet. *Aug*. 66, 3; *Tib*. 10, 1; Tac. *Ann*. 14, 53, 3.
4 In a similar vein, see e.g. Syme 1939: 342 (note 7); Roddaz 1984: 323; Rich 1990: 167–168; Richardson 2012: 98–99; Levick 2013: 86.
5 Joseph. *AJ*. 15, 350.
6 As discussed above.
7 Jameson 1969: 219.
8 Magie 1908: 148–152. So Rich 1990: 168; Kienast 2009: 109.
9 On that subject, see esp. Zanker 1990: 188–196.
10 Cass. Dio 53, 32, 1. See also Rich 1990: 168.
11 See Richardson 2012: 98; Levick 2013: 86.
12 Joseph. *AJ*. 15, 350–351. Reinhold 1933: 84–85.
13 See Halfmann 1986: 163.
14 On dating Agrippa's second eastern journey, see Reinhold 1933: 106; Halfmann 1986: 163–164.
15 On Agrippa's role in Augustus's succession plans, see Sawiński 2018: 31–46.
16 *IG* III 575; *CIG* II 1878, *CIL* III 491; *IG* V^1 1166, *CIL* III 494. See also Reinhold 1933: 107; Roddaz 1984: 441–444.
17 So e.g. Reinhold 1933: 106; Halfmann 1986: 164–165.
18 An observation for which I would like to thank Adam Ziółkowski.
19 Thompson 1950: 31–141; Sartre 1997: 173, 255; Zanker 1990: 261.
20 Reinhold 1933: 108.
21 Rose 1997: 151 (no. 83).
22 *RPC* I 1106.
23 Roddaz 1984: 446.
24 Reinhold 1933: 110; Roddaz 1984: 431–432.
25 *IG* IV 1363; Reinhold 1933: 108.
26 Plin. *HN*. 23, 58.
27 See Reinhold 1933: 110; Roddaz 1984: 432.
28 Strab. 16, 2, 19. See Reinhold 1933: 110–111; Roddaz 1984: 432–433; Millar 1993: 36.
29 *CIL* III 156: *I. O. M. PRO SAL[U]TE AGRIP[PAE]*.
30 Reinhold (1933: 111, note 36) thought the first of the two visits mentioned by the Byzantine chronicler may have taken place during Agrippa's first stay in the East, in 23 BC.
31 Mal. 9, 222; 225. See also Roddaz 1984: 434–435; Sartre 1997: 379.
32 Joseph. *AJ*. 16, 12–15.
33 Joseph. *BJ*. 1, 416.
34 Halfmann 1986: 163.
35 According to Dio (54, 28, 2), later on, revolting Pannonian tribes reacted in the same way, giving up at the mere news of Agrippa's arrival; see above.
36 Cass. Dio 54, 24, 4–6; Joseph. *AJ*. 16, 21–23; Reinhold 1933: 113–115; Roddaz 1984: 463–468; Rich 1990: 201–202.
37 *RPC* I 1865; Reinhold 1933: 115.
38 Cass. Dio 54, 24, 7.
39 Joseph. *AJ*. 16, 23.
40 See Reinhold 1933: 117 (note 74).
41 Rose 1997: 172–174 (no. 112); Boschung 2002: 146.
42 Joseph. *AJ*. 16, 27–30; 167–170. I have written on those decrees in more detail above (in Section 1.3.2).
43 See Halfmann 1986: 164.
44 Sartre 1997: 27–28.
45 Gaius was born in 20 BC, and so, in 6 BC, he was only 14 and had not yet assumed his *toga virilis*.

46 There is much literature on Gaius Caesar's eastern mission; see primarily Zetzel 1970: 259–266; Romer 1974: *passim*; *id.* 1979: 199–214; Halfmann 1986: 166–168; Dąbrowa 1998: 203–205; Luther 2010: 103–127.
47 The whole discussion is reported on in detail by A. Luther (2010: 106, note 18).
48 See esp. Romer 1978: 187–202; Rose 2005: 45 (note 132).
49 See Herz 1980: 287–288. This date is also accepted by Halfmann 1986: 166; Kienast, Eck, Heil 2017: 67.
50 Ovid. *Ars am.* 1, 177–178; Plin. *HN.* 6, 141. See also Luther 2010: 111.
51 Vell. Pat. 2, 102, 1; Tac. *Ann.* 3, 48, 1; Suet. *Tib.* 12, 3. See Luther 2010: 114–115.
52 See Romer 1974: 97; Bowersock 1984: 173; Rose 1997: 18; Zanker 1990: 224, 261.
53 *IG*^{2}, II, 3250; Ehrenberg, Jones 1955: 68 (no. 64).
54 Ovid. *Ars am.* 1, 177–228. On that subject, see esp. Romer 1974: 95–98; Syme 1978: 8–11; Bowersock 1984: 173; Rose 1997: 17–18. In an inscription from Messene (*SEG* XXIII, 206, ll. 10–12), Gaius's eastern expedition was painted as "fought for the salvation of all people from barbarians" ("ὑπὲρ τᾶς ἀνθρώπων πάντων σωτηρίας τοῖς βαρβάροις μαχόμενον").
55 Suet. *Tib.* 12, 2. Differently Cassius Dio (55, 10, 19), who reports the meeting with Tiberius took place on Chios. However, considering where Rhodes is relative to those two islands, Samos seems more likely. See Halfmann 1986: 166–167; Swan 2004: 117.
56 *IGR* IV 248; Merkelbach 1974: 186.
57 Vell. Pat. 2, 101, 1; Cass. Dio 55, 10a, 4.
58 The only author to report on Gaius Caesar's visit to Egypt is Orosius (7, 3, 5), but he offers no details regarding Gaius's actions there.
59 Weingärtner 1969: 39.
60 Plin. *HN.* 2, 168; 6, 141; elsewhere in his text (*HN.* 6, 160), he says that, in the end, Gaius did not enter Arabia. Halfmann (1986, 167) supposes there is also an allusion to Gaius's Arabian expedition in the inscription from Messene quoted above, which mentions a successful campaign of his against barbarians, but that is only a guess, as the mention could just as well refer to Gaius's campaign in Armenia and Parthia. For a detailed interpretation of that inscription, see Zetzel 1970: 259–266; Herz 1993: 272–288; Kantiréa 2007: 162–163, 208. On Gaius's Arabian expedition, see Romer 1974: 161–169; Hurlet 1997: 134–136, among others.
61 Mentioned in Pliny (*HN.* 6, 141).
62 See Luther 2010: 111.
63 Suet. *Aug.* 93.
64 Vell. Pat. 2, 101, 1–3. See also Woodman 1977: 126.
65 Cass. Dio 55, 10a, 4–5. See also Swan 2004: 127–128; Luther 2010: 122.
66 *RGDA* 27, 2; Tac. *Ann.* 2, 4, 1.
67 Strab. 11, 14, 6; Vell. Pat. 2, 102, 2; Cass. Dio 55, 10a, 6–7. See also Swan 2004: 130–131.
68 Vell. Pat. 2, 102, 3.
69 Vell. Pat. 2, 102, 3; Suet. *Aug.* 65, 1.
70 For information on that monument, see Borchhardt 1974: 217–241; Ganzert 1984. Gaius Caesar also received numerous posthumous honours, both in Rome and the provinces. On that subject, see Sawiński 2018, 71–81.
71 *RPC* I 2361.
72 The connection between Juba and Augustus's son comes up in Pliny (*HN.* 6, 141), who writes that the king authored a treatise on Gaius's *expeditio Arabica*, which did not survive.
73 Zanker 1990: 225–226.

74 For Germanicus's eastern mission, see esp. Koestermann 1958: 331–375; Pani 1987: 1–23; Kehne 1998b: 445–446; Rivière 2016: 277–338.
75 Tac. *Ann.* 2, 5, 1.
76 *SCPP* ll. 30–32.
77 Tac. *Ann.* 2, 43, 1.
78 Detailed information on the situation in Armenia and the Parthian Kingdom at the time is to be found in Tacitus (*Ann.* 2, 1–4).
79 Tac. *Ann.* 2, 42, 3–5; Joseph. *AJ*. 18, 53; *TS* fr. 1, ll. 15–16. See also Drogula 2015a: 145.
80 The route of Germanicus's eastern journey has been reconstructed in detail by Hoët-van Cauwenberghe, Kantiréa 2013: 148–151.
81 See Hurlet 1997: 198.
82 Tac. *Ann.* 2, 53, 1; Halfmann 1986: 168; Shaw 1990: 177–178.
83 Tac. *Ann.* 2, 53, 1–3; Suet. *Cal.* 1, 2. For the honours accorded Germanicus by the Athenians, see Blonce, Gangloff 2013: 114–119.
84 Tac. *Ann.* 2, 54, 1.
85 Tac. *Ann.* 2, 54, 2–4.
86 Tac. *Ann.* 2, 56, 1–3. On Zeno of Pontus, see Rivière 2016: 302.
87 See Hurlet 1997: 201.
88 *RPC* I 3629; 3630. For various suggestions on how to date that emission, see the commentary on it by the editors of the *RPC* and Olbrycht 2016: 625–626.
89 Tac. *Ann.* 2, 58, 1–2; *SCPP* ll. 39–45.
90 Halfmann 1986: 169–170. On Germanicus's visit to Egypt, see Van Ooteheghem 1959: 241–251; Weingärtner 1969: *passim*; Hennig 1972: 349–365; Rivière 2016: 315–338.
91 Some researchers also see Germanicus's journey to Egypt in terms of *imitatio Alexandri*. See e.g. Hennig 1972: 364–365.
92 Tac. *Ann.* 2, 59, 1; Suet. *Tib.* 52, 2; Hurlet 1997: 203.
93 For an edition and detailed commentary, see Weingärtner 1969: 108–119.
94 For that trip, which was mostly about sightseeing, see Weingärtner 1969: 136–159; Rivière 2016: 329–338.
95 Tac. *Ann.* 2, 60–61.
96 Halfmann 1986: 169.
97 *TS* fr. 1, ll. 37–38; Tac. *Ann.* 2, 83, 2. The circumstances of Germanicus's death are not quite clear. Ancient authors imply he was poisoned by someone persuaded to do so by Calpurnius Piso, then the governor of Syria. See Plin. *HN*. 11, 187; *Tac. Ann.* 2, 69, 1; Suet. *Tib.* 52, 3; *Cal.* 2; Cass. Dio 57, 18, 10. For a detailed account of Germanicus's illness and death, see Tac. *Ann.* 2, 70–72.
98 Tac. *Ann.* 2, 83, 2; *TS* fr. 1, ll. 35–38. Unfortunately, those portions of the *Tabula Siarensis* that used to contain information about the objects survive in fragments. See Sánchez, Gutiérrez 1999: 164–178; Lott 2012: 223–224. For more on the many posthumous honours granted Germanicus in Rome and the provinces, see Sawiński 2018: 128–142.
99 As mentioned in an inscription from Olympia (*IvO*, 221) commissioned by one M. Antonius Pisanus. On the statue, see Rose 1997: 25; 146–147 (no. 79).
100 Rose 1997: 154–155 (no. 89).
101 Rose 1997: 189 (no. 130); Boschung 2002: 108.

4 Honours accorded to members of the *domus Augusta*

4.1 Imperatorial acclamations

Under the Republic, a victorious commander could be hailed *imperator* and receive the right to a triumph or ovation if he met certain specific conditions. The basic criteria were having held independent *imperium* and having led the campaign under one's own auspices (*suis auspiciis*). The principate brought with it significant changes in that regard. Although holding independent *imperium* was still necessary for the right to an acclamation or triumph and ovation, no commander fought *suis auspiciis* anymore, as every war was now waged under the auspices of the emperor as the commander-in-chief of the whole army.[1] After Augustus established the principate, the circle of people who had independent *imperia* while conducting their military campaigns, and so could be hailed *imperator* or granted a triumph, shrank considerably. Also relevant was the principle, introduced by the first princeps, that those honours were in practice reserved exclusively for the emperor and members of his family.[2]

The first member of the imperial family to receive the title of *imperator* for his military efforts was M. Agrippa. Its appearance in Agrippa's titulature is confirmed by epigraphical sources, which unfortunately do not discuss the circumstances of the acclamation,[3] although we can, with high probability, see it as connected to his actions in Spain and to the suppression in 19 BC of the insurrection of the Cantabri and Astures.[4]

Later, successes in the fight against Germanic tribes gave the title of *imperator* to Drusus the Elder. The acclamation most likely took place in 10 or 9 BC, when he conducted campaigns in Germania as a commander holding independent *imperium*. In R. Syme's view, Augustus's stepson was actually hailed *imperator* twice.[5] His opinion rests on a very uncertain reconstruction of an inscription fragment from a city gate in Saepinum, where Drusus features in the text as *imp. II*; moreover, it is in sharp contrast to other epigraphical sources, primarily coins: an inscription from the Forum of Augustus bearing a eulogy of Drusus, another inscription from Vicenza, and series of *aurei* and *denarii* minted by Claudius all mention only a single acclamation.[6] It seems improbable that Claudius would not have highlighted a double one on coins produced in honour of his famous father.

Tiberius was winning his first military decorations around the same time. R. Syme thought he was first hailed *imperator* for his victories over Pannonian and Dalmatian tribes in the years 10–9, dating his first acclamation to 10 BC;[7] other researchers believe it only took place in 9 BC.[8] After Drusus died, Tiberius finished his brother's work in Germania, for which, in 8 BC, he received the title again;[9] then, in AD 4–6, he was in charge of campaigns in Germania again, which earned him his third acclamation. Cassius Dio reports it happened in 6, in a sense crowning Tiberius's 3 years of fighting Germanic tribes.[10]

Suppressing the dangerous uprising in Pannonia and Dalmatia in the years 6–9 meant he was hailed *imperator* for the fourth and fifth times, but we do not know exactly when those acclamations took place. Cassius Dio only mentions one of them, placing it in AD 9, right after the capture of Andretium, which sealed the fate of the revolt in Dalmatia;[11] he probably means the fifth.[12] D. Faoro convincingly demonstrates the fourth must have occurred in the previous year, after the rebelled Pannonian tribes surrendered, which in turn happened on 3 August AD 8 on the River Bathinus.[13]

Regrettably, ancient authors do not say when or under what circumstances Tiberius attained the title for the sixth and seventh times. We only know there was a sixth time from coin emissions minted at Lugdunum, where the IMP VI appears in his titulature.[14] The coins are usually dated to AD 11, permitting the assumption that Tiberius's sixth acclamation was a result of his campaigns in Germania, where he was sent to stabilize the situation after Varus's defeat. According to D. Faoro, Tiberius's sixth acclamation coincides with Augustus's twentieth, commemorated in a coin emission from Rome, which can be dated with precision to AD 11–12 owing to a mention of the emperor's thirty-fourth *tribunicia potestas*.[15] On those grounds, he believes Tiberius's sixth *acclamatio* was held towards the end of 11 or at the beginning of 12.[16] Things are the same in the case of Tiberius's seventh acclamation, likewise only mentioned on coins minted at Lugdunum. Those include series of *asses* and *dupondii* dated to 12–14.[17] On that basis, we may assume it was occasioned by Germanicus's victorious campaign in Germania; as a result, Augustus received his twenty-first, and last, acclamation, and Tiberius received his seventh as the emperor's *collega imperii*. Barnes and Syme date those two acclamations to AD 13; Faoro dates them to the summer of the year 14. In their opinion, Germanicus was awarded his first acclamation at the same time.[18] Unfortunately, with the sources silent on that, we do not know which campaign of Germanicus was involved or when it happened.[19] When it comes to imperatorial acclamations, we may regard Tiberius as the real record-holder of the reigning dynasty; before becoming emperor, he won that honour seven times.

Gaius Caesar, in turn, was hailed *imperator* for his actions in the East. Our main source here is Cassius Dio, who claims the acclamation took place because of Gaius's victorious campaign in Armenia, which ended in the capture of Artagira in AD 3. That is confirmed by epigraphical sources, which do attest to the title of *imperator* having been part of Gaius's titulature.[20]

In AD 13, Germanicus assumed the general command of the Rhine army, and the campaigns to be fought in the region opened for him, as for Drusus and Tiberius before, the prospect of winning high-prestige rewards and military fame. Epigraphical sources do confirm he was hailed *imperator* twice, but dating his first acclamation is problematic.[21] Some information can be gleaned from an inscription honouring Fabricius Tuscus, an equestrian officer from the colony of Alexandreia Troas, which lists the various military functions he served in Augustus's reign,[22] including a mention of Fabricius receiving prestigious army awards (the *hasta pura* and the *corona aurea*) for his deeds during a German campaign (*bello Germanico*), apparently granted him *a Germanico Caesare imp*.[23] The fact the epithet *divus* is missing in the mention of Augustus makes some researchers assume the inscription was set up before the first princeps died,[24] but, although I find their argument strong, it is certainly not decisive. Still, if we do accept that limitation on the date of the inscription, we can conclude that, as it explicitly calls Germanicus an *imperator*, then his first imperatorial acclamation took place in Augustus's reign.[25] The exact date, however, is quite controversial. D. Timpe and F. Goodyear favour AD 11; T. Barnes and R. Syme favour AD 13, F. Hurlet favours AD 13 or the beginning of AD 14, whereas D. Faoro supposes it came as a result of Germanicus's victorious campaign of the summer of the year 14.[26] The last suggestion appears to me the least likely, as Tacitus implies that, in the final weeks of Augustus's life, the legions stationed in Germania were not involved in any major military operations: he writes the soldiers sat idle in their summer camp when the news reached them that Augustus was dead.[27] We also know that, towards the end of Augustus's life, Germanicus mostly stayed in the Gallic provinces, carrying out various administrative tasks, and it was there that he learned of the emperor's death.[28] Therefore, with the sources silent, we cannot ascertain either the circumstances or the precise date of Germanicus's first acclamation and can only assume it took place in the final years of Augustus's principate.

It is only with his second acclamation, which took place in 15, that we are back on solid ground: Tacitus mentions that Germanicus was granted the title *imperator* for a successful operation that freed the Roman ally Segestes, held captive by Arminius's followers. The novel factor is that the honour was not conferred by the will of the army, but rather on Tiberius's explicit orders.[29]

In the vast majority of cases, the granting of the title was initiated by the army, but the final decision of whether to approve its initiative was up to the emperor. Cases are known where the princeps refused; Augustus did, once, with Tiberius and Drusus. Specifically, he did not agree to his stepsons receiving the titles for their successes in 12 and 11 BC in Pannonia and Germania;[30] his decision was not motivated by any personal hostilities and neither did it mean the princeps failed to appreciate their achievements. The actual reason was that Drusus and Tiberius had conducted that campaign as *legati Augusti* and had not held independent *imperium*.[31] Instead, Augustus agreed to confer on both his stepsons *ornamenta triumphalia* as a substitute of a sort for triumph. The reward gave the young men the right to wear a triumphator's attire and laurel wreath during various games, as with those who had been awarded actual triumphs.[32]

Military successes of members of the *domus Augusta* and the imperatorial acclamations following them were also a great opportunity for the princeps himself, as, by claiming his part in those victories, he could increase the number of his own acclamations. Tiberius's campaigns in Pannonia and Germania earned Augustus the title of *imperator* five times.[33] After Gaius Caesar captured Artagira, the princeps was hailed *imperator* together with his son. It was his sixteenth acclamation.[34] Tiberius, after he became emperor, owed his eighth and last to Germanicus's victorious campaign of AD 16 against the Cherusci.[35]

4.2 Triumphs and ovations

Granting a victorious commander the title of *imperator* was a prerequisite for him holding a triumph, the most prestigious reward for military success there was.[36] Formally, the decision was taken by the senate, but ultimately it was always up to the emperor, who could accept or reject the decree. During Augustus's reign, only Tiberius celebrated a triumph; under Tiberius, only Germanicus did. That confirms the high rank of the honour in question, which, after 19 BC, was *de facto* only available to the princeps and the most prominent members of the *domus Augusta*.[37]

The first commander from the imperial family to receive the honour was Tiberius: in 7 BC, he triumphed in recognition of the successes he had had the previous year in Germania.[38] From Cassius Dio, it can be deduced that, after his return from Germania, Tiberius awaited his triumph, as was traditional, outside the pomerium, because, according to that historian, as he assumed his second consulship, Tiberius convoked the senate in the Portico of Octavia (*porticus Octavia*), which was outside the pomerium. Evidently, he did not want to lose his *imperium* before he held the triumph.[39] Cassius Dio says that, when the ceremony was over, Tiberius threw a festive banquet for senators on the Capitoline, while Livia held a similar party for the Roman matrons.[40]

For the second time, Tiberius received the right to triumph after suppressing the uprising in Pannonia and Dalmatia in AD 9,[41] but, as Rome was in mourning following the *clades Variana*, he had to postpone celebrating it. Suetonius reports that the festivities actually organized at the time were much more modest. Tiberius entered Rome on foot wearing the *toga praetexta* and a laurel wreath and went to the Campus Martius where, in the presence of standing senators, he ascended a specially prepared tribunal to take his seat beside Augustus and between the two consuls.[42] The triumph proper only took place 3 years later, after Tiberius's return from Germania—to be exact, on 23 October AD 12, according to the *Fasti Praenestini*.[43] We find a fairly detailed description of the proceedings in Velleius Paterculus and especially in Suetonius;[44] the former actually took part in person. We read in those authors that, after Tiberius, the key role in the triumphal procession fell to his legates, who were awarded *ornamenta triumphalia*; it is logical to assume that first among those was Germanicus, who had won his first military experience at Tiberius's side in the Pannonian–Dalmatian campaign. The most important chiefs of the defeated tribes were paraded; Suetonius writes that one of the leaders of the Pannonian rebellion, called Bato, was generously rewarded by Tiberius and then settled in Ravenna, in a sense in return for Bato letting Tiberius and his troops withdraw from unfavourable positions at one point during the war. We also learn from Suetonius that the ceremony was presided over by Augustus in person. Before heading for the Capitoline, which was the final point of each triumphal procession, Tiberius paid homage to the princeps, dedicating his victories to him. The whole ceremony culminated in a feast for the Roman plebs, members of whom were also paid 300 sesterces each. Thus, in the light of the accounts of the sources adduced here, we may assume the ceremony contained all the most vital elements traditionally featured in most Roman triumphal processions.

No doubt Tiberius's second triumph needs to be seen also in the context of Augustus's dynastic policy, as it was a splendid opportunity for him to present his future successor to the inhabitants of Rome. Framing him as a conqueror of dangerous barbarian tribes and the author of Rome's most important military successes was meant to reinforce the public's opinion that he deserved to soon take Augustus's place. Tiberius's victories indicated the gods favoured him, which in turn guaranteed prosperity and stability for the Empire under his future rule.[45]

It is most likely to Tiberius's second triumph that some *aurei* and *denarii* refer that were produced in the years 13–14 in the mint at Lugdunum. On the obverse of that emission, there is Augustus's head in the laurel wreath with the legend "CAESAR AUGUSTUS DIVI F PATER PATRIAE"; on the reverse is Tiberius in a triumphal quadriga, holding the attributes of a triumphator—that is, a laurel branch and a *sceptrum*, the legend reading "TI CAESAR AUG F TR POT XV" (Figure 4.1).[46]

Some researchers suspect that the triumph in question (and Tiberius's victories) are also referred to by the image on one of the two silver *skyphoi* discovered in Boscoreale near Pompeii.[47] The first vessel depicts the sacrifice before an expedition of war and a triumphal procession centred on a figure in a quadriga, identified as Tiberius. On the chariot, there is an image of two Victories holding a shield (Figure 4.2). The subject matter and message fit those of the images on the other cup. It is generally thought that the main character in those is Augustus. In the first image, the princeps is shown seated on the *sella curulis* in the company of lictors and soldiers, accepting homage from barbarians, who humble themselves before him (Figure 4.3). In the other, he is likewise seated on the curule chair, while the goddess

Figure 4.1 Aureus (AD 13–14)—Lugdunum. Obverse legend: CAESAR AUGUSTUS DIVI F PATER PATRIAE; head of Augustus. Reverse legend: TI CAESAR AUG F TR POT XV; Tiberius in a triumphal quadriga.

Source: *RIC*, I[2], *Aug*. 221.

Figure 4.2 A silver skyphos, Boscoreale. A depiction of Tiberius's triumph.

Source: S. Reinach, *Repertoire des reliefs Grecs et Romains*, Paris 1909.

Venus sets on the globe he holds up a statuette of Victoria, presenting him with symbolic permanent victory. To one side, there can be seen the Genius of the Roman People, holding the horn of plenty, and the goddess Roma, her foot on the enemy's weaponry; on the other, Mars leads towards Augustus personifications of the conquered provinces.[48] The ideological message of

Figure 4.3 A silver skyphos, Boscoreale. An image of Augustus receiving barbarians' tribute.

Source: S. Reinach, *Repertoire des reliefs Grecs et Romains*, Paris 1909.

those images was extremely clear: Augustus was depicted as the unquestioned ruler of the world, whose reign, thanks to the support of the most important Roman deities, ensured universal security and the might of the state. Meanwhile, Tiberius was shown as his right-hand, most important commander, who confirmed through his successive victories that he would make a worthy successor.

Zanker thought the image cycle on the *skyphoi* may have reflected the images on the unpreserved victory monument erected on the senate's initiative in order to celebrate and commemorate Tiberius's second triumph.[49] Ann L. Kuttner was of a similar opinion, thinking that the iconography on the *skyphoi* had been modelled on or inspired by reliefs decorating a public monument raised to celebrate Tiberius's triumph. In her opinion, the monument was probably the plinth of an honorific column with a statue of Augustus on top, most likely placed in the Forum of Caesar. Unlike Zanker, however, she believed the occasion was Tiberius's first triumph.[50] However, any such discussion is purely speculative. First, we do not know when the cups were made[51] and so cannot tell the period of their iconographic model either; second, we have no information on the type of monument involved; and, third, it is not really known whether any such monument even existed, as ancient authors do not mention the senate deciding to have any structure built in Rome in reference to or in connection with a triumph of Tiberius. In fact, Cassius Dio writes that the only material commemoration of Tiberius's victories was a triumphal arch, which was, however, erected in Pannonia.[52]

Some scholars also read allusions to Tiberius's second triumph into the scenes pictured on the *gemma Augustea* (Figure 4.4). It is generally supposed the *gemma* was made after AD 10.[53] The top strip depicts Augustus seated in

Figure 4.4 The *gemma Augustea* (c. AD 10). Tiberius's triumph(?).

Source: © akg-images/Erich Lessing.

the company of the goddess Roma, holding in his right hand a *lituus*, which, Zanker believed, in that context stood for the highest military command.[54] Immediately behind the emperor, there can be seen personifications of the pacified and prospering provinces, and, in front of him, one can see Tiberius getting off a triumphal quadriga. A young soldier stands before it, most often identified as Germanicus. The *lituus* the princeps holds indicates that Tiberius's victories were won under Augustus's auspices. The bottom part of the gemstone shows Roman legionaries setting up a *tropaeum* with bound captives sitting under it. Off to the right, personified provinces lead more barbarians towards the *tropaeum*.[55] Of course, the theory that the image on the cameo does refer to Tiberius's victories on the Pannonian–Dalmatian front and the triumph held as a reward for those cannot be simply rejected; however, considering Roman art was essentially not documentary in nature, I am inclined to treat the images on the *gemma Augustea* in symbolic terms, not as an allusion to specific events during Augustus's reign. In my opinion, the scenes chiefly highlighted the exceptional role played by the *domus*

Augusta in ensuring Rome's unending military success, which in turn guaranteed the stability and might of the Empire.

Another member of the reigning dynasty to triumph was Germanicus. As Tacitus notes, he received the honour in AD 15, when the war in Germania was still continuing.[56] Present-day researchers disagree on which of Germanicus's campaigns was the direct reason for the decree granting him a triumph. In Syme's opinion, the decision was taken at the beginning of 15—that is, shortly after the victorious expedition against the Marsi, resulting directly from Germanicus's first imperatorial acclamation, which the scholar dates to AD 13.[57] D. Timpe approached the issue differently, seeing the triumphal decree in connection with the summer campaign of 15, which would mean Germanicus's triumph was decided on at the same time as his legates' *ornamenta triumphalia*—that is, in autumn of 15, once the campaign was over.[58] However, his view needs to be verified; the relevant passage in Tacitus clearly indicates the triumphal decree was adopted early in AD 15, before Germanicus began the offensive operations in Germania planned for the year. Thus, I share Syme's opinion cited above that the senate awarded Germanicus his triumph after the successful campaign against the Marsi.

From a note preserved in the *Fasti Amiternini* and Tacitus's account, we know Germanicus's triumph took place exactly on 26 May 17.[59] Among the tribes whose defeat was celebrated, the historian lists the Chatti, Cherusci, and Angrivarii,[60] which leads to the assumption that, although the triumph was granted in AD 15, the victories it commemorated included those of the following year's campaign, and so was a reward for the entirety of Germanicus's achievements in the years 14–16. We also read in Tacitus that the triumph included all the most important elements typically featured in triumphal processions. Spoils were paraded, as were paintings of the places where the battles had been fought in Germania, as well as of the battles themselves. Germanicus's children participated;[61] in addition, Strabo tells us the procession showed off well-known Germanic chiefs and their family members.[62] No doubt the ceremony was a marvellous occasion to publicly showcase one of the major candidates for succession, who had, after 4 years, returned to Rome in the glory of the conqueror of the Germans and the avenger of Varus's defeat, having recovered the legions' eagles lost by that commander.[63] As B. Severy aptly observed, Germanicus showed himself "as the perfect imperial heir endowed with both military and familial authority."[64] It is worth noting that Germanicus was, after Tiberius, the second member of the *domus Augusta* to hold a triumph after 19 BC, when Augustus virtually reserved that honour exclusively for the emperor. Tacitus writes that, on the occasion of the triumph, the princeps ordered every plebeian to be paid 300 sesterces in Germanicus's name,[65] which was certainly intended to win his potential successor the affection and support of the people of Rome.

Germanicus's triumph and his Rhine victories are commemorated in a series of *dupondii*, usually dated to the reign of Caligula, who very often referred to his father's achievements on the coins minted during his rule.

The obverse of those emissions shows Germanicus in a quadriga, wearing a military cloak (*paludamentum*) and holding a *sceptrum* in his left hand. There is an image of Victory in the triumphal chariot, and the whole is complemented by a legend reading "GERMANICUS CAESAR." On the reverse, Germanicus has a *lorica* on and holds a legion's eagle (*aquila*) in his left hand. The legend is "SIGNIS RECEPT DEVICTIS GERM SC" (Figure 4.5).[66] That is, the reverse highlights one of the most crucial achievements of that commander during the Germanic campaign—the recovery of the legions' standards lost by Roman units owing to the defeat sustained in AD 9 in the Teutoburg Forest.[67]

It is probably Germanicus's Rhine victories and the triumph granted to him that are referred to in the images on the sheath of the so-called Sword of Tiberius found in Germany; the images provide important information on how the commander was depicted. It is supposed the artefact was made some time after AD 16, and the interpretation dominant in scholarship identifies the figures shown in one of the scenes as Tiberius and Germanicus.[68] The princeps is shown after the manner of Jupiter enthroned: one hand rests on a shield with a sign saying, "FELICITAS TIBERII." In front of him stands Germanicus, presenting him with a *victoriola* (a figurine of Victory), thus dedicating his victories to the emperor. In the background can be seen Mars Ultor and Victoria, who holds a shield. On this one, the sign reads, "VICTORIA AUGUSTI." Thus, Germanicus is shown as Tiberius's most important commander, who, with his military successes, proved himself a worthy candidate to take over as emperor one day. The deities present in

Figure 4.5 Dupondius (Caligula's time)—Rome. Obverse legend: GERMANICUS CAESAR; a depiction of Germanicus in the triumphal quadriga. Reverse legend: SIGNIS RECEPT DEVICTIS GERM SC; Germanicus in armour with an eagle (*aquila*) in his left hand.

Source: *RIC* I^2, *Cal.* 57.

the scene are, in a way, patrons of victories won by the *domus Augusta*, and their support means that the reigns of Tiberius and his future successors will continue the period of power and stability of the Empire initiated by Augustus's principate.[69]

Members of the *domus Augusta* could also receive a less prestigious reward and a substitute of a kind for a triumph—that is, an ovation. The first to be granted the honour was Tiberius,[70] whose ovation was held in 9 BC in recognition of his victorious campaign against Pannonian and Dalmatian tribes.[71] Cassius Dio reports that Tiberius celebrated the occasion by holding banquets for the people at various locations in Rome, while Livia and Julia arranged similar feasts for women.[72] Some researchers believe that Tiberius, like Drusus the Elder (on which issue see below), received the reward not for military success already won, but, rather in advance, so to speak, for his expected victories on the Pannonian front,[73] a view I find completely erroneous. First, Cassius Dio clearly writes that Augustus's stepsons were both granted the ovations for their *earlier* achievements in Pannonia and Germania,[74] and, second, the whole practice of rewarding members of the *domus Augusta* with such honours demonstrates they were granted for military and diplomatic missions once they had been accomplished.

In AD 19, the senate granted Drusus the Younger an ovation for his successes in Illyricum, although Tacitus tells us Drusus did not celebrate it immediately after his return to Rome from Illyricum, deferring it instead to a later date,[75] as Rome was in mourning following Germanicus's death. From epigraphical sources, we know that Drusus's ovation took place in the end on 28 May 20.[76]

Cases are also known where the senate did grant a member of the imperial family a triumph or ovation, but it was not held. Diverse reasons could have been involved. In 19 BC, Agrippa received the right to hold a triumph for suppressing the uprising of the Spanish Cantabri[77] and then, in 14, for stabilizing the situation in the Rome-dependent Bosporan Kingdom. Cassius Dio mentions that solemn sacrifices were made in Rome to celebrate that success of Agrippa's,[78] but, in each case, Augustus's son-in-law refused the high-prestige honour. It would be difficult to determine for certain what his reasons were. Cassius Dio sees his behaviour as an expression of *moderatio*,[79] but I do not think that is explanation enough, as Dio's opinion is in contrast to Agrippa's actions both earlier and later, all of which demonstrate he was quite eager to accept various prestigious honours granted to him. C. J. Simpson pointed out two possible causes for Agrippa's rejecting the triumph in 19. One of them was supposedly his offended pride: Agrippa felt unappreciated by the senate, which had granted him the honour, not freely, but only, as Dio says, on Augustus's explicit orders. The other cause would have been the desire to create precedent, so to speak, by which only the princeps could hold a triumph.[80] However, I find Simpson's first explanation unconvincing; Agrippa could not possibly have expected the senators to grant him a triumph themselves, when he had sent his report on the

Spanish campaign directly to Augustus and not to the senate.[81] The second potential reason put forward by that researcher appears more likely to me: it is no accident that Agrippa's refusal came at the same time that L. Cornelius Balbus held his triumph. As I have mentioned above, Balbus was the last triumphator from outside the narrow circle of the *domus Augusta*. A simpler solution was proposed by J. Rich, who believed that Agrippa refused the triumph granted to him under the influence of Augustus's actions, as the princeps rejected, first, the triumph granted him for his victorious campaign in Spain (in 26–25 BC) and then the ovation awarded him in 19 after the legions' eagles had been recovered from the Parthians.[82] As Rich rightly emphasized, in that situation, by holding his own triumph, Agrippa would have committed a severe faux pas.[83]

In 12 BC, the senate, for the first time, granted Tiberius a triumph for his successes in Pannonia, but, in this case, Augustus forbade its celebration, only agreeing to his stepson receiving *ornamenta triumphalia*.[84] His reasons were that Tiberius had conducted the campaigns in Pannonia as *legatus Augusti* and so had not held independent *imperium*.[85]

The following year, Drusus the Elder was granted an ovation for his successes in Germania;[86] it bears pointing out he received that honour even though, in 11 BC, he had led campaigns in the rank of *legatus Augusti*, and so without independent *imperium*.[87] In Cassius Dio, we read that all due preparations had been made in Rome, and the ceremony was to be held as soon as Drusus was back from Germania. It would have taken place during the *Feriae Latinae*, making it special;[88] before his ovational entry into Rome, Drusus was first to hold a triumph on the Mons Albanus, which would have culminated in a procession to the temple of Jupiter Latiaris there.[89] None of those festivities ever took place owing to Drusus's unexpected death.[90]

The situation was the same in the case of Germanicus, who was awarded an ovation for his diplomatic success in Armenia in AD 19. As he then died in the East, the ovation was cancelled.[91]

4.3 Triumphal and honorific arches

Triumphal and honorific arches erected in the honour of the several members of the *domus Augusta* were a physical form of commemoration of their military and diplomatic victories.[92] They were erected both in Rome and in those places in the Empire that had a connection to those people's actions. They were meant to remind the inhabitants of the provinces about the successes and power of the reigning dynasty.

To begin with, I would like to focus on those objects that were erected in connection with a triumph or ovation ceremony and commemorated specific military or diplomatic achievements of members of the *domus Augusta*. Then, I shall move on to monuments that were erected posthumously and were accompanied by a number of other posthumous honours. The first member of the imperial family other than the princeps to be granted a triumphal arch was Tiberius. The honour in question fell to him in AD 9, after he suppressed the great anti-Roman insurrection in Pannonia and Dalmatia. The senate then granted both Augustus and Tiberius the right to hold a triumph complete with two arches, which were to stand in Pannonia.[93] As they were to be built in order to celebrate and commemorate a specific victory and triumph held on its occasion, the arches can be treated as triumphal in the proper sense of the word. Unfortunately, we lack any information on statues or sculptures that might have decorated them. Nor do we know when they were set up, as the mourning in force in Rome owing to Varus's defeat caused Tiberius's triumph to be postponed,[94] and it is likely that the same happened to the construction of the arches.[95] It is worth noting that Tiberius was probably the first person in the imperial family, not counting Augustus, who was thus honoured in his lifetime and during that emperor's reign.[96]

In AD 16, another arch was consecrated next to the temple of Saturn in the Forum Romanum, dedicated to Tiberius and Germanicus.[97] Tacitus suggests the arch was mostly meant to commemorate Germanicus getting back the legions' eagles lost by Varus—one of his greatest achievements in Germania. The only piece of information found in literary sources on its location is the mention in Tacitus, which places it *propter aedem Saturni*.[98] In 1900, foundations were uncovered near the temple to Saturn that were regarded as likely remnants of the arch of Tiberius and Germanicus.[99] Based on that discovery, it was assumed the monument stood exactly between the Rostra and the Basilica Julia and was oriented towards the arch of Augustus erected in 19 BC, to the south of the Temple of Caesar, after he recovered the legions' eagles from the Parthians.[100] A slightly different spot was put forward by F. Coarelli, who believed the uncovered foundation was in fact a remnant of a fountain (the *Lacus Servilius*). In that archaeologist's opinion, the arch of Tiberius and Germanicus stood in the *vicus Iugarius*, between the temple of Saturn and the Basilica Julia; two brick pillars had been discovered there, which he thought were part of the arch.[101] Regardless of which of the proposed locations we should accept, the fact remains that the arch was situated on the route traditionally taken by triumphal processions ultimately seeking the Capitoline Hill.[102]

Based on the foundations discovered—assuming they do in fact belong to the structure in question—and a depiction of the monument preserved on a frieze on the Arch of Constantine, it can be said the arch had one passageway.[103] We have virtually no data on any statuary that may have decorated it, but, taking into account the circumstances under which it was built, we may assume the iconographic pattern could have been modelled on the Parthian arch of Augustus, images of which survive on coins. From those, we know that, on the attic above the central passage, there was a statue of the emperor in a quadriga, and, above the archways to the sides, statues of Parthians were set, facing Augustus and returning the eagles.[104] Another model could have been provided by the scene depicted on Augustus's lorica in the famous statue from Prima Porta or the images featured on coins minted after 19 BC to commemorate Augustus's recovering the legions' standards from the Parthians. With that context in mind, the decorations on the arch constructed next to the temple of Saturn could have been as follows: centrally, statues of Tiberius and Germanicus in the triumphal quadriga; to the sides, Germans in attitudes of submission, kneeling and returning the legions' eagles (*signa militaria*) looted before.[105] If that theory is accurate, then Germanicus will have been the first member of the reigning dynasty, not counting the emperor, whose image in a quadriga was placed on top of an arch. Until then, only Augustus had been depicted in that style. Statues of him in a triumphal chariot had adorned, first, the Actium monument and, then, the Parthian arch.[106]

In AD 19, the senate issued a decree on erecting two triumphal arches in honour of Germanicus and his adoptive brother, Drusus the Younger, also awarding them an ovation. The achievements thus recognized were the diplomatic successes Tiberius's sons had had in Armenia and Illyricum, respectively.[107] Tacitus writes that the arches were to be placed in the Forum of Augustus, flanking the temple to Mars Ultor.[108] Based on uncovered fragments, it can be determined the arches had one passageway each. They were situated in the northern part of the forum, near the exit towards the district of Subura.[109] Also in Tacitus, we read that statues of the emperor's sons were to be placed on top of the arches,[110] but we do not have any more detailed information on their appearance.[111] What we do know is that they were in excellent company, next to statues of the most eminent members of the *gens Iulia* and the most famous Romans (*summi viri*), which were placed in adjacent porticoes on both sides of the temple.[112] Of Drusus's arch, small fragments remain of the honorific inscription, reconstructed by G. Alföldy.[113] Thus, based on Alföldy's hypothetical reconstruction, we may suppose it listed the most important stages of Drusus's *cursus honorum* and emphasized one of his greatest achievements in politics—normalizing the situation in Illyricum.

The first member of the *domus Augusta* honoured with an arch posthumously was Drusus the Elder. The monument was one of the many honours granted him by the senate in 9 BC and was primarily intended to commemorate Drusus's successes in his campaign in Germania. From Suetonius, we know the arch was to stand in Rome, be made of marble, and be adorned with *tropaea*.[114] The choice of construction site was not an accident either, as it was to be placed by the road built three centuries earlier by the great Appius Claudius Caecus, one of the most prominent members of the *gens Claudia*, to which Drusus also belonged. The intention of the funders was to sharply highlight the dead man's *gens* ties, drawing on the glorious tradition of one of Rome's oldest aristocratic houses. It should also be remembered that the via Appia, commonly referred to as the queen of roads, was among the most important Roman communication arteries and Rome's most important connection to southern Italy. Therefore Drusus's arch was to be built in a prestigious and busy spot.[115] Along the same road stood sepulchral monuments of Roman aristocracy, including the famous tomb of the Scipios, which was also meaningful, considering that the arch was posthumous. The precise location of the monument remains unknown, because Suetonius does not specify the place along the via Appia. According to some historians, the arch stood near the temple of Mars, between the first and second milestone, outside porta Appia, a view based solely on a late mention preserved in the *Mirabilia Urbis Romae (de arcubus)* of an *arcus triumphalis foris portam Appiam ad templum Martis.*[116] However, in actuality, the passage probably refers to the arcade of Aqua Antoniniana, the remains of which can be found to this day in front of the porta Appia, looking from Rome, as the object was long misidentified as the *arcus Drusi*. Another argument against the site having been next to that temple to Mars is that the temple was too distant from the city. Considering that, later, other arches were erected along the Appian road, it seems Drusus's monument, which started the tradition, was placed closer to the city—most likely somewhere near porta Capena, where the via Appia began.[117]

Information about the statuary decorating the arch and its architectural form is primarily provided by coins. Images of the arch of Drusus have been preserved on, among other coins, *aurei* and *denarii* minted by Emperor Claudius between AD 41 and 45.[118] They reveal a single-passageway arch with a statue on top of Drusus on horseback between two *tropaea* (Figure 4.6). Interestingly, Augustus's stepson is shown in a dynamic pose—his

Figure 4.6 Denarius (c. AD 41–45)—Rome. Obverse legend: NERO CLAUDIUS DRUSUS GERMANICUS IMP; head of Drusus. Reverse legend: DE GERMANIS; a triumphal arch surmounted by an equestrian statue between two trophies.

Source: *RIC* I^2, *Claud.* 72.

horse galloping, his spear raised and ready to strike. In other words, he was depicted in combat, as a conqueror of the dangerous Germanic tribes, confirming his *virtus* in service to the state.[119] Thus, the funders' intention was to showcase the special role played by the imperial family, emphasizing that it was to the actions of its members that Rome owed all the most important victories outside its borders. There was also a dedicatory inscription on the arch, listing Drusus's most important achievements.[120]

The senate's decision to posthumously commemorate Drusus with an arch started a new tradition of honouring subsequent members of the imperial family in that way. In AD 4, the authorities of the Italian colony of Pisa ruled that an honorific arch would be constructed in honour of Gaius Caesar, who had recently died in the East. The decree was inspired by an earlier *senatus consultum* on posthumously honouring Augustus's son. We find detailed information on the appearance and location of that monument in an inscription from Pisa, which contains the text of the honorific decree of the local authorities, issued after Gaius's premature death:

> 34 *Utique [arc]us celeberrimo coloniae nostrae loco constituatur orna-*
> 35 *tu[s sp]oleis devictarum aut in fidem receptarum ab eo gentium, super*
> 36 *eu[m st]atua pedestris ipsius triumphali ornatu circaque eam duae*
> 37 *e[questr]es inauratae Gai et Luci Caesarum statuae ponantur.*
>
> (*CIL* XI 1421, ll. 34–37)

> and that an arch should be placed in the most frequented place in our colony, decorated with the spoils of nations conquered or received in alliance by him, and on the arch should be placed a statue of him on foot in triumphal dress and two gilded equestrian statues of Gaius and Lucius Caesar should be placed on either side.[121]

The structure was to be erected in the most visited and most prestigious part of the town, which allows for the assumption that it was built in the local forum, where it then acted as a gate to that venue.[122] It was to be decorated with the standards and weapons (*spolia*) of peoples who had been conquered or had agreed to acknowledge Rome's power over them as a result of Gaius's eastern expedition. On top was placed a statue of the deceased commander wearing the robe of triumph (*toga picta*), flanked by gilded mounted statues of Gaius and his brother Lucius, who had died 2 years earlier.[123] It ought to be stressed here that placing two sculptures of the same person on an arch was a rare exception, and this is, in fact, the first documented instance of the practice.[124] C. B. Rose suspects that the central statue of Gaius was placed in a quadriga to make its height proportional to that of the equestrian statues at its sides,[125] but I have to disagree, as the Pisan inscription quite clearly mentions a *statua pedestris*.[126] W. Lebek pointed out that the message conveyed by the ornamental statuary on the arch carried some extra, even some double extra, meaning; in his opinion, the gilded mounted statues were a clear reference to the dead brothers having received from the equites the honorary title of *princeps iuventutis*. Beginning in Augustus's time, it became the unofficial title of prospective successors of emperors.[127] Gaius received it in 5 BC; Lucius, 3 years later.[128] Bearing that context in mind, the founders of the monument chiefly wanted to posthumously commemorate the brothers as deceased successors to the purple—hardly a trivial matter for the Pisans, as we know both young men had special ties to the colony (Lucius was even its patron), and its inhabitants had great expectations for when one of them succeeded Augustus.[129] Moreover, the two mounted statues of Augustus's sons evoked obvious associations with the divine brothers Dioscuri.[130] Meanwhile, depicting Gaius in a triumphator's garb and decorating the arch with trophies won in the East were actions intended as commemorative of his military achievements during the Parthian expedition.[131] The *spolia* of the defeated barbarians, which included primarily armour, weapons, and standards, were probably depicted on the relief decorating the monument.[132] That the inhabitants of the colony decided on an arch for Gaius and a number of other high-prestige, posthumous honours for both prematurely dead brothers was not only an expression of loyalty to the *domus Augusta*, but also emphasized the special character of the relationship the Italian town had with the reigning dynasty.

Germanicus's death during his mission in the East in AD 19 gave the senate another opportunity to honour the emperor's family in the person of a deceased member, who had been generally regarded as the major candidate for succeeding Tiberius. Among the posthumous honours awarded him were honorific arches (*iani*), to be erected in Rome, but also in Syria and on the Rhine—that is, parts of the Empire with a particular connection to his actions.[133] Invaluable information on their location and appearance can be found in the *Tabula Siarensis*, significantly supplementing Tacitus's account, which is reticent on the matter.

The arch in Rome

9 *Placere uti ianus marmoreus extrueretur in circo Flaminio pe[cunia publica, posi-]*

10 *tus ad eum locum, in quo statuae divo Augusto domuique Augus[tae publicae positae es-]*

11 *sent ab G(aio) Norbano Flacco, cum signis devictarum gentium in a[ngulis tituloque]*

12 *in fronte eius iani, senatum populumque Romanum id monum[entum aeternae dedi-]*

13 *casse memoriae Germanici Caesaris, cum i{i}s Germanis bello superatis et [deinceps]*

14 *a Gallia summotis receptisque signis militaribus et vindicata fraud [ulenta clade]*

15 *exercitus p(opuli) R(omani), ordinato statu Galliarum, proco(n)s(ul) missus in transmarinas pro[vincias]*
16 *in conformandis iis regnisque eiusdem tractus ex mandatis Ti(berii) Caesaris Au[g(usti), dato re-]*
17 *ge Armeniae, non parcens labori suo, priusquam decreto senatus [ovans urbem ingre-]*
18 *deretur, ob rem p(ublicam) mortem obisset; supraque eum ianum statua Ger[manici Caesaris po-]*
19 *neretur in curru triumphali et circa latera eius statuae D[rusi Germanici patris ei-]*
20 *us, naturalis fratris Ti(berii) Caesaris Aug(usti) et Antoniae matris ei[us et Agrippinae uxoris et Li-]*
21 *viae sororis et Ti(berii) Germanici fratris eius et filiorum et f[iliarum eius.]*

(*Tabula Siarensis*, fr. 1, ll. 9–21; ed. Sánchez, Gutiérrez 1999: 52, 54)

It was pleasing that a marble arch should be built at public expense in the circus Flaminius, set at that place where the statues for the divine Augustus and the statues for the *domus Augusta* had been set up at public expense by Gaius Norbanus Flaccus, decorated with representation of conquered peoples in the corners and with an inscription on the front of the arch stating that the senate and people of Rome had dedicated this monument to the eternal memory of Germanicus Caesar because, after he had conquered the Germans in war and driven them out from Gaul and recovered the lost military standards and avenged the dishonest defeat of an army of the Roman people and arranged the affairs of the Gauls, and after he had then been sent as proconsul to the overseas provinces to also arrange them and the kingdoms of that same area according to the orders of Tiberius Caesar Augustus, and after he installed a new king of Armenia, not sparing in his own labor and before he could return to the city victorious by decree of the senate, he died on behalf of the state; and (they directed) that on top of this arch should be placed a statue of Germanicus Caesar in a triumphal chariot and that at his sides should be placed statues of his natural father Drusus Germanicus, brother of Tiberius Caesar Augustus, and of his mother Antonia and his wife Agrippina and his sister Livia and his brother Tiberius Germanicus and his sons and daughters.[134]

One *ianus* dedicated to Germanicus was to be built *in circo Flaminio*,[135] not an accidental location. The Circus Flaminius was situated at the start of the route taken by triumphal processions, and triumphators exhibited their war trophies there.[136] That area of Rome also contained various buildings closely connected to the imperial family, such as the Portico of Octavia and the statuary group that Gaius Norbanus Flaccus dedicated to Augustus and the *domus Augusta*, mentioned in the *Tabula Siarensis*.[137] Another structure close to the Circus was the Theatre of Marcellus, also built in honour of a member of the reigning dynasty.

We know from the *TS* that an elaborate statue group was to be put on the attic. At the centre of the composition, there was a statue of Germanicus in a triumphal quadriga, surrounded by those of his parents—Drusus the Elder and Antonia the Younger—his wife Agrippina, sister Julia Livia (or Livilla), brother Tiberius Germanicus (the later Emperor Claudius), and his sons and daughters (Figure 4.7).[138] Despite certain allusions to Germanicus's triumph of AD 17—depicting the dead man in a quadriga and decorating the *ianus* with the standards of defeated peoples—the statues referred to that event only indirectly. Their other purpose was to fix in the public imagination the image of an exceptional family, its members worthy of imitation by other Romans.[139] Germanicus was represented as a model father of a family. With his many children, whose images made it on to the arch too, he had more than carried out the recommendations of Augustus's marriage legislation. It was no accident that, during public spectacles or games, the emperor showcased Germanicus surrounded by his children; the point was to encourage other citizens to follow his example.[140] Women had a no less important role to play in Germanicus's family—thus statues of Antonia, Agrippina, and

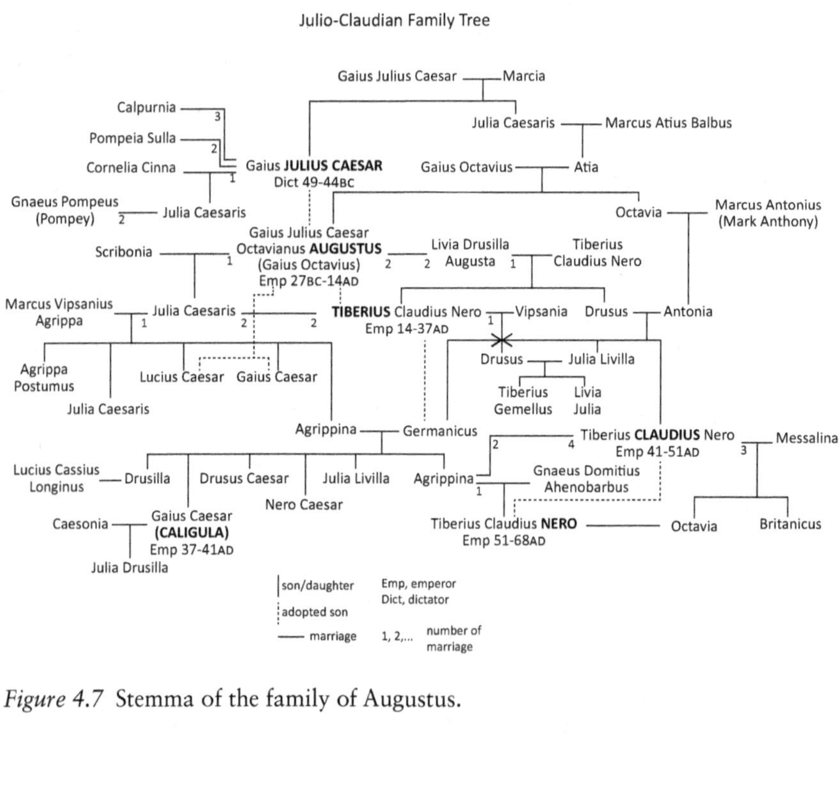

Figure 4.7 Stemma of the family of Augustus.

Livilla were placed on the arch too. As the mothers and wives of potential successors to the purple, they guaranteed the stability of the dynasty and smooth succession within the reigning family. B. Severy stresses that the presence of images of women and children on Germanicus's arch was a significant innovation when compared with the Republican tradition; she assumes that only male members of the *gens* of the person to whom an arch was dedicated were depicted on the fornices built under the Republic, and only if they had had specific achievements in the public arena.[141] Although that is the first documented arch with women and children on it, we do not have enough knowledge on the statuary decorating Republican fornices to arbitrarily claim they had only been decorated with images of men. At first glance, it may seem puzzling that there were no statues on the arch of either Tiberius or Drusus the Younger, but their absence was deliberate, as the funders intended to show the dead man surrounded exclusively by his immediate family and so had his adoptive father and adoptive brother omitted. It is also interesting that the arch featured statues of both dead and living relatives of Germanicus, spanning three generations of his family.

The standards or emblems (*signa*) of the peoples defeated as a result of Germanicus's campaigns were another important element of the ornamentation of the *ianus*. As Rose supposes, they may have included not merely standards, but also images of the vanquished barbarians, probably in relief.[142] There was also an inscription detailing Germanicus's achievements in Gaul, Germania, and the East,[143] which, therefore, commemorated all his successes abroad.

The question whether Germanicus's arch in *Circo Flaminio* had one or three archways remains unanswered. Lebek favoured the former option, arguing that the term *ianus* which the *Tabula Siarensis* uses to refer to the monument, was only used to mean single-archway structures, whereas the term *arcus* could, in his opinion, indicate both single-passageway and triple-passageway arches.[144] That theory is purely speculative, however, as there is no way to be certain the arches referred to as *iani* all had only one archway. With the sources being so terse, it would be hard to unambiguously determine the distinction between objects called *ianus* and *arcus*, especially as the context in which those terms come up in sources shows they could be used interchangeably, to refer to the same monuments. The arch of Augustus built in Ossigi in Spain may serve as a good example; in Augustan-era inscriptions, it was referred to as *ianus*, whereas, in inscriptions from Domitian's time, the term *arcus* is used.[145] With Germanicus's arches, the situation is similar: they are called *iani* in the text of the *TS*, but *arcus* by Tacitus.[146] In any case, F. Kleiner was of a different opinion to Lebek: he believed such an elaborate statuary group could only have fitted on a triple-archway object. Kleiner based his view on an analysis of diverse coin emissions bearing images of arches and demonstrating that such multi-statue groups were put on monuments with three archways.[147] I do not think Kleiner's interpretation of the matter solves the problem either, as it is the size of a structure that was crucial rather than the number of passageways, and so the arch of Germanicus in Rome may have had one of those or three.

The arch in the East

22 *Alter ianus fieret in montis Amani iugo, quod est in [finibus provinciae Syriae, sive qui]*
23 *alius aptior locus Ti(berio) Caesari Aug(usto) principi nostro [videretur in iis regionibus quarum*
24 *curam et tutelam Germanico Caesari ex auctori[tate huius ordinis ipse mandasset;]*
25 *item statua eius poneretur et titulus conve[niens rebus ab eo gestis fronti eius iani in-]*
26 *sculperetur.*

(*Tabula Siarensis*, fr. 1, ll. 22–26; ed. Sánchez-Gutiérrez 1999: 54)

and that a second arch should be built on the ridge of Mount Amanus in Syria or in some other place, if any other location within the areas that he had assigned to the care and protection of Germanicus Caesar in accordance with the will of the senate should seem more appropriate to Tiberius Caesar Augustus our *princeps*; and likewise that a statue of him should be set up there and an inscription assembling the deeds of Germanicus Caesar should be inscribed on the front of the arch.[148]

The second of the three arches dedicated to Germanicus was to be constructed in the mountain range of Amanus on the Cilician–Syrian border—or in some other place in the East that had a connection to the actions of Tiberius's adopted son; the senate left the choice of the location up to the emperor.[149] According to Lebek, the arch was most likely built in the pass or gorge on the main route from Cilicia to Syria—that is, in a busy spot.[150] The sources say nothing detailed on the decoration of that *ianus*; all we know is that a statue of Germanicus was to be placed on top.[151] Lebek suspected the depiction was similar to that on the Roman arch, in a triumphal chariot.[152] The monument also featured an inscription commemorating Germanicus's greatest achievements.[153] Considering where the arch was set up (in the eastern part of the Empire), the text was most likely in Greek.[154]

The arch on the Rhine

26 *Tertius ianus vel ap[ud ripam Rheni vel prope eum tumulum fieret]*
27 *quem Druso, fratri Ti(beri) Caesaris Aug(usti), pr[rimo sua sponte excitare coepisset totus exerci-]*
28 *tus, deinde permissu divi Aug(usti) perf[ecisset, supraque eum ianum statua Germanici Cae-]*

29 *saris constitueretur recipientis[signa militaria a Germanis; et praeciperetur Gal-]*
30 *lis Germanisque qui citra Rhen[um incolerent, quorum civitates iussae essent a divo]*
31 *Aug(usto) rem divinam ad tumulu[m Drusi facere ut eodem loco facerent publice alterum simi-]*
32 *le sacrificium parentant[es quotannis eo die quo Germanicus Caesar decessisset]*
33 *et cum esset in ea region[e, ubi is tumulus est, exercitus et hiberna ageret nata-]*
34 *li Germanici Caesar[is, is eo die decurreret per eum ianum qui ex hoc s(enatus) c(onsulto) factus esset.]*

(*Tabula Siarensis*, fr. 1, ll. 26–34; ed. Sánchez-Gutiérrez 1999: 54, 56, 58)

and that a third arch should be either placed on the bank of the Rhine or next to the burial mound which the whole army had first begun of its own accord to build for Drusus the brother of Tiberius Caesar Augustus and then had completed with the permission of the Divine Augustus; and that on this arch should be set a statue of Germanicus Caesar receiving back the military standards from the Germans; and that the Gauls and Germans who live on this side of the Rhine, whose communities had been ordered by the divine Augustus to conduct cult at the burial mound of Drusus, should be ordered to make a second similar public sacrifice, giving funeral offerings annually on that day on which Germanicus Caesar had died; and that when the army should be in the area of the burial mound of Drusus and be in winter quarters on the birthday of Germanicus Caesar, it should parade through the arch constructed in accordance with this decree of the senate.[155]

Tacitus reports that the third of Germanicus's *iani* was to be erected on the Rhine,[156] although he does not specify where exactly. Unfortunately, the text of the *Tabula Siarensis* is badly damaged in the portions to do with its location and the celebrations to be held nearby, so that we only have hypotheses to rely on. In the light of the reconstruction of that part of the text proposed by Lebek, which is generally accepted in scholarship, the arch must have been located in what is today Mainz, near Drusus's cenotaph (the *tumulus Drusi*).[157] As P. Herz supposes, it could have been the entrance to the holy precinct centred on that symbolic tomb.[158]

On the arch, a statue of Germanicus was placed, shown as he retrieved legions' eagles from the Germans.[159] The depiction was most likely modelled on the statue pattern found in the arch of Tiberius and Germanicus mentioned above, consecrated a few years earlier next to the temple to Saturn in the Forum Romanum: it was primarily meant to glorify the dead commander and fix in the memory of posterity the belief that, thanks to his achievements, the disgrace of Varus defeat was effaced, and Rome's prestige in Germania was restored. Thus, the monument celebrated one of Germanicus's most important deeds in Germania, especially as seen from the perspective of the soldiers: loss of eagles was seen as shameful, and so recovering them was of huge psychological importance to the troops. Taking that aspect of the matter into account, it seems likely that the arch showcasing Rome's great victory and humiliation of the barbarians stood somewhere along the road that led from the legion camp (Mainz-Kästrich) to Drusus's cenotaph—in a busy spot, that is, passed often, in particular by the legionaries stationed there. Such a location would have been of great importance to reinforce in the Rhine army loyalty towards the imperial family and to improve the soldiers' morale. Erecting the *ianus* near the *tumulus Drusi*, next to which representatives of Gallic and Germanic tribes gathered each year to sacrifice in Drusus's and Germanicus's honour, also helped fix in the minds of the local population the conviction that Rome's power and rule were all-encompassing.[160]

Even though the *Tabula Siarensis* contains no information about an honorific inscription on the German *ianus*, we may regard it as certain that one was in fact put up. That is confirmed by Tacitus, who mentions that all the arches decided on by the senate after Germanicus's death bore texts informing about his achievements,[161] and, in any case, a commemorative monument could hardly have been built without a fitting inscription.

In 1986, the foundations of a triple-passageway arch were uncovered in Mainz (in Mainz-Kastel). Not far away, fragments of architectural decoration were found, which had probably once been part of the object.[162] On the stone slabs that formed the foundations, there were stamps of the 14th legion, stationed in the area twice: first between 13 BC and AD 43, and second, after a short break, in AD 70–92.[163] The discovery led to some heated discussion in scholarship, as voices spoke in favour of identifying the Mainz-Kastel arch as the *ianus* of Germanicus described by the *Tabula Siarensis*. In the opinion of H. Frenz, one argument for that interpretation is the styling of the preserved architectural details of the structure, which he thought characteristic of the Julio-Claudian period. Therefore, he believed the foundations discovered in Mainz-Kastel to be the remains of the arch of Germanicus.[164] H. Bellen disagreed, believing the Romans could not have, at the time, decided to build an arch on the right bank of the Rhine, as, in Tiberius's time, the area was only under Roman control to a small extent and so was vulnerable to frequent attacks from the Germans. In his view, that location would also have been a major obstacle to the yearly military parade in Germanicus's honour, which supposedly passed under the *ianus*, as the army would have had to cross the river. Instead, Bellen believed the *ianus* must have stood in the immediate vicinity of Drusus's cenotaph, on the left bank.[165] Not all of his arguments are convincing; also in 1986, a wooden bridge pier was lifted from the bottom of the Rhine. As it was dated to Tiberius's reign, Mainz may well have already had a permanent crossing then, which, in turn, indicates that both banks of the Rhine at this point in its course were under Roman control at the time.[166] A permanent bridge would have also made the *decursio* easy, even if troops had to be moved to the right bank. In my opinion, the crucial argument in the discussion about where the Rhine *ianus* was situated is its location relative to Drusus's cenotaph. If we accept the *communis opinio* essentially prevalent in research that the so-called *Drusus-stein* in left-bank Mainz is a remnant of Drusus's symbolic tomb, then the arch in Germanicus's honour is quite likely to have been erected near the monument to his father. That location would also have been justified if we consider the religious celebrations held near both those objects, mentioned in both the *Tabula Siarensis* and Suetonius.[167] To sum up that particular discussion, I believe attempts to identify the Mainz-Kastel arch with the *ianus* of Germanicus are mistaken; instead, the monument was probably built only under Domitian, in connection with his victorious campaign against the Chatti.[168]

The death of Drusus the Younger in AD 23 was another opportunity for the senate to emphasize their respect for and loyalty to the ruling dynasty by appropriately honouring the dead man. In Tacitus, we read that honours were decreed for him similar to those that had been conferred on Germanicus, with extra ones added.[169] Based on that, we may assume there were honorific arches among those posthumous honours, an assumption potentially confirmed by the inscription containing the text of the senate's decree issued after Tiberius's son died, fragments of which have been found in Rome.[170] Regrettably, the part of the inscription that most likely held information on arches to be constructed in Drusus's honour only survives in fragments, so that, again, all we can do is speculate. An attempt to reconstruct the missing parts of the inscription was undertaken by W. Lebek:

> *[Tertius (?) ianus fieret apud (eam) aram, quae - - -, cum titulo in fronte eius iani senatum populumque Romanum id monumentum posuisse et dedicasse memoriae Drusi Caesaris, cum is imposito rege Suebis et]*
>
> 1 *[ordinato statu Illyrici ex mandatis Ti(beri) Caesaris Augusti pa]tris sui*
> 2 *[- - - mortem obisset, supraque eum ianum statua Dru]si Caesaris in cur-*
> 3 *[ru triumphali poneretur - - - et statua Ti(beri)] Caesaris Augusti*
> 4 *[patris eius - - -, et praeciperetur Illyriis, ut ad eam aram q(uae) s(upra) s(cripta) e(st) publice facerent re]m divinam paren-*
> 5 *[tantes quotannis eo die, quo Drusus Caesar decessisset.]*
>
> (*CIL* VI 31200 B col. I 1–5; ed. Lebek 1989b: 87)

that a third arch should be built at that altar which ... with an inscription on the front of the arch stating that the senate and Roman people had erected this monument and dedicated it to the memory of Drusus

> Caesar, since he, with a king having been imposed on the Suebi and with the organization of Illyricum having been arranged according to the instructions of his father Tiberius Caesar Augustus, ... had died, and that on top of this arch a statue of Drusus Caesar in a triumphal chariot should be placed ... and a statue of Tiberius Caesar Augustus, his father ... and that orders should be given to the people of Illyricum that they make public funeral sacrifices at the altar described above annually on the day that Drusus Caesar had died.[171]

Assuming, then, that the honours granted Drusus were similar to those decided on earlier for Germanicus, then one of Drusus's arches should have been erected in Rome. According to Lebek, on top, there was a statue of Drusus in a triumphal quadriga, and, on the attic, there was an inscription detailing the achievements of the deceased.[172] Perhaps, as had been the case with the arch of Germanicus *in circo Flaminio*, statues of Drusus's closest family were placed next to his.

Another arch might have been built somewhere in Illyricum—that is, in the region where Drusus had carried out his mission. According to Lebek's reconstruction, there was a statue of him on top in a quadriga with a statue of Tiberius next to it, with a commemorative inscription.[173] Showing Tiberius's son styled as a triumphator would have been interesting in that he had never held a triumph. One must agree with Lebek that the image may have simply been modelled on that of Germanicus, whose statues in quadrigas had adorned the arch in the Circus Flaminius and the *ianus* in Syria; the emperor's son—who, with Germanicus dead, was the first candidate for succession—could hardly have been honoured in a less prestigious manner than his adoptive brother had been a few years earlier.[174]

Notes

1 *Contra* Schumacher (1985: 218), who believed the proconsuls of public provinces had *imperium cum auspiciis*, a claim unconfirmed by the sources, which quite clearly demonstrate proconsuls, like imperial legates, conducted campaigns under the emperor's auspices. Vell. Pat. 2, 129, 4; Ehrenberg, Jones 1955: 63 (no. 43): *Marti Augusto sacrum / auspiciis Imp(eratoris) Caesaris Aug(usti), / pontificis maxumi, patris / patriae, ductu Cossi Lentuli / co(n)s(ulis), XVviri sacris faciundis, / proco(n)sulis, provincia Africa / bello Gaetulico liberata, / civitas Lepcitana.* See also Syme 1978: 62.

2 The last triumphator from outside the imperial family was L. Cornelius Balbus, who held a triumph for his victories in 19 BC in Africa. See Schumacher 1985: 212. In addition, only two cases are known of the title of *imperator* being accorded to commanders who were not members of the *domus Augusta* in Augustus's and Tiberius's times—to L. Passienus Rufus and Iunius Blaesus, who owed their acclamations to successful campaigns in Africa. *CIL* VIII 16456: *Iunoni Liviae Augusti sacrum / L(ucio) Passieno Rufo imperatore / Africam obtinente / Cn(aeus) Cornelius Cn(aei) f(ilius) Cor(nelia) Rufus / et Maria C(ai) f(ilia) Galla Cn(aei) / conservati vota l(ibentes) m(erito) solvont.* Vell. Pat. 2, 125, 5; Tac. *Ann.* 3, 74, 4. See also Syme 1978: 62; Schumacher 1985: 215: 218–219; Woodman, Martin 1996: 489; Havener 2016: 354–355.

3 As mentioned in inscriptions from Corcyra, Gnathia, and Ephesus. See *CIG* II 1878; *CIL* IX 262; *IK* 17.1, 3006.

4 See Daniel 1933: 68; Hanslik 1961: 1256. *Contra* Kienast, Eck, Heil (2017: 66), who claim Agrippa was not hailed *imperator* in his lifetime.

5 Syme 1979: 313 (note 25). So Hurlet 1997: 91–92; Kienast, Eck, Heil 2017: 62. *Contra* Rich (1999: 549), who believes Drusus was only granted one acclamation, which took place in 9 BC. A completely different perspective has been offered recently by Vervaet (2020: 157). In his opinion, after Drusus's death, the senate approved his two earlier acclamations, which Vervaet thinks took place in 12 and 11 BC, but were rejected by Augustus at the time. He believes they were among the honours the senate accorded Drusus after his unexpected death, but no sources support that hypothesis, and Dio (54, 33, 5) says Augustus only refused to approve Drusus's salutation once. The refusal occurred in 11 BC.

6 *CIL* IX 2443: *Nero Claudius Ti(berii) f(ilius) Drusus Germ[anicus] augur, c[o(n)s(u)l], imperator [II]*. For an interpretation of the inscription, see esp. Bernecker 1976: 185–192. See also Rich (1999: 550, note 29), in whose opinion the number of Drusus's acclamations listed in this inscription is an error. Rich believes it cannot be ruled out that the Saepinum inscription takes into account Drusus's acclamation of 11 BC too, even though Augustus did not confirm it. *Inscr. It.* XIII.3, 15–16 (no. 9): *[Nero] Cl[a]udiu[s]Tib(erii) f(ilius)/[Dru]sus Ge[r]man[i]cus, /[co(n)s(ul)], pr(aetor) urb(anus), q(uaestor), aug(ur), imp(erator)/[app]ella[t]us in Germania*; *CIL* V 3109: *[Nero]ni Claudio [Druso---]/[co(n)]s(uli) imp(eratori)*; *RIC* I^2, *Claud.* 70–73. For an interpretation of the inscription, see Vassileiou 1983: 213–214.

7 Syme 1979: 312–314.

8 See Barnes 1974: 22; Rich 1999: 549; Kienast, Eck, Heil 2017: 72.

9 Cass. Dio 55, 6, 5; Syme 1979: 313.

10 Cass. Dio 55, 28, 6. Dio's chronology was accepted by Barnes 1974: 23, and Schumacher 1985: 216–217. Not so Syme (1979: 316), who dated Tiberius's third acclamation to AD 5. In his opinion, it was then that Tiberius achieved his most spectacular successes, predisposing him to the title of *imperator*. D. Faoro (2016: 209, 212) allows for both possibilities, assuming Tiberius's third acclamation could have taken place either late in 5 or early in 6.

11 Cass. Dio 56, 17, 1.

12 See Barnes 1974: 24; Swan 2004: 248.

13 Faoro 2016: 209.

14 *RIC* I^2, *Aug.* 242–243.

15 *RIC* I^2, *Aug.* 471.

16 Faoro 2016: 210.

17 *RIC* I^2, *Aug.* 244–248.

18 Barnes 1974: 25–26; Syme 1978: 58; Faoro 2016: 210–212.

19 Unfortunately, Dio's account, which might have mentioned it, is cut short at the summer of AD 13, and the gap extends as far as the events surrounding Augustus's death. It is also difficult to determine which campaign of Germanicus is intended in a short epigram preserved in the *Palatine Anthology* and attributed to Crinagoras. See *Anth. Pal.* 9, 283. For any analysis of the epigram, see Barnes 1974: 25; Syme 1978: 58–59; 1979: 318.

20 Cass. Dio 55, 10a, 7. *CIL* V 6416 (an inscription on an arch at Ticinum, erected for the *domus Augusta* in the years 7–8). On the subject of that acclamation, see also Syme 1979: 315; Schumacher 1985: 216; Swan 2004: 132; Faoro (2016: 208, 212) dates Gaius's acclamation to late AD 3 or early 4.

21 Among the sources confirming that Germanicus was hailed *imperator* twice, there is an inscription set up in his honour in Rome by the *plebs urbana* (*CIL* VI 909) and an inscription on the arch at Mediolanum Santonum dedicated to Tiberius, Germanicus, and Drusus the Younger by C. Iulius Rufus, a priest of

the cult of Roma and Augustus at Lugdunum. See *CIL* XIII 1036; Rose 1997: 130. Goodyear (1981: 83) is incorrect, however, in his claim that Germanicus is also referred to as "IMP. II" on coins, as all we have is a single emission from Caesarea in Cappadocia (*RPC* I 3623), which does refer to him as an *imperator* ("IMP."), but without specifying the number of salutations.

22 *Contra* Faoro 2016: 2010 (note 33).

23 *AE* 1973: 501.

24 Brunt 1974: 174; Barnes 1974: 25. *Contra* Orth (1978: 58–59), who favours a date early in Tiberius's reign. In Orth's opinion, the *German war* mentioned in the inscription, which brought Fabricius Tuscus the honours mentioned above, refers to Germanicus's campaigns on the Rhine led already under Tiberius.

25 That would be a strong argument in favour of Germanicus having been granted his first independent *imperium* in AD 11, as Cassius Dio suggests. As we know, holding independent *imperium* was among the main preconditions for being awarded imperatorial acclamation. On that subject, see above.

26 Timpe 1968: 36–37 (note 34); 45; Goodyear 1981: 84; Barnes 1974: 25–26; Syme 1979: 317–320. Hurlet 1997: 169–172; Faoro 2016: 212.

27 Tac. *Ann.* 1, 31, 3–4.

28 Tac. *Ann.* 1, 31, 2–3; 33, 1; 34, 1.

29 Tac. *Ann.* 1, 58, 5–6. See also Timpe 1968: 45; Syme 1979: 321–322.

30 Cass. Dio 54, 33, 5.

31 See Kehne 1998a: 206–207; Rich 1990: 213.

32 Suet. *Tib.* 9, 2; *Claud.* 1, 3; Cass. Dio 54, 33, 5; Rich 1999: 548–549.

33 Faoro 2016: 212.

34 Cass. Dio 55, 10a, 7. Syme 1979: 315; Swan 2004: 132; Faoro 2016: 209, 212.

35 Tac. *Ann.* 2, 18, 2; Syme 1979: 322. Kienast, Eck, Heil 2017: 72.

36 See Syme 1979: 310.

37 See Hickson 1991: 128.

38 Vell. Pat. 2, 97, 4; Suet. *Tib.* 9, 2. Flower (2020: 17) is wrong in believing that granting Tiberius the triumph means he led the campaign in Germania under his own auspices. As I have mentioned above, all of Augustus's commanders, including members of the imperial family, conducted campaigns under his auspices. The same applies to Germanicus, who held a triumph in AD 17, even though his campaigns in Germania were waged *auspiciis Tiberii*; see Tac. *Ann.* 2, 41, 1.

39 Cass. Dio 55, 8, 1; See also Richardson 2012: 143.

40 Cass. Dio 55, 8, 2. See also Rich 1990: 226.

41 Cass. Dio 56, 17, 1.

42 Suet. *Tib.* 17, 2.

43 *Inscr. It.* XIII.2, 134–135; Vell. Pat. 2, 121, 2; Suet. *Tib.* 20.

44 Vell. Pat. 2, 121, 3; Suet. *Tib.* 20.

45 That aspect of Tiberius's triumph was pointed out by Hickson 1991: 129–130; Beard 2007: 296; and Flower 2020: 17.

46 *RIC*, I^2, *Aug.* 221–224; Mlasowsky 1996: 313–315; Vout 2013: 69. *Contra* Kuttner (1995: 153), who unconvincingly ties that emission to Tiberius's first triumph.

47 See Zanker 1990: 229. For a detailed analysis of the artefact, see Kuttner 1995: *passim*, although the book must be used with care owing to the errors it contains regarding various events from Augustus's principate: the author persistently dates Octavian's (*sic!*) triumph to 27 BC, even though it is common knowledge it actually took place 2 years earlier than that; she also places Tiberius's departure for Rhodes in 4 BC instead of in 6 BC. See Kuttner 1995: 85, 147–148, 150, 173, 177, 195.

48 See Kuttner 1995: 94–98; Zanker 1990: 230–231.

49 Zanker 1990: 229. See also Kleiner 1997: 377–380.

50 Kuttner 1995: 151–153; 193–197. In her opinion, the scene on one of the *skyphoi* depicting a triumphal procession refers to Tiberius's first triumph.
51 Dating them is a controversial issue. Some even believe they were only made in Claudius's reign. See Zanker (1990: 349), who presents various researchers' views on the matter.
52 Discussed below.
53 Zanker 1990: 232–233.
54 Zanker 1990: 232–233.
55 For a description of the images on the cameo, see e.g. Zanker 1990: 232–234.
56 Tac. *Ann.* 1, 55, 1.
57 Syme 1979: 322.
58 Timpe 1968: 44–46.
59 *Inscr. It.* XIII.2, 187: [*Fer(iae) ex s(enatus) c(onsulto), quod*] *eo die* [*Germanicus C*]*aesar* [*triumphans in urbem*] *inv*[*e*]*ctus est*; Tac. *Ann.* 2, 41, 2: *Germanicus Caesar a.d. VII. Kal. Iunias triumphavit.*
60 Tac. *Ann.* 2, 41, 2.
61 Tac. *Ann.* 2, 41, 2–3; Vell. Pat. 2, 129, 2; Suet. *Cal.* 1, 1; see also Rose 1997: 24; Hurlet 1997: 179–180.
62 Strab. 7, 1, 4.
63 That was the way Germanicus's achievements were expressed in the text of the *TS* (fr. 1, ll. 13–15).
64 Severy 2003: 226.
65 Tac. *Ann.* 2, 42, 1.
66 *RIC*, I[2], *Cal.* 57; *HCC*, I, *Cal.* 37. For a recent discussion of that emission, see Suspène 2013: 179–180.
67 Germanicus recovering legions' eagles is mentioned in Tacitus (*Ann.* 1, 60, 3; 2, 25, 1–2), Cassius Dio (57, 18, 1), and *TS* fr. 1, ll. 13–14.
68 Another interpretation exists, according to which the scene shows Tiberius presenting an image of Victory to Augustus seated in the *sella curulis*. See Vout 2013: 69.
69 Schrömbges 1986: 186–187; Mlasowsky 1996: 337–338; Rose 1997: 24; Zanker 1990: 234–235.
70 Who most likely received it in 11 BC, the same as Drusus the Elder. See Cass. Dio 54, 34, 3; Rich 1999: 549.
71 Vell. Pat. 2, 96, 3; Suet. *Tib.* 9, 2; Ehrenberg, Jones, 1955: 45: *Ti. Caesar ex Pan[onia ovans urbem intr]avit*. See also Miltner 1937: 223. Rich (1999: 550) thinks the ovation took place soon after Drusus's funeral.
72 Cass. Dio 55, 2, 4.
73 See Syme 1979: 311; Rich 1999: 549.
74 Cass. Dio 54, 33, 5; 34, 3.
75 Tac. *Ann.* 2, 64, 1; 3, 11, 1; Shaw 1990: 182–185.
76 *CIL* XIV 244: *V k Iun Drusus [Caesar] triumphavit ex Ill[yrico]*; *Inscr. It.* XIII.2, 187. Tacitus (*Ann.* 3, 19, 3) also reports it was held in the end.
77 Cass. Dio 54, 11, 6.
78 Cass. Dio 54, 24, 7.
79 Cass. Dio 54, 11, 6.
80 Simpson 1991: 137–138.
81 Cass. Dio 54, 11, 6. See commentary on that passage in Rich 1990: 188. The senators' attitude could also have been influenced by their widely known dislike of Agrippa.
82 Cass. Dio 53, 26, 5; 54, 8, 3. See the commentary in Rich 1990: 182.
83 Rich 1990: 188; *id.* 1999: 547.
84 Cass. Dio 54, 31, 4.
85 See Rich 1990: 210.

86 Suet. *Claud.* 1, 3; Cass. Dio 54, 33, 5.

87 *Contra* Vervaet 2020: 168, in whose opinion granting Augustus's two stepsons an ovation in 11 BC means they had led campaigns in Pannonia and Germania and held independent *imperium* since as early as 12 BC. One did have to hold independent *imperium* to receive an ovation, but, in Tiberius's and Drusus's case, the accolade may have been meant to make up for Augustus earlier refusing Tiberius the triumph accorded him by the senate and rejecting imperatorial acclamations for his stepsons. Granting the two brothers an ovation can also be seen as indicating a change in their standing in advance. In 11 BC, they received proconsular powers and, from then on, were to command legions as holders of independent *imperium*. It also bears stressing that a case is known of an ovation being granted to a commander who was *legatus Augusti pro praetore*, namely Aulus Plautius, a legate of Claudius in Britain, who was awarded the honour for his achievements during the conquest of the island. See Suet. *Claud.* 24, 6; *Vesp.* 4, 1; Tac. *Ann.* 13, 32, 2.

88 Cass. Dio 55, 2, 5.

89 See Rich 1999: 551–552.

90 See Syme 1979: 311; Rich 1990: 213; *id.* 1999: 549; Hurlet 1997: 92 (note 69). Some scholars incorrectly believe Drusus held the ovation in 11 BC; so, among others, Havener 2016: 335; Itgenshorst 2017: 66 (note 27), 71; Flower 2020: 15. However, no sources support their claim. What is more, Dio (55, 2, 5) clearly writes that Drusus's death prevented him from celebrating the ovation he was awarded. Suetonius (*Claud.* 1, 4) also suggests Drusus was going to apply for the right to offer *spolia opima* in the temple of Jupiter Feretrius on the Capitoline. Rich (1999: 552–554) believes that, if Augustus's stepson had not died young, he would have obtained that exceptional, very rare honour. On this subject, see also Kehne 1998a: 187–211.

91 Tac. *Ann.* 2, 64, 1; *TS* fr. 1, ll. 17–18.

92 I count as triumphal arches all those objects that were put up on the occasion of a triumph or ovation of a member of the *domus Augusta*, using the term "honorific arch" to refer to monuments erected as part of their posthumous honours.

93 Cass. Dio 56, 17, 1. See also Swan 2004: 248–249.

94 As mentioned above.

95 Considering Tiberius's triumph over Pannonia and Dalmatia did take place, we may assume those arches were also built at a later time, although Kleiner (1985a: 51) disagrees.

96 Some scholars think Gaius and Lucius Caesar had been honoured in that way before, and the arch dedicated to them was placed to the north of the temple of divus Caesar in the Forum Romanum, but it is not known whether it was erected in their lifetime or, as some researchers would have it, only after their death. On that subject, see Coarelli 1985: 271–273; Rose 1997: 19; Roehmer 1997: 104–109; Zanker 1990: 223.

97 Tac. *Ann.* 2, 41, 1. Some researchers classify the structure as an arch of Tiberius. See Coarelli 1993: 107–108; Roehmer 1997: 113. Others assumed it was dedicated to Tiberius and Germanicus; so e.g. Kleiner 1985a: 51, 70; Rose 1997: 24.

98 Tac. *Ann.* 2, 41, 1.

99 Kleiner 1985a: 51.

100 Kleiner 1985a: 51; Rose 1997: 24; on the Parthian arch of Augustus and its location, see esp. Nedergaard 1988: 224–239; Rich 1998: 97–115.

101 Coarelli 1993: 107–108.

102 For the route taken by triumphal processions and the location of the *porta triumphalis*, see Coarelli 1985: 363–414; Beard 2007: 92–105; 335 (a map).

103 Kleiner 1985a: 52.

104 *RIC* I², *Aug.* 131, 359. See also Kleiner 1985a: 26–27.
105 Images of a barbarian kneeling and humbly returning eagles were, for example, placed on *denarii* issued after 19 BC in Rome; see *RIC* I², *Aug.* 287–289. The motif also appeared on gemmas. Thus, the decoration of the arch of Tiberius and Germanicus used an iconographic pattern worked out before, legible and widely understandable. As Paul Zanker (1990: 191) aptly put it, "Der kniende Barbar blieb auch künftig eine ausserordentlich erfolgreiche Bildformel und prägte weitgehend die Vorstellung der Römer von ihrem Verhältnis zu den and den Grenzen des Imperiums wohnenden Völkern." There was also a depiction of Germanicus taking legions' standards back from Germans on the Rhine arch dedicated to him posthumously, for which see below.
106 Kleiner 1985a: 24, 26.
107 Discussed above.
108 Tac. *Ann.* 2, 64, 1. On those objects, see chiefly Zanker 1968: 24; Ganzert 1997: 193–206; Rose 1997: 108.
109 Kleiner 1985a: 53.
110 Tac. *Ann.* 2, 64, 1.
111 Taking into account the context in which the construction of the two monuments was decided on, we can be nearly certain both sons of Tiberius were styled triumphators, with triumphal togas and possibly in quadrigas.
112 Zanker 1990: 197 (fig. 149).
113 The inscription may have run as follows: *[Senatus populu]sque [Romanus]/ [Druso Caesari Ti(beri) Caesaris Aug]usti [f(ilio) Divi Augusti nepoti]/ [Divi Iuli pron]ep[oti, co(n)s(uli), pontifici, auguri, sodali Augustali]./[Hunc f]iliu[m Ti(berius) Caesa]r D[ivi Augusti f(ilius) Augustus]/[in Illyricum misit, ubi virtute e]ius [pax imperii ita confirmata est],/[ut ei una cum Germanico C]aesa[re fratre ovatio decerneretur]*. See Alföldy 1992: 108.
114 Suet. *Claud.* 1, 3: *Praeterea senatus inter alia complura marmoreum arcum cum tropaeis via Appia decrevit.* Cass. Dio 55, 2, 3.
115 Lebek 1991a: 74.
116 See Rich 1990: 219; Lebek 1991a: 73–74 (note 49); Pisani Sartorio 1993: 93; Roehmer 1997: 102.
117 Later, the arches of Trajan and Lucius Verus were constructed on the via Appia, the construction of which was decided on by the senate after their deaths. See Pisani Sartorio 1993: 93.
118 *RIC* I², *Claud.* 69–72; Kleiner 1985a: 34.
119 See Lebek 1991a: 75–76.
120 Lebek 1991a: 77–78.
121 Translated by J. B. Lott 2012: 75.
122 *DPG* l. 34. Kleiner 1985b: 158; Rose 1997: 99–100; Segenni 2011: 104–105.
123 *DPG* ll. 35–37. Kleiner 1985b: 159; Rose 1997: 100; Galsterer 2000: 183.
124 Kleiner 1985b: 35.
125 Rose 1997: 100.
126 *DPG* l. 36.
127 *RGDA* 14, 2; the title is also confirmed for Lucius by an inscription from Pisa (*DPL* ll. 7–8). See Lebek 1991a: 65.
128 Kienast, Eck, Heil 2017: 67–68.
129 *DPL* l. 8: *patronus coloniae nostrae* (Lucius), whereas Gaius was referred to in an inscription (*DPG* ll. 13–14) as *coloniaeque nostrae unicum praesidium*.
130 Segenni 2011: 105.
131 Lebek 1991a: 64–65.
132 See Kleiner 1985b: 162–163; Rose 1997: 100.
133 Tac. *Ann.* 2, 83, 2; *TS* fr. 1, ll. 9; 22; 26. For information on posthumous arches of Germanicus, see esp. Lebek 1987: 129–148; *id.* 1991: 67–71;Trillmich 1988: 51–60; Schmitt 1997: 73–137; Roehmer 1997: 132–147.

134 Translated by J. B. Lott 2012: 89, 91.
135 *TS* fr. 1, l. 9. On a marble city map of Rome from the 3rd century AD (*Forma Urbis Romae*), the monument stands between the portico of Octavia and the Theatre of Marcellus, and that location has been generally accepted by historians, See Lebek 1991a: 67 (note 36); Rodríguez Almeida 1993: 94–95; Zanker 1990: 150 (fig. 118).
136 An example is provided by Lucullus, who, during his triumph, held an exhibition there of weapons and engines of war captured in his campaigning in the East. See Plut. *Luc.* 37, 2.
137 *TS* fr. 1, ll. 10–11. See also Castagnoli 1984: 330–331; Lebek 1987: 136; on the statuary group set up by G. Norbanus Flaccus, consul of AD 15, in honour of the *domus Augusta*, see Flory 1996: 287–306.
138 *TS* fr. 1, ll. 18–21.
139 See Lebek 1991a: 67–68.
140 Suet. *Aug.* 34, 2. See also Carter 2003: 144–145.
141 Severy 2000: 324.
142 Rose 1997: 110. Cf. also Castagnoli 1984: 331.
143 *TS* fr. 1, ll. 12–18.
144 See Lebek 1991a: 48, 59–61.
145 *CIL* II 4701–4703; 4721.
146 *TS* fr. 1, ll. 9, 22, 26; Tac. *Ann.* 2, 83, 2.
147 Cf. Kleiner 1989: 200–201; in a similar tone, Rose 1997: 110.
148 Translated by J. B. Lott 2012: 91.
149 *TS* fr. 1, ll. 22–24; Tac. *Ann.* 2, 83, 2.
150 Lebek 1987: 140–141.
151 *TS* fr. 1, l. 25.
152 Lebek 1991a: 69.
153 *TS* fr. 1, ll. 25–26.
154 Lebek 1987: 142.
155 Translated by J. B. Lott 2012: 91.
156 Tac. *Ann.* 2, 83, 2.
157 *TS* fr. 1, ll. 26–28; Lebek 1987: 147; *id.* 1989a: 57–62.
158 Herz 2001: 106, 108. See also Bellen 1989: 78.
159 *TS* fr. 1, ll. 28–29.
160 *TS* fr. 1, ll. 30–32; Suet. *Claud.* 1, 3. See also Bellen 1984: 385–396.
161 Tac. *Ann.* 2, 83, 2.
162 Frenz 1989: 69–70.
163 Frenz 1989: 69; Lebek 1989a: 77.
164 Frenz 1989: 69–75.
165 Bellen 1989: 77–78; see also Lehmann 1991: 94.
166 See Klein 2002: 12–13.
167 *TS* fr. 1, ll. 30–34; Suet. *Claud.* 1, 3.
168 See Lebek 1989a: 79–82; Bellen 1989: 80–81; Roehmer 1997: 267–270.
169 Tac. *Ann.* 4, 9, 2.
170 As was the case with Germanicus before, the text of Drusus's honorific decree was probably inscribed on bronze tablets set up in Rome and the most vital locations in the Empire; see Lebek 1989b: 83–84.
171 Translated by J. B. Lott 2012: 165.
172 Lebek 1989b: 89, 91.
173 Lebek 1989b: 89–90; *id.* 1991: 54–55, 71.
174 Lebek 1989b: 89; *id.* 1991a: 71.

Conclusion

All the persons acting as extraordinary commanders on Augustus's and Tiberius's orders belonged to the small circle of the imperial family and were potential candidates for succession. The importance and nature of the missions entrusted to them varied. In the West of the Empire, they were mostly serious military undertakings or reorganization of the areas recently conquered by Augustus—for instance, Tiberius establishing the *Ara Ubiorum* in Germania or the reorganization of the provincial structure in Pannonia after the great uprising of the local tribes was suppressed in AD 9—actions crucial for the Romanization and unification of the newly annexed regions. In the East, members of the *domus Augusta* mostly carried out diplomatic missions and inspected the provinces.

Generally speaking, those commanders did well at the tasks entrusted to them, being well prepared for them. Agrippa had won the requisite military experience in the civil wars during the second triumvirate, Drusus and Tiberius had had their first taste of war in Raetia, and Germanicus had fought at Tiberius's side in Pannonia before assuming general command in Germania. There can be no doubt that it was thanks to their military talent that Augustus was able to actualize his far-reaching plans for conquest of lands on the Rhine and the Danube.

The motives of Augustus, and later Tiberius, as they gave those special tasks to members of their immediate family, varied as well. Because of the sheer number and extent of duties involved in ruling the Empire, they could not make it to each place where their presence was needed, and, in Augustus's case, his lack of military talent mattered too. But members of the reigning dynasty, equipped with a small portion of the emperors' *auctoritas*, could represent them before the people in the provinces, the army, and foreign monarchs, and so they went wherever the intervention of mere governors failed or the situation called for the presence of the princeps himself. Examples include Agrippa being sent to suppress the dangerous uprising of the Cantabri and Astures, Tiberius being despatched to Germania after Varus's defeat, and Germanicus's eastern expedition. In addition, the scale of the military campaigns carried out at the time involved large military forces, which in turn needed to be commanded by experienced and talented generals. That is, of course, not to say there were no such generals among ordinary legates and governors, but entrusting large armies to people from outside the narrow circle of the *domus Augusta* could have created a grave threat to the emperor's position, especially with the new political order and regime only recently forming. It would have also been inadvisable for the glory of victories and of annexing new territories to fall to someone from outside the dynasty. Furthermore, the conquest and later organization of the captured territories by members of the imperial family were of considerable importance to the process of forming in the conquered population loyalty towards the princeps and the family centred on him. Meanwhile, diplomatic talks and negotiations had to be conducted by persons worthy of representing the majesty of Rome and its emperor. With that perspective in mind, members of the reigning family were perfectly qualified for carrying out the policy of conquest and representing Rome internationally.

Comparing the *imperia* of the several members of the imperial family and their relative standing in the *domus Augusta* points to a specific hierarchy within that group. That standing certainly differed between Drusus the Elder, who held *imperium proconsulare* in Gaul and Germania and was only another candidate to succession, and Agrippa, who held *imperium maius* relative to that of provincial governors throughout the Empire as Augustus's second-in-command and *collega imperii*. The type of *imperium* accorded members of the *domus Augusta* depended chiefly on the status of the province and the significance of the mission entrusted to them. If they led a military campaign in Germania or on the Danube, they did so as proconsuls, whereas those carrying out special missions in the East, excluding Gaius Caesar, received the greater proconsular *imperium* (*imperium maius quam*). In the former case, granting such broad prerogatives was unnecessary, as members of the *domus Augusta* operated in imperial provinces, the governors of which held *imperia pro praetore*, ranked below the *imperium* of a proconsul, whereas, in the East, the special commanders were active in areas governed by both imperial legates and senate-nominated proconsuls. Under those circumstances, their superior *imperium* let them intervene freely in the affairs of those public provinces.

The origins of the extraordinary *imperia* of the members of the emperor's family must no doubt be sought in the late Republican era, as we know of several striking examples of special powers being granted to commanders of the time (such as to Pompey in 77 and 67 BC or to Cassius in 43). Those powers were actually very similar to those provided later by the *imperia* held by members of the *domus Augusta*. The similarity mostly lay in the type and territorial scope of the *imperium*, which was *proconsulare* and applied, not in a single province, but in much larger territory. Besides, in both cases, the *imperium* was separate from the office it nominally accompanied; both the aforementioned Republican commanders and the members of the imperial family held their *imperia* without holding at the time any magistracy *cum imperio*.

It is also in the late Republic that we should look for the roots of the so-called *imperium maius*, only held within the *domus Augusta* by the princeps, Agrippa, and Germanicus. Under the Republic, the only case was that of Cassius, who received that kind of power over other governors in the East in 43 BC. We have to remember, of course, that the situation was unusual and forced by the ongoing civil war, which made the senate "sanction" the status quo. We also know of attempts to grant the same prerogatives to other commanders under the Republic (to Pompey in 57). In the end, Messius's bill did not pass, but the situation proves the late Republic already knew, in the abstract, the mode of *imperium* that Augustus and his family would later use to control the provinces.

Clearly, specifying the nature and scope of the *imperia* held by members of the *domus Augusta* was to make it possible for them to smoothly co-operate with the provincial administration, but was of little significance to the ordinary inhabitants of the provinces they were active in, as those were neither too familiar with nor overly interested in the legal standing or the exact powers of those emissaries. In the eyes of the provincials, their exceptional position was mostly determined by their being highest-ranking members of the emperor's family and the main candidates for succession.

Analyzing the careers of members of the *domus Augusta* reveals important differences between their *cursus honorum*. For instance, Drusus the Elder and Tiberius started their military careers as ordinary imperial legates, conducting campaigns in Raetia, and then in Germania and Pannonia. They only rose to independent *imperium* after praetorship and consulship. That is in sharp contrast with the case of Gaius Caesar, who was granted *imperium proconsulare* having skipped all possible steps of the *cursus honorum*. Naturally, that was because, as Augustus's son and the main candidate for succession, he enjoyed a very different status in the imperial family to that of the emperor's stepsons.

The special rank of the emperor's relatives active in the provinces was due not simply to their extraordinary *imperia*, but also to the high-prestige honours they were awarded. Especially worthy of note among them were those granted for military achievements—that is, triumphs, ovations, and imperatorial acclamations. Augustus's consistent actions in this area caused those honours, which at the beginning of his reign could still fall to many commanders, to become virtually reserved for the princeps and the most important members of his *domus*, making them particularly prestigious.

That Augustus and Tiberius entrusted members of their families with the most important military campaigns and various diplomatic missions should also be seen through the lens of the first two emperors' dynastic policy: the missions provided an excellent opportunity for those family members to be introduced and advertised to the legions and inhabitants of provinces, while the prospective successors had a chance to gain the necessary military and administrative experience. In addition, by carrying out their tasks successfully, they could prove they were worthy candidates to wield the highest power in the state. Visiting diverse provinces of the Empire gave members of the *domus Augusta* ample opportunity to emphasize to the locals how generous the princeps and his family were, resulting in the establishment or funding of many public buildings—see Agrippa's public works programme during his two missions in the East. For the inhabitants of a province, the arrival of a member of the *domus Augusta* was an occasion to express their loyalty and devotion to the reigning family by granting them numerous prestigious honours.

As a phenomenon, entrusting special missions to people who were then immediately granted extraordinary powers hardly took shape for the first time under Augustus. As I have written above, the practice had its roots in the late-Republic era. Still, it was a novelty that, during Augustus's and Tiberius's principates, the circle of persons who were granted such special prerogatives and who could carry out special undertakings dwindled considerably, having been limited solely to members of the emperor's immediate family. That remained closely related to the process Augustus had started of building a dynasty centred on him, as the new elite in power. Conferring extraordinary prerogatives on family members, entrusting them with important state missions, and awarding them high-prestige honours were a significant part of that process, which concentrated all the power and honours within a single family.

Solving serious military and diplomatic problems through the actions of the most important members of the imperial family was characteristic of Augustus's and Tiberius's principates, but disappeared—in that particular form—under the later emperors of the Julio-Claudian dynasty. I think that, on the one hand, that may have been because the new order had by then settled, and the position of the princeps in the state had grown stronger, whereas Augustus's situation had not been so comfortable. During his reign, the new regime was not yet fixed, and the foundations of the emperor's power and position were still taking shape. Under the circumstances, placing large military forces under the command of people unrelated to him could have created a group of ambitious generals who enjoyed the support of the army and could have become undesirable competition for the *domus Augusta*. Therefore, the imperial family gained the monopoly for commanding large armies. During the early stages of his reign, Tiberius continued along the course set by Augustus. On the other hand, another factor resulted in special commanders never being nominated from among the imperial family during the second half of Tiberius's reign or under the later rulers of the Julio-Claudian dynasty: this was, quite simply, the dearth of appropriate candidates, which was in turn due to several circumstances coinciding. The potential candidates—after the death of Drusus the Younger, Germanicus's sons, and, under Caligula and Nero, Tiberius Gemellus and Britannicus, respectively—were all killed on those emperors' explicit orders. In addition, Britannicus and Nero were too young for Claudius to entrust them with military undertakings such as the conquest of Britain or the annexation of Thrace.

Of course, with that category of commanders gone, the problems they used to be nominated to solve did not go away: Rome still waged wars and continued to conduct diplomatic talks with other countries. However, those duties began to be entrusted to commanders from outside the reigning family, who now no longer held special *imperium*, instead acting as ordinary imperial legates. It is worth noting here a few more spectacular cases of military problems being solved under the later emperors of the Julio-Claudian dynasty. In AD 43, Claudius began the conquest of Britain, the greatest military undertaking of his reign. He gave the command to Aulus Plautius, sent to the front in the rank of *legatus Augusti pro praetore*. For his successes, Plautius was, in AD 47, allowed an ovation—an extraordinary distinction, considering he was not part of the imperial family and had not held independent *imperium*.[1]

In AD 63, Nero again faced the as yet unsolved Armenian–Parthian conundrum and decided to give the high command of the campaign in the East to the experienced general Domitius Corbulo. In order to avoid any misunderstandings between him and the governors of the eastern provinces, Corbulo received special prerogatives. In E. Dąbrowa's opinion, he was granted *imperium maius* then,[2] a view that I believe goes too far, as it is contradicted by our sources. From Tacitus, our best source on the matter, it would appear the rulers of client states and governors of imperial provinces in the East merely received instructions from the princeps to obey Corbulo during his campaign,[3] so that their subordination to him resulted not from his superior *imperium*, but rather from the emperor's orders to that effect that had been sent to those governors. A sharp contrast can be observed with the procedure implemented earlier regarding Agrippa and Germanicus, who acted in the East with the mandate of the senate and the people, holding the greater proconsular *imperium*. In the context of this discussion, another important passage in Tacitus is the one where the historian mentions the functions of the governor of Syria being divided between G. Cestius and Corbulo: the former was entrusted with civilian administration of the province; the latter, with military matters and the command of the Syrian legions, which were to be employed in the Armenian campaign.[4] On those grounds, we may assume Corbulo's legal standing had not changed, and he remained an imperial legate. Even though his position stood out compared with that of other imperial commanders, his powers were not as extensive as those accorded members of the *domus Augusta* active in the East under Augustus and Tiberius. To illustrate that clearly, unlike Gaius Caesar or Germanicus, who, as members of the emperor's family, could enthrone Armenian kings in his name, Corbulo was not granted that right. Indeed, it is here worth citing another passage in Tacitus, this one on a meeting between Corbulo and Tiridates, a candidate for the Armenian throne. The author reports that the king elect laid his regal tiara before an image of Nero set on a *sella curulis*, pledging to only receive the crown from the emperor's hands.[5]

The adduced examples confirm that the practice of nominating special commanders from within the *domus Augusta* was specific to the principates of Augustus and Tiberius: only then were persons from the imperial family granted extraordinary powers and rewarded with such high-prestige honours. The cases of the senators Plautius and Corbulo demonstrate that, under the later Julio-Claudian emperors, few commanders stood out from among the governors in general, and their legal status and rank were not comparable with those of members of the reigning dynasty active in the provinces under the first and second princeps.

Notes

1 See Suet. *Claud.* 24, 6; *Vesp.* 4, 1; Tac. *Ann.* 13, 32, 2; Vervaet 2020: 155.
2 Dąbrowa 1998: 55.
3 Tac. *Ann.* 15, 25, 3.
4 Tac. *Ann.* 15, 25, 3.
5 Tac. *Ann.* 15, 29, 1–3.

Appendix 1

The *imperia* of members of the *domus Augusta*

Marcus Agrippa

Type of power held: *imperium proconsulare maius quam …*
Territorial range: all the provinces of the Roman Empire
Date when granted: 23 BC (?) (extended twice, in 18 and 13 BC)
Sources:

> καὶ εἰς {ς} ἅς δήποτέ σε ὑπαρχείας τὰ κοινὰ τῶν Ῥωμαίων ἐφέλκοιτο, μηθενὸς ἐν ἐκείναις ἐξουσίαν μείζω <εἶναι> τῆς σῆς ἐν νόμωι ἐκυρώθη […]
>
> (P. Colon. inv. no 4701)

> Κἀν τούτῳ τὸν Ἀγρίππαν ἐκ τῆς Συρίας ἐλθόντα τῇ τε δημαρχικῇ ἐξουσίᾳ αὖθις ἐς ἄλλα ἔτη πέντε ἐμεγάλυνε καὶ ἐς τὴν Παννονίαν πολεμησείουσαν ἐξέπεμψε, μεῖζον αὐτῷ τῶν ἑκασταχόθι ἔξω τῆς Ἰταλίας ἀρχόντων ἰσχῦσαι ἐπιτρέψας.
>
> (Cass. Dio 54, 28, 1)

Drusus the Elder

Type of power held: *imperium proconsulare*
Territorial range: Germania and the Gallic provinces
Date when granted: 11 BC
Sources:

> διὰ μὲν οὖν ταῦτα τάς τε ἐπινικίους τιμὰς καὶ τὸ ἐπὶ κέλητος ἐς τὸ ἄστυ ἐσελάσαι, τῇ τε τοῦ ἀνθυπάτου ἐξουσίᾳ, ἐπειδὰν διαστρατηγήσῃ, χρήσασθαι ἔλαβε.
>
> (Cass. Dio 54, 33, 5)

Tiberius

Type of power held: *imperium proconsulare*
Territorial range: Pannonia and Germania

Date when granted: 11 BC (renewed in 6 BC and then in AD 4)
Sources:

> ὥστε καὶ τῶν ἄθλων τῶν αὐτῶν τῷ Δρούσῳ τυχεῖν.
>
> (Cass. Dio 54, 34, 3)

Type of power held: *imperium proconsulare maius quam …*
Territorial range: all the provinces of the Roman Empire
Date when granted: AD 12 or 13
Sources:

> senatus populusque Romanus postulante patre eius ut aequum ei ius in omnibus provinciis exercitibusque esset quam erat ipsi, decreto complexus est.
>
> (Vell. Pat. 2, 121, 1)

> ac non multo post lege per consules lata, ut provincias cum Augusto communiter administraret.
>
> (Suet. *Tib.* 21, 1)

Gaius Caesar

Type of power held: *imperium proconsulare*
Territorial range: the eastern provinces (*transmarinae provinciae*)
Date when granted: 1 BC
Sources:

> ἀνάγκης δ' ἐπικειμένης τὸν Γάιον εἵλετο, καὶ τήν τε ἐξουσίαν αὐτῷ τὴν ἀνθύπατον καὶ γυναῖκα ἔδωκεν, ἵνα κἀκ τούτου τι προσλάβῃ ἀξίομα, καί οἱ καὶ συμβούλους προσέταξε.
>
> (Cass. Dio 55, 10, 18)

> praepositus Orientis
>
> (Suet. *Tib.* 12, 2)

Germanicus

Type of power held: *imperium proconsulare*
Territorial range: Germania and the Gallic provinces
Date when granted: AD 11 (extended for another 5 years in AD 14)
Sources:

> Μάρκου δὲ Αἰμιλίου μετὰ Στατιλίου Ταύρου ὑπατεύσαντος, Τιβέριος μὲν καὶ Γερμανικὸς ἀντὶ ὑπάτου ἄρχων ἔς τε τὴν Κελτικὴν ἐσέβαλον.
>
> (Cass. Dio 56, 25, 2)

at Germanico Caesari proconsulare imperium petivit, missique legati qui deferrent, simul maestitiam eius ob excessum Augusti solarentur.

(Tac. *Ann.* 1, 14, 3)

Type of power held: *imperium proconsulare maius quam ...*
Territorial range: the eastern provinces (*transmarinae provinciae*)
Date when granted: AD 17
Sources:

lex ad populum lata esset, ut in quamcumq(ue) provinciam venisset, maius ei imperium quam ei qui eam provinciam proco(n)s(ule) optineret, esset, dum in omni re maius imperium Ti. Caesari Aug(usto) quam Germ(anico) Caesar(i) esset, tamquam ipsius arbitri et potestatis omnia esse deberent.

(*SCPP* ll. 34–37)

tunc decreto patrum permissae Germanico provinciae, quae mari dividuntur, maiusque imperium, quoquo adisset, quam iis qui sorte aut missu principis obtinerent.

(Tac. *Ann.* 2, 43, 1)

proco(n)s(ul) missus in transmarinas pro[vinicias]

(*TS.* fr. 1, l. 15)

Drusus the Younger

Type of power held: *imperium proconsulare*
Territorial range: Illyricum (Raetia, Noricum, Pannonia, and Dalmatia)
Date when granted: AD 17
Sources:

nec multo post Drusus in Illyricum missus est, ut suesceret militiae studiaque exercitus pararet.

(Tac. *Ann.* 2, 44, 1)

Appendix 2

Missions of members of the imperial family in the provinces

A2.1 Missions of members of the imperial family in the provinces

Person	*Place*	*Years*	*Aim of the mission*	*Sources*
M. Agrippa	The eastern provinces	23–22 BC	Regulating Rome's relationship with the Parthians; inspecting the Roman East before Augustus's visit	Joseph. *AJ*, 15, 350 Cass. Dio 53, 32, 1
	Gaul	20/19 BC	Suppressing the revolt of the Gallic tribes	Cass. Dio 54, 11, 1–2 Strab. 4, 6, 11
	Spain	19 BC	Suppressing the uprising of the Cantabri and Astures	Cass. Dio 54, 11, 2–6
	The eastern provinces	17/16–13 BC	Inspecting the Roman provinces and vassal kingdoms in the East; consolidating Rome's influence in the Bosporan Kingdom	Joseph. *AJ*, 16, 12–15; 21–23; *BJ*, 1, 416 Cass. Dio 54, 24, 4–6 Strab. 16, 2, 19 Mal. 9, 225
	Pannonia	12 BC	Suppressing the rebellion of the Pannonian tribes	Cass. Dio 54, 28, 2
Drusus the Elder	Germania	10–9 BC	Military campaigns against Germanic tribes	Liv. *Per.* 141; Vell. Pat. 2, 97, 2–3; Suet. *Claud.* 1, 2; Cass. Dio 54, 36, 3; 55, 1, 2–4; Flor. 2, 30

Tiberius	Pannonia	11–9 BC	Military campaigns against Pannonian and Dalmatian tribes	*RGDA* 30,1; Liv. *Per*. 141; Cass. Dio 54, 36, 2–3; 55, 2, 4
	Germania	8–7 BC	Finalizing the conquest of Germanic tribes	Vell. Pat. 2, 97, 4; Suet. *Tib*. 9, 2; Cass. Dio 55, 6, 5
	Germania	AD 4–6	Campaigns against Germanic tribes	Vell. Pat. 2, 104–109; Cass. Dio 55, 28, 5
	Pannonia	AD 6–9	Suppressing the uprising of Pannonian and Dalmatian tribes	Vell. Pat. 2, 110–115; Suet. *Tib*. 16, 1–2; Cass. Dio 55, 29–32; 33, 1; 34, 4–7; 56, 12–16
	Germania	AD 10–12	Normalizing the situation in Germania after Varus's defeat	Vell. Pat. 2, 120–121; Suet. *Tib*. 18, 1–2; Cass. Dio 56, 24, 6; 25, 2–3
	Gaul	AD 11/12	Suppressing the rebellion of the Gallic tribes	Vell. Pat. 2, 121, 1
Gaius Caesar	The eastern provinces	1 BC–AD 4	Normalizing the situation in Armenia; regulating Rome's relationships with the Parthians	*RGDA* 27, 2; Vell. Pat. 2, 101–102; Cass. Dio 55, 10a, 4–9; Tac. *Ann*. 2, 4, 1
Germanicus	Gaul	AD 13/14	Inspecting the Gallic provinces	Tac. *Ann*. 1, 31, 2–3; 33, 1; *TS*, fr. 1, l. 15
	Germania	AD 14–16	Suppressing the mutiny of the Rhine legions; campaigns against Germanic tribes	Tac. *Ann*. 1, 34–45; 48–51; 56–71; 2, 5–26; *TS*, fr. 1, ll. 13–15
	The eastern provinces	AD 17–19	Enthroning Armenia's new king; renewing the alliance with the Parthian kingdom; inspecting the eastern provinces	Vell. Pat. 2, 129, 3; Tac. *Ann*. 2, 53–61; 64; 68–69; *TS*, fr. 1, ll. 15–17; *SCPP* (ll. 30–31)
Drusus the Younger	Illyricum	AD 17–20	Strengthening Roman influence in Germania, Pannonia, and Dalmatia	Vell. Pat. 2, 129, 3; Tac. *Ann*. 2, 44–46; 62–63; 3,7,1; 11, 1

Appendix 3

Imperatorial acclamations of members of the *domus Augusta*

A3.1 Imperatorial acclamations of members of the *domus Augusta*

Person	*Number of salutations*	*Reason for the honorification*	*Date*	*Sources*
M. Agrippa	Imp. I	Suppressing the uprising of the Cantabri and Astures	19 BC (?)	*CIG* II 1878; *CIL* IX 262
Drusus the Elder	Imp. I	Victories in Germania	10 or 9 BC (?)	Tac. *Ann.* 1, 3, 1 *Inscr. It.* XIII.3, 15–16 (no. 9) *RIC* I^2, Claud. 70–73
Tiberius	Imp. I	Victories over the Pannonian and Dalmatian tribes	10 or 9 BC (?)	Tac. *Ann.* 1, 3, 1
	Imp. II	Victories over the Germanic tribes	8 BC	Cass. Dio 55, 6, 5
	Imp. III	Successes fighting the Germanic tribes	AD 5 or 6 (?)	Cass. Dio 55, 28, 6
	Imp. IV–V	Suppressing the insurrection in Pannonia and Dalmatia	AD 8–9	Cass. Dio 56, 17, 1
	Imp. VI	Stabilizing the situation in Gemania after Varus's defeat	AD 11–12 (?)	*RIC* I^2, Aug. 242–243
	Imp. VII	Germanicus's victorious campaign in Germania	AD 13–14 (?)	*RIC* I^2, *Tib.* 1
Gaius Caesar	Imp. I	Victorious campaign in Armenia and Parthia	AD 3	Cass. Dio 55, 10a, 7 *CIL* V 6416
Germanicus	Imp. I	Victorious campaign in Germania	AD 11–14 (?)	*AE* 1973, 501
	Imp. II	Successes fighting the Germanic tribes	AD 15	Tac. *Ann.* 1, 58, 5–6

Appendix 4

Triumphs and ovations of members of the *domus Augusta*

A4.1 Triumphs and ovations of members of the *domus Augusta*[1]

Person	*Type of honour granted*	*Reason the honour was granted*	*Date when celebrated*	*Sources*
Tiberius	Ovation	Victories in Pannonia and Dalmatia	9 BC	Vell. Pat. 2, 96, 3 Suet. *Tib.* 9, 2 Cass. Dio 55, 2, 4
	Triumph	Military successes in Germania	7 BC	Vell. Pat. 2, 97, 4 Cass. Dio 55, 8, 2 Suet. *Tib.* 9, 2
	Triumph	Suppressing the rebellion in Pannonia and Dalmatia	AD 12	Vell. Pat. 2, 121, 2 Suet. *Tib.* 20 *Inscr. It.* XIII.2, 134–135
Germanicus	Triumph	Victories in Germania	AD 17	Vell. Pat. 2, 129, 2 Tac. *Ann.* 2, 41, 2 Suet. *Cal.* 1, 1 *Inscr. It.* XIII.2, 187
Drusus the Younger	Ovation	Diplomatic successes in Illyricum	AD 20	Tac. *Ann.* 2, 64, 1; 3, 11, 1; 19, 3 *CIL* XIV 244

Note

1 The Appendix 4 table omits the triumphs and ovations that members of the imperial family did receive, but that never happened for various reasons.

Bibliography

Abramenko, A. 1994. "Drusus' Umkehr an der Elbe und die angebliche Opposition gegen seine germanischen Feldzüge: Zum literarischen Vorbild für Cass.Dio 55, 1, 1–4 und Suet. Claud. 1, 2." *Athenaeum* 82.2: 371–383.

Akveld, V. F. 1961. *Germanicus*. Groningen.

Alföldy, G. 1992. "L'iscrizione dell'arco di Druso nel Forum Augustum." In G. Alföldy (ed.), *Studi sull'epigrafia augustea e tiberiana di Roma*, Rome: 101–110.

Alföldy, G. 2000. "Das neue Edikt des Augustus aus El Bierzo in Hispanien." *ZPE* 131: 177–205.

Ameling, W. 1994. "Augustus und Agrippa: Bemerkungen zu PKöln VI 249." *Chiron* 24: 1–28.

Arnaud, P. 1994. "Transmarinae provinciae: Réflexions sur les limites géographiques et sur la nature des pouvoirs en Orient des 'corégents' sous les règnes d'Auguste et de Tibère." *CCG* 5: 221–253.

Atkinson, K. M. T. 1958. "The Governors of the Province Asia in the Reign of Augustus." *Historia* 7.3: 300–330.

Baar, M. 1990. *Das Bild des Kaisers Tiberius bei Tacitus, Suetonius und Cassius Dio*. Stuttgart.

Badian, E. 1980. "Notes on the Laudatio of Agrippa." *CJ* 76.2: 97–107.

Baltrusch, E., Hegewisch, M., Meyer, M., Puschner, U., and Wendt, C. (eds.) 2012. *2000 Jahre Varusschlacht: Geschichte – Archäologie – Legenden (Topoi)*. Berlin.

Barnes, T. 1974. "The Victories of Augustus." *JRS* 64: 21–26.

Beard, M. 2007. *The Roman Triumph*. Cambridge, MA; London.

Bellen, H. 1984. "Das Drususdenkmal apud Mogontiacum und die Galliarum civitates." *JRGZM* 31: 385–396.

Bellen, H. 1989. "Der römische Ehrenbogen von Mainz-Kastel: Ianus Germanici aut Domitiani?" *Arch. Kor. RGZM* 19: 77–84.

Béranger, J. 1953. *Recherches sur l'aspect idéologique du Principat*. Basel.

Bernecker, A. 1976. "Zur Tiberius-Inschrift von Saepinum." *Chiron* 6: 185–192.

Bernecker, A. 1989. *Die Feldzüge des Tiberius und die Darstellung der unterworfenen Gebiete in der "Geographie des Ptolemaeus."* Bonn.

Bickel, E. 1943–44. "Der Mythus um die Adler der Varusschlacht." *RhM* 92: 302–318.

Bird, H. W. 1987. "Tiberius, Piso and Germanicus: Further Considerations." *Acta Classica* 30: 72–75.

Bleicken, J. 1993. "Imperium consulare/proconsulare im Übergang von den Republik zum Prinzipat." In J. Bleicken (ed.), *Colloquium aus Anlass des 80. Geburtstages von Alfred Heuss*, Kallmünz Opf.: 117–133.

Bleicken, J. 1998. *Augustus: Eine Biographie*. Berlin.

Blonce, C., Gangloff, A., 2013. "Mémoire du voyage de Germanicus en Orient." *CCG* 24: 113–134.

Bodel, J. 1999. "Punishing Piso." *AJP* 120.1: 43–63.

Bogue, J. F. 1970. *Tiberius in the Reign of Augustus*. Dissertation, University of Illinois. Urbana.

Bonamente, G., Segoloni, M. P. (eds.) 1987. *Germanico: La persona, la personalità, il personaggio nel bimillenario della nascita*. Atti del Convegno (Macerata–Perugia 1986). Rome.

Borchhardt, J. 1974. "Ein Kenotaph für Gaius Caesar." *JDAI* 89: 217–241.

Borszák, I. 1969. "Das Germanicusbild des Tacitus." *Latomus* 28: 588–600.

Borszák, I. 1970. "Zum Verständnis der Darstellungskunst des Tacitus: Die Veränderungen des Germanicus-Bildes." *Act. Ant.* 18.3–4: 279–292.

Boschung, D. 2002. *Gens Augusta: Untersuchungen zu Aufstellung, Wirkung und Bedeutung der Statuengruppen des julisch-claudischen Kaiserhauses*. Mainz.

Bowersock, G. W. 1984. "Augustus and the East: The Problem of the Succession." In F. Millar and E. Segal (eds.), *Caesar Augustus: Seven Aspects*, Oxford: 169–188.

Bringmann, K. 1977. "Imperium proconsulare und Mitregentschaft im frühen Prinzipat." *Chiron* 7, 219–238.

Broughton, T. R. S. 1951–1952. *The Magistrates of the Roman Republic*. I–II. New York.

Brunt, P. A. 1974. "C. Fabricius Tuscus and an Augustan Dilectus." *ZPE* 13: 161–185.

Brunt, P. A. 1977. "Lex de imperio Vespasiani." *JRS* 67: 95–116.

Callies, H. 1993. "Zur augusteisch-tiberianischen Germanenpolitik." In J. Bleicken (ed.), *Colloquium aus Anlass des 80. Geburtstages von A. Heuss*, Kallmünz Opf.: 135–141.

Capponi, L. 2013. "Aegyptus." In R. S. Bagnall, K. Brodersen, C. B. Champion, A. Erskine, S. R. Huebner (eds.), *The Encyclopedia of Ancient History*, Malden: 117–120.

Carter, J. M. 2003. *Suetonius: Divus Augustus*, edited with commentary. London.

Castagnoli, F. 1984. "L'Arco di Germanico in Circo Flaminio." *Arch. Class* 36: 329–332.

Castellvi, G. 2015. "Les trophées-tours romains: Permanences et évolutions des trophées de bataille, du IIe s. av. J.-C. au IIe s. apr. J.-C." In C. C. Petolescu, M. Galinier, F. Matei-Popescu (eds.), *Colonne trajane et trophées romains*, Bucharest: 207–258.

Ceresa-Gastaldo, A. (ed.) 1990. *Il bimillenario di Agrippa*. Le XVII Giornate filologiche genovesi si sono svolte ... il 20 e 21 febbraio 1989. Genoa.

Christ, K. 1956. *Drusus und Germanicus: Der Eintritt der Römer in Germanien*. Paderborn.

Christ, K. 1977. "Zur augusteischen Germanienpolitik." *Chiron* 7: 149–205.

Coarelli, F. 1985. *Il Foro Romano, II: Periodo repubblicano e augusteo*. Rome.

Coarelli, F. 1992. *Il Foro Boario: Dalle origini alla fine della repubblica*. Rome.

Coarelli, F. 1993. "Arcus Tiberii (Forum)." *LTUR* I: 107–108.

Cooley, A. E. 2009. *Res gestae divi Augusti: Text, Translation, and Commentary*. Cambridge.

Dąbrowa, E. 1998. *The Governors of Roman Syria from Augustus to Septimius Severus*. Bonn.

Dalla Rosa, A. 2014. *Cura et tutela: Le origini del potere imperiale sulle province proconsolari*. Stuttgart.

Damon, C. 1999. "The Trial of Cn. Piso in Tacitus Annals and the Senatus Consultum de Cn. Pisone Patre: New Light on Narrative Technique." *AJP* 120.1: 143–162.

Daniel, R. 1933. *Marcus Vipsanius Agrippa: Eine Monographie*. Breslau.

Deininger, J. 1965. *Die Provinziallandtage der römischen Kaiserzeit von Augustus bis zum Ende des dritten Jahrhunderts n. Chr*. Munich, Berlin.

Deininger, J. 2000. "Germaniam pacare: Zur neueren Diskussion über die Strategie des Augustus gegenüber Germanien." *Chiron* 30: 749–773.

Dettenhofer, M. H. 2000. *Herrschaft und Widerstand im augusteischen Principat: Die Konkurrenz zwischen Res publica und domus Augusta*. Stuttgart.

Drogula, F. 2015a. "Who Was Watching Whom? A Reassessment of the Conflict Between Germanicus and Piso." *AJP* 136: 121–153.

Drogula, F. 2015b. *Commanders and Command in the Roman Republic and Early Empire*. Chapel Hill.

Eck, W. 1985. *Die Statthalter der germanischen Provinzen von 1.–3. Jahrhundert*. Cologne.

Eck, W. 1995. "Plebs und Princeps nach dem Tod des Germanicus." In I. Malkin, Z. W. Rubinsohn (eds.), *Leaders and Masses in the Roman World: Studies in Honor of Zvi Yavetz*, Leiden, New York, Cologne: 1–10.

Eck, W. 1997. "Die Täuschung der Öffentlichkeit: Der Prozess gegen Cnaeus Calpurnius Piso im Jahre 20 n. Chr." In U. Manthe, J. von Ungern-Sternberg (eds.), *Grosse Prozesse der römischen Antike*, Munich: 128–145.

Eck, W. 2007. *The Age of Augustus* (2nd edn). Oxford.

Eck, W. 2010. "Die Donau als Ziel römischer Politik: Augustus und die Eroberung des Balkans." In L. Zerbini (ed.), *Roma e le province del Danubio*, Soveria Manelli: 19–33.

Eck, W. 2018. "Augustus–Tiberius–Varus: Eine römische Erfolgsgeschichte in Germanien und ihr Scheitern." *Geschichte in Köln: Zeitschrift für Stadt und Regionalgeschichte* 65: 7–30.

Eck, W. 2019. "Die Bürgerrechtskonstitutionen als serielle Quellengattung und Proconsul als Element in der Titulatur der römischen Kaiser." In A. Heller, C. Muller, A. Suspene (eds.), *Philorhômaios kai philhellèn: Hommage à Jean-Louis Ferrary*, Geneva: 481–499.

Eck, W., Caballos, A., Fernández, F., 1996. *Das senatus consultum de Cn. Pisone patre*. Munich.

Ehrenberg, V. 1953. "Imperium maius in the Roman Republic." *AJP* 74.2: 113–136.

Ehrenberg, V., Jones, A. H. M. 1955. *Documents Illustrating the Reigns of Augustus and Tiberius* (2nd edn). Oxford.

Faoro, D. 2016. "Nota sulla cronologia delle acclamazioni imperatorie XV–XXI di Augusto e III–VII di Tiberio Cesare." *ZPE* 199: 208–212.

Ferrary, J. L. 2001. "À propos des pouvoirs d'Auguste." *CCG* 12: 101–154.

Fishwick, D. 1987. *The Imperial Cult in the Latin West: Studies in the Ruler Cult of the Western Provinces of the Roman Empire*. Leiden.

Flory, M. B. 1996. "Dynastic Ideology, the Domus Augusta, and Imperial Women: A Lost Statuary Group in the Circus Flaminius." *TAPhA* 126: 287–306.

Flower, H. 2020. "Augustus, Tiberius, and the End of the Roman Triumph." *CA* 39.1: 1–28.

Fraschetti, A. 1988. "Osservazioni sulla Tabula Siarensis (frg. I, ll. 6–8)." *Epigraphica* 50: 47–60.

Fraschetti, A. (ed.) 2000. *La commemorazione di Germanico nella documentazione epigrafica*. Rome.

Frenz, H. G. 1985. "Drusus Maior und sein Monument zu Mainz." *JRGZM* 32: 394–421.

Frenz, H. G. 1988. *Der römische Ehrenbogen von Mainz-Kastel: Ein imperiales Monument der frühen Kaiserzeit apud ripam Rheni*. Wiesbaden.

Frenz, H. G. 1989. "Zur Zeitstellung des römischen Ehrenbogens von Mainz-Kastel." *Arch. Kor. RGZM* 19: 69–75.

Galinsky, K. 2012. *Augustus: Introduction to the Life of an Emperor*. Cambridge.

Gallotta, B. 1981. "Germanico oltre il Reno." *Acme* 34.2: 293–316.

Gallotta, B. 1987. *Germanico*. Rome.

Galsterer, H. 2000. "Die Trauer der Städte um verstorbene Prinzen in der frühen Kaiserzeit." In A. Fraschetti (ed.), *La commemorazione di Germanico nella documentazione epigrafica: Convegno Internazionale di Studi Cassino 21–24 ottobre 1991*, Rome: 173–187.

Ganzert, J. 1984. *Das Kenotaph für Gaius Caesar in Limyra: Architektur und Bauornamentik*. Tübingen.

Ganzert, J. 1997. "Zu den Ehrenbögen für Germanicus und Drusus auf dem Augustusforum: 'arcus circum latera templi Martis Ultoris'." *MDAI(R)* 104: 193–206.

Giovannini, A. 1999. "Les pouvoirs d'Auguste de 27 à 23 av. J.-C.: Une relecture de l'ordonnance de Kymè de l'an 27 (IK 5, No 17)." *ZPE* 124: 95–106.

Girardet, K. M. 1990. "Die Entmachtung des Konsulates im Übergang von der Republik zur Monarchie und die Rechtsgrundlagen des augusteischen Prinzipats." In W. Görler, S. Koster (eds.), *Pratum Saraviense: Festschrift für P. Steinmetz*, Stuttgart: 89–126.

Girardet, K. M. 1992. "Imperium und provinciae des Pompeius seit 67 v. Chr." *CCG* 3: 177–188.

Girardet, K. M. 1993. "Die Rechtsstellung der Caesarattentäter Brutus und Cassius in den Jahren 44–42 v. Chr." *Chiron* 23: 207–232.

Girardet, K. M. 2000. "Imperium 'Maius': Politische und verfassungsrechtliche Aspekte. Versuch einer Klärung." In A. Giovannini (ed.), *La Révolution Romaine après Ronald Syme: Bilans et perspectives*, Vandoeuvres, Geneva: 167–236.

Girardet, K. M. 2001. "Imperia und provinciae des Pompeius 82 bis 48 v. Chr." *Chiron* 31: 153–209.

Goodyear, F. R. D. 1972. *The Annals of Tacitus, Books 1–6*, edited with a commentary. Vol. 1: *Annals 1.1–54*. Cambridge.

Goodyear, F. R. D. 1981. *The Annals of Tacitus, Books 1–6*, edited with a commentary. Vol. 2: *Annals 1.55–81 and Annals 2*. Cambridge.

Gray, E. W. 1970. "The Imperium of M. Agrippa." *ZPE* 6: 227–238.

Gruen, E. 1996. "The Expansion of the Empire under Augustus." In A. K. Bowman, E. Champlin, A. Lintott (eds.), *The Cambridge Ancient History, vol. X, The Augustan Empire, 43 B.C.–A.D. 69*, Cambridge: 147–197.

Gruen, E. 2005. "Augustus and the Making of the Principate." In K. Galinsky (ed.), *The Cambridge Companion to the Age of Augustus*, Cambridge: 33–51.

Halfmann, H. 1986. *Itinera principum: Geschichte und Typologie der Kaiserreisen im Römischen Reich*. Stuttgart.

Hanslik, R. 1961. "Marcus Vipsanius Agrippa." *RE* IX A1. col. 1226–1275.

Haslam, M. W. 1980. "Augustus Funeral Oration for Agrippa." *CJ* 75: 193–199.

Havener, W. 2016. *Imperator Augustus: Die diskursive Konstituierung der militärischen persona des ersten römischen Princeps*. Stuttgart.

Hennig, D. 1972. "Zur Ägyptenreise des Germanicus." *Chiron* 2: 349–365.

Herz, P. 1980. "Der Aufbruch des Gaius Caesar in den Osten." *ZPE* 39: 285–290.

Herz, P. 1993. "Die Adoptivsöhne des Augustus und der Festkalender: Gedanken zu einer Inschrift aus Messene." *Klio* 75: 272–288.

Herz, P. 2001. "Das römische Heer und der Kaiserkult in Germanien." In W. Spickermann, H. Cancik, J. Rüpke (eds.), *Religion in den germanischen Provinzen Roms*, Tübingen: 91–116.

Hickson, F. V. 1991. "Augustus Triumphator: Manipulation of the Triumphal Theme in the Political Program of Augustus." *Latomus* 50.1: 124–138.

Hoët-van Cauwenberghe, C., Kantiréa, M. 2013. "La popularité de Germanicus en Orient: Les figures d'un prince héritier sous Tibère." *CCG* 24: 135–156.

Hurlet, F. 1994. "Recherches sur la durée de l'imperium des 'co-régents' sous les principats d'Auguste et de Tibère." *CCG* 5: 255–289.

Hurlet, F. 1997. *Les collègues du prince sous Auguste et Tibère: De la légalité républicaine à la légitimité dynastique*. Rome.

Hurlet, F. 2000. "Auspiciis Imperatoris Caesaris Augusti, ductu proconsulis: L'intervention impériale dans le choix et les compétences du proconsul d'Afrique sous les Julio-Claudiens." *L'Africa Romana* 13: 1513–1540.

Hurlet, F. 2006. *Le proconsul et le prince d'Auguste à Dioclétien*. Bordeaux.

Hurlet, F. 2015. *Auguste: Les ambiguïtés du pouvoir*. Paris.

Hurlet, F. 2016. "De Pompée à Auguste: Les mutations de l'imperium militiae; Les réalités institutionnelles." In V. Fromentin, E. Bertrand, M. Coltelloni-Trannoy, M. Molin, G. Urso (eds.), *Cassius Dion: Nouvelles lectures*, vol. 2, Bordeaux: 582–593.

Itgenshorst, T. 2017. "Die Transformation des Triumphes in augusteischer Zeit." In F. Goldbeck, J. Wienand (eds.), *Der römische Triumph in Prinzipat und Spätantike*, Berlin: 59–81.

Jameson, S. 1969. "22 or 23?" *Historia* 18.2: 204–229.

Jashemski, W. F. 1950. *The Origins and History of the Proconsular and the Propraetorian Imperium to 27 B.C.* Chicago.

Kantiréa, M. 2007. *Les Dieux et les Dieux Augustes: Le culte impériale en Gréce sous les Julio-claudiens et les Flaviens. Etudes épigraphiques et archéologiques*. Athens.

Kehne, P. 1998a. "Augustus und seine spolia opima: Hoffnungen auf den Triumph des Nero Claudius Drusus?" In T. Hantos, G. A. Lehmann (eds.), *Althistorisches Kolloquium aus Anlass des 70. Geburstags von Jochen Bleicken*, Stuttgart: 187–211.

Kehne, P. 1998b. "Germanicus." *RGA* 11: 438–448.

Kehne, P. 2018. "Zur Erforschung der Germanicusfeldzüge, zu den Ursachen für die Unmöglichkeit ihrer Rekonstruktion und zu den Problemen des Germanicus-Bildes." In S. Burmeister, S. Ortisi (eds.), *Phantom Germanicus: Spurensuche zwischen historischer Überlieferung und archäologischem Befund*. Symposium vom 2.–3. Juli 2015, Museum und Park Kalkriese/Universität Osnabrück, Rahden/Westf.: 31–95.

Kienast, D. 2009. *Augustus: Prinzeps und Monarch* (4th edn). Darmstadt.

Kienast, D., Eck, W., Heil, M., 2017. *Römische Kaisertabelle: Grundzüge einer römischen Kaiserchronologie* (6th edn). Darmstadt.

Klein, M. J. 2002. "Rzymska Moguncja w świetle najnowszych badań" [Roman Mainz in the light of recent research]. In K. Ilski, L. Mrozewicz, M. Musielak (eds.), *Xenia Posnaniensia XIII*. Poznań.

Kleiner, F. S. 1985a. *The Arch of Nero in Rome: A Study of the Roman Honorary Arch before and under Nero*. Rome.
Kleiner, F. S. 1985b. "The Arch of Gaius Caesar at Pisa (CIL, XI, 1421)." *Latomus* 44: 156–164.
Kleiner, F. S. 1989. "The Study of Roman Triumphal and Honorary Arches 50 Years after Kähler." *JRA* 2: 195–206.
Kleiner, F. S. 1997. "The Boscoreale Cups: Copies of a Lost Monument?" *JRA* 10: 377–380.
Kloft, H. 1977. *Prorogation und außerordentliche Imperien 326–81 v. Chr.: Untersuchung zur Verfassung der römischen Republik*. Meisenheim am Glan.
Knoke, F. 1922. *Die Kriegszüge des Germanicus in Deutschland*. Berlin.
Koch, M. 1979. "M. Agrippa und Neukarthago." *Chiron* 9: 205–214.
Koehn, C. 2010. "Pompeius, Cassius und Augustus: Bemerkungen zum *imperium maius*." *Chiron* 40: 301–322.
Koenen, L. 1970. "Die laudatio funebris des Augustus für Agrippa auf einem neuen Papyrus (P. Colon. inv. no 4701; vgl. Taf. VIIIa)." *ZPE* 5: 217–283.
Koestermann, E. 1953. "Der pannonisch-dalmatinische Krieg 6–9 n. Chr." *Hermes* 81: 345–378.
Koestermann, E. 1957. "Die Feldzüge des Germanicus 14–16 n. Chr." *Historia* 6: 429–479.
Koestermann, E. 1958. "Die Mission des Germanicus im Orient." *Historia* 7: 331–375.
Kuntze, K. 1985. *Zur Darstellung des Kaisers Tiberius und seiner Zeit bei Velleius Paterculus*. Frankfurt.
Kuttner, A. L. 1995. *Dynasty and Empire in the Age of Augustus: The Case of the Boscoreale Cups*. Berkeley.
Lacey, W. K. 1996. *Augustus and the Principate: The Evolution of the System*. Leeds.
Last, H. 1947. "Imperium maius: A Note." *JRS* 37: 157–164.
Lebek, W. D. 1987. "Die drei Ehrenbögen für Germanicus: Tab. Siar. Frg. I 9–34; CIL VI 31199a 2–17." *ZPE* 67: 129–148.
Lebek, W. D. 1989a. "Die Mainzer Ehrungen für Germanicus, den älteren Drusus und Domitian (Tab. Siar. I.26–34; Suet. Claud. 1.3)." *ZPE* 78: 45–82.
Lebek, W. D. 1989b. "Die Postumen Ehrenbögen und der Triumph des Drusus Caesar (CIL VI 31200 b col. I, 1–4; Tac. Ann. 4, 9, 2)." *ZPE* 78: 83–91.
Lebek, W. D. 1991a. "Ehrenbögen und Prinzentod: 9 v. Chr.–23 n. Chr." *ZPE* 86: 47–78.
Lebek, W. D. 1991b. "Der Proconsulat des Germanicus und die auctoritas des Senats: Tab. Siar. Frg. I 22–24." *ZPE* 87: 103–124.
Lebek, W. D. 1999. "Das senatus consultum de Cn. Pisone patre und Tacitus." *ZPE* 128: 183–211.
Lehmann, G. A. 1989. "Zum Zeitalter römischen Okkupation Germaniens: Neue Interpretationen und Quellenfunde." *Boreas. Münsterische Beiträge zur Archäologie* 12: 207–230.
Lehmann, G. A. 1991. "Das Ende der römischen Herrschaft über das 'Westelbische' Germanien: Von der Varus-Katastrophe zur Abberufung des Germanicus Caesar 16/7 n. Chr." *ZPE* 86: 79–96.
Levick, B. 1999. *Tiberius the Politician*. London, New York.
Levick, B. 2013. *Augustus: Image and Substance*. London, New York.
Lott, J. B. 2012. *Death and Dynasty in Early Imperial Rome: Key Sources, with Text, Translation, and Commentary*. Cambridge.

Luther, A. 2010. "Zum Orientfeldzug des Gaius Caesar." *Gymnasium* 117: 103–127.
Magie, D. 1908. "The Mission of Agrippa to the Orient in 23 B.C." *CPh* 3: 145–152.
Marquardt, J. 1873. *Römische Staatsverwaltung*. I. Leipzig.
Merkelbach, R. 1974. "Gaius Caesar, *princeps iuventutis* in Assos." *ZPE* 13: 186.
Millar, F. 1966. "The Emperor, the Senate and the Provinces." *JRS* 56: 156–166.
Millar, F. 1989. "Senatorial Provinces: An Institutionalized Ghost." *Ancient World* 20: 93–97.
Millar, F. 1993. *The Roman Near East 31 BC–AD 337*. Cambridge, MA; London.
Miltner, F. 1937. "Augustus' Kampf um die Donaugrenze." *Klio* 30: 200–226.
Mlasowsky, A. 1996. "Nomini ac fortunae Caesarum proximi: Die Sukzessionspropaganda der römischen Kaiser von Augustus bis Nero im Spiegel der Reichsprägung und der archäologischen Quellen." *JDAI* 111: 249–388.
Mommsen, T. 1888. *Römisches Staatsrecht* (3rd edn). Leipzig.
Nedergaard, E. 1988. "Zur Problematik der Augustusbögen auf dem Forum Romanum." In W. D. Heilmeyer, E. La Rocca, H. G. Martin (eds.), *Kaiser Augustus und die verlorene Republik: Eine Ausstellung im Martin-Gropius-Bau, Berlin 7. Juni–14. August 1988*, Mainz: 224–239.
Olbrycht, M. J. 2016. "Germanicus, Artabanos II of Partia, and Zeno Artaxias in Armenia." *Klio* 98.2: 605–633.
Orth, W. 1978. "Zur Fabricius-Tuscus-Inschrift aus Alexandreia/Troas." *ZPE* 28: 57–60.
Pani, M. 1987. "La missione di Germanico in oriente: Politica estera e politica interna." In G. Bonamente, M. P. Segoloni (eds.), *Germanico: La persona, la personalità, il personaggio nel bimillenario della nascita*. Atti del Convegno (Macerata, Perugia 1986), Rome: 1–23.
Parsi, B. 1963. *Désignation et investiture de l'empereur romain (I et II siècles après J.-C.)*. Paris.
Pisani Sartorio, G. 1993. "Arcus Drusi (via Appia)." *LTUR* I: 93.
Pucci Ben Zeev, M. 1998. *Jewish Rights in the Roman World: The Greek and Roman Documents Quoted by Josephus Flavius*. Tübingen.
Reinhold, M. 1933. *Marcus Agrippa: A Biography*. New York.
Rich, J. W. 1990. *Cassius Dio: The Augustan Settlement (Roman History 53–55.9)*. Warminster.
Rich, J. W. 1998. "Augustus's Parthian Honours, the Temple of Mars Ultor and the Arch in the Forum Romanum." *PBSR* 66: 71–128.
Rich, J. W. 1999. "Drusus and the *spolia opima*." *CQ* 49.2: 544–555.
Rich, J. W. 2012. "Making the Emergency Permanent: Auctoritas, Potestas and the Evolution of the Principate of Augustus." In Y. Rivière (ed.), *Des réformes augustéennes*, Rome: 37–121.
Rich, J. W. 2015. "Consensus, Rituals and the Origins of the Principate." In J. L. Ferrary and J. Scheid (eds.), *Il princeps romano: Autocrate o magistrato? Fattori giuridici e fattori sociali del potere imperiale da Augusto a Commodo*, Pavia: 101–138.
Richardson, J. S. 1996. *The Romans in Spain*. Oxford.
Richardson, J. S. 2002. "The New Augustan Edicts from Northwest Spain." *JRA* 15: 411–415.
Richardson, J. S. 2012. *Augustan Rome 44 BC to AD 14: The Restoration of the Republic and the Establishment of the Empire*. Edinburgh.
Ridley, R. T. 1981. "The Extraordinary Commands of the Late Republic: A Matter of Definition." *Historia* 30.3: 280–297.

Rivière, Y. 2016. *Germanicus: Prince romain 15 av. J.-C. – 19 apr. J.-C.* Paris.

Roddaz, J. M. 1984. *Marcus Agrippa.* Rome.

Roddaz, J. M. 2005. "Culte impérial et fidélité dynastique: Agrippa et l'ile Lesbos." *Studia Historica: Historia Antigua* 23: 401–412.

Rodríguez Almeida, E. 1993. "Arcus Germanici in Circo Flaminio." *LTUR* I: 94–95.

Roehmer, M. 1997. *Der Bogen als Staatsmonument: Zur politischen Bedeutung der römischen Ehrenbögen des 1. Jhs. n. Chr.* Munich.

Rogers, R. S. 1943. *Studies in the Reign of Tiberius: Some Imperial Virtues of Tiberius Drusus Iulius Caesar.* Baltimore.

Romer, F. E. 1974. *G. and L. Caesar in the East.* Dissertation (Microfilms). Ann Arbor.

Romer, F. E. 1978. "A Numismatic Date for the Departure of C. Caesar?" *TAPhA* 108: 87–202.

Romer, F. E. 1979. "Gaius Caesar's Military Diplomacy in the East." *TAPhA* 109: 199–214.

Rose, C. B. 1997. *Dynastic Commemoration and Imperial Portraiture in the Julio-Claudian Period.* Cambridge.

Rose, C. B. 2005. "The Parthians in Augustan Rome." *AJA* 109: 21–75.

Rowe, G. 2002. *Princes and Political Cultures: The New Tiberian Senatorial Decrees.* Ann Arbor.

Salmon, E. T. 1956. "The Evolution of Augustus' Principate." *Historia* 5.4: 456–478.

Salvo, D. 2010. "Germanico e la rivolta delle legioni del Reno." *Ricerche di Storia Antica* 2: 138–156.

Sánchez, A., Gutiérrez, O. 1999. *Tabula Siarensis: Edición, traducción y comentario.* Pamplona. [Cit. as *TS.*]

Santos, F. D. 1975. "Die Integration Nord- und Nordwestspaniens als römische Provinz in der Reichspolitik des Augustus. Von der konsularischen zur hispanischen Ära." *ANRW* 2.3: 523–571.

Sartre, M. 1997. *Wschód rzymski: Prowincje i społeczeństwa prowincjonalne we wschodniej części basenu Morza Śródziemnego w okresie od Augusta do Sewerów (31 r. p.n.e.–235 r. n.e.).* Wroclaw: L'Orient romain: Provinces et sociétés provinciales en Méditerranée orientale d'Auguste aux Sévères, 31 avant J.-C.–235 après J.-C. (Paris, 1991).

Šašel Kos, M. 2011. "The Roman Conquest of Dalmatia and Pannonia under Augustus: Some of the Latest Research Results." In G. Moosbauer, R. Wiegels (eds.), *Fines imperii—imperium sine fine? Römische Okkupations- und Grenzpolitik im frühen Principat: Beiträge zum Kongress Fines imperii—imperium sine fine? in Osnabrück vom 14. Bis 18. September 2009*, Rahden/Westf.: 107–117.

Sawiński, P. 2004. "Agrippa's Mission in the East." *Eos* 91.2: 242–250.

Sawiński, P. 2005. *Specjalni wysłannicy cesarscy w okresie od Augusta do Tyberiusza: Studium nad początkami pryncypatu.* Poznań.

Sawiński, P. 2010. "Some Comments on the Character and Scope of the Power of Proconsuls During the Time of the Republic: *Imperium Consulare* or *Proconsulare*?" *Eos* 97.1: 29–44.

Sawiński, P. 2018. *The Succession of Imperial Power under the Julio-Claudian Dynasty (30 BC–AD 68).* Berlin.

Schleiermacher, W. 1960. "Die Besetzung Germaniens durch Drusus." *Analecta Archaeologica*: 231–236.

Schmitt, T. 1997. "Die drei Bögen für Germanicus und die römische Politik in frühtiberischer Zeit." *RSA* 27: 73–137.

Schrömbges, P. 1986. *Tiberius und die Res Publica Romana: Untersuchungen zur Institutionalisierung des frühen römischen Principats*. Bonn.

Schumacher, L. 1985. "Die imperatorischen Akklamationen der Triumvirn und die auspicia des Augustus." *Historia* 34.2: 191–222.

Schumacher, L. 1988. *Römische Inschriften*. Stuttgart.

Seager, R. 2005. *Tiberius* (2nd edn). London.

Segenni, S. 2011. *I Decreta pisana: Autonomia cittadina e ideologia imperiale nella colonia Opsequens Iulia Pisana*. Bari.

Severy, B. 2000. "Family and State in the Early Imperial Monarchy: The Senatus Consultum de Pisone Patre, Tabula Siarensis, and Tabula Hebana." *CPh* 95.3: 318–337.

Severy, B. 2003. *Augustus and the Family at the Birth of the Roman Empire*. New York, London.

Shaw. M. L. G. 1990. *Drusus Caesar: The Son of Tiberius*. Dissertation, University of British Columbia.

Sherk, R. K. 1969. *Roman Documents from the Greek East: Senatus Consulta and Epistulae to the Age of Augustus*. Baltimore.

Shotter, D. C. A. 1968. "Tacitus, Tiberius and Germanicus." *Historia* 17.2: 194–214.

Shotter, D. C. A. 1992. *Tiberius Caesar*. London.

Siber, H. 1940. *Das Führeramt des Augustus*. Leipzig.

Simon, H. G. 1982. "Eroberung und Verzicht: Die römische Politik in Germanien zwischen 12 v.Chr. und 16 n. Chr." In D. Baatz, F. R. Herrmann (eds.), *Die Römer in Hessen*, Stuttgart: 38–57.

Simpson, C. J. 1991. "Agrippa's Rejection of a Triumph in 19 B.C." *LCM* 16: 137–138.

Stevenson, T. 2013. "The Succession Planning of Augustus." *Antichthon* 47: 118–139.

Sumner, G. V. 1967. "Germanicus and Drusus Caesar." *Latomus* 26.2: 413–435.

Suspène, A. 2013. "Germanicus: Les témoignages numismatiques." CCG 24: 175–195.

Swan, P. M. 2004. *The Augustan Succession: An Historical Commentary on Cassius Dio's Roman History Books 55–56 (9 B.C.–A.D. 14)*. Oxford.

Syme, R. 1939. *The Roman Revolution*. Oxford (paperback edn 2002).

Syme, R. 1978. *History in Ovid*. Oxford.

Syme, R. 1979. "Some Imperatorial Salutations." *Phoenix* 33.4: 308–329.

Telschow, K. 1975. "Die Abberufung des Germanicus (16 n. Chr.): Ein Beispiel für die Kontinuität römischer Germanienpolitik von Augustus zu Tiberius." In E. Levèvre (ed.), *Monumentum Chiloniense: Studien zur augusteischen Zeit; Kieler Festschrift für E. Burck zum 70. Geburstag*, Amsterdam: 148–182.

Thompson, H. A. 1950. "The Odeion in the Athenian Agora." *Hesperia* 19: 31–141.

Timpe, D. 1962. *Untersuchungen zur Kontinuität des frühen Prinzipats*. Wiesbaden.

Timpe, D. 1967a. "Drusus' Umkehr an der Elbe." *RhM* 110: 289–306.

Timpe, D. 1967b. "Zur Geschichte und Überlieferung der Okkupation Germaniens unter Augustus." *Saeculum* 18.3: 278–293.

Timpe, D. 1968. *Der Triumph des Germanicus: Untersuchungen zu den Feldzügen der Jahre 14–16 n. Chr. in Germanien*. Bonn.

Timpe, D. 1971. "Der römische Verzicht auf die Okkupation Germaniens." *Chiron* 1: 267–284.

Timpe, D. 1975. "Zur Geschichte der Rheingrenze zwischen Caesar und Drusus." In E. Levèvre (ed.), *Monumentum Chiloniense: Studien zur augusteischen Zeit; Kieler Festschrift für E. Burck zum 70. Geburstag*, Amsterdam: 124–147.

Timpe, D. 2012. "Die 'Varusschlacht' in Ihren Kontexten: Eine Kritische Nachlese zum Bimillennium." *HZ* 294: 593–652.

Trillmich, W. 1988. "Der Germanicus-Bogen in Rom und das Monument für Germanicus und Drusus in Leptis Magna: Archäologisches zur Tabula Siarensis (I, 9–21)." In J. González, J. Arce (eds.), *Estudios sobre la Tabula Siarensis*, Madrid: 51–60.

Van Ooteheghem, J. 1959. "Germanicus en Égypte." *LEC* 27: 241–251.

Vassileiou, A. 1983. "Drusus imperator appelatus in Germania (Ergänzung des Drususelogiums auf dem Forum Augusti)." *ZPE* 51: 213–214.

Vervaet, F. J. 2014. *The High Command in the Roman Republic: The Principle of the "summum imperium auspiciumque" from 509 to 19* BCE. Stuttgart.

Vervaet, F. J. 2020. "*Subsidia dominationi*: The Early Careers of Tiberius Claudius Nero and Nero Claudius Drusus Revisited." *Klio* 102.1: 121–201.

Vout, C. 2013. "Tiberius and the Invention of Succession." In A. G. G. Gibson (ed.), *The Julio-Claudian Succession: Reality and Perception of the "Augustan Model"*, Leiden, Boston: 59–77.

Weingärtner, D. G. 1969. *Die Ägyptenreise des Germanicus*. Dissertation, Bonn.

Weinstock, S. 1966. "The Posthumous Honours of Germanicus." In R. Chevallier (ed.), *Mélanges d'archéologie et d'histoire offerts à A. Piganiol*, Paris: 891–898.

Wells, C. M. 1972. *The German Policy of Augustus: An Examination of the Archaeological Evidence*. Oxford.

Welwei, K. W. 1986. "Römische Weltherrschaftsideologie und augusteische Germanienpolitik." *Gymnasium* 93.2: 118–137.

Wesch-Klein, G. 2016. *Die Provinzen des Imperium Romanum: Geschichte, Herrschaft, Verwaltung*. Darmstadt.

Wolters, R. 1989. *"Tam diu Germania vincitur": Römische Germanensiege und Germanensieg-Propaganda bis zum Ende des 1. Jahrhunderts n. Chr.* Bochum.

Wolters, R. 1990a. "Der Germanicus-Dupondius, die Tabula Siarensis und der römische Verzicht auf die Okkupation Germaniens." *NZ* 101: 7–15.

Wolters, R. 1990b. *Römische Eroberung und Herrschaftsorganisation in Gallien und Germanien: Zur Entstehung und Bedeutung der sogenannten Klientel-Randstaaten*. Bochum.

Wolters, R. 2000. *Die Römer in Germanien*. Munich.

Wolters, R. 2009. *Die Schlacht im Teutoburger Wald: Arminius, Varus und das römische Germanien* (2nd edn). Munich.

Wolters,R. 2014–15. "Germanicusfeldzüge vor den Germanicusfeldzügen? Annalistische Rekonstruktionen ante excessum divi Augusti." *Palamedes* 9/10: 197–209.

Woodman, A. J. 1977. *Velleius Paterculus: The Tiberian Narrative (2.94–131)*. Cambridge.

Woodman, A. J. 1983. *Velleius Paterculus: The Caesarian and Augustan Narrative (2.41–93)*. Cambridge.

Woodman, A. J., Martin, R. H. 1996. *The Annals of Tacitus, Book 3*, edited with commentary. Cambridge.

Zanker, P. 1968. *Forum Augustum: Das Bildprogramm*. Tübingen.

Zanker, P. 1990. *Augustus und die Macht der Bilder*. Munich.

Zetzel, J. E. G. 1970. "New Light on Gaius Caesar's Eastern Campaign." *GRBS* 11: 259–266.

Ziółkowski, A. 2004. *Historia Rzymu*. Poznań. Originally published as *Storia di Roma* (Rome, 2000).

Index of persons

Note: The index only lists persons mentioned in the main body of the text, not counting the footnotes.

Index of peoples and places

Note: The index only lists peoples and places mentioned in the main body of the text, not counting the footnotes.

For Product Safety Concerns and Information please contact our EU representative GPSR@taylorandfrancis.com
Taylor & Francis Verlag GmbH, Kaufingerstraße 24, 80331 München, Germany

www.ingramcontent.com/pod-product-compliance
Lightning Source LLC
LaVergne TN
LVHW021130300926
849160LV00010B/944
* 9 7 8 0 3 6 7 7 2 5 3 4 1 *